Soups

Practical Cookery

Soups

p

This is a Parragon Book
This edition published in 2002

Parragon
Queen Street House
4 Queen Street
Bath BA1 1HE, UK

ISBN: 0-75258-314-X (Hardback)
ISBN: 0-75258-320-4 (Paperback)

Printed in China

NOTE

Cup measurements in this book are for American cups.
Tablespoons are assumed tobe 15ml. Unless otherwise stated,
milk is assumed to be full fat, eggs are medium
and pepper is freshly ground black pepper.

Recipes using uncooked eggs should be
avoided by infants, the elderly, pregnant women and anyone
suffering from an illness.

Contents

Introduction 10

Vegetable Soups

Hot & Spicy Soups

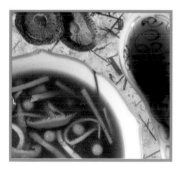

Oriental Soups (continued)

European Soups

International Soups

Traditional British Soups

Low Fat

Special Occasion Soups

Introduction

Soup is one of the fundamental forms of food. Its traditions go back to the earliest days of civilised man with the advent of fire. It remains a favourite source of nourishment and pleasure today and homemade soup has become a special treat.

The benefits of soups are numerous. It is nutritious, satisfying to eat and generally lean. It is economical to make, especially using abundant seasonal produce, but even expensive ingredients go further when made into soups.

Making soup can be a very creative endeavour, as well as satisfying for the cook as for the recipients. Practice hones skills and promotes confidence. This book offers an array of different styles of soup, using a variety of ingredients and techniques. Consider the recipes as a framework of proportions, and experiment with alternative ingredients if you wish.

Equipment

Soup-making requires little in the way of basic equipment. A good knife or two and a large saucepan with a lid are essential. A stockpot or soup kettle, or a large-capacity cast-iron casserole is also useful. Other things required to expedite your efforts are probably already in your kitchen – a cutting board,

colander, sieves, vegetable peeler, scissors, ladle and spoons. A fat-separator or de-greasing jug (pitcher) is helpful, as is a large-capacity measuring container.

A wide range of specialised equipment is available but not necessarily essential to making soups. For puréeing soups, the various options produce differing results. A food mill, the most economical choice, will do the basic job of producing relatively smooth soups and it also sieves at the same time. For the smoothest and best texture, nothing beats a blender. A food processor may be used for chopping and slicing ingredients as well as puréeing cooked soups, so it performs a variety of functions. A hand-held blender can purée right in the saucepan, as long as the depth of liquid is appropriate.

These pieces of equipment may each have a role to play in soup-making, but it is best to experiment first and see what you really need for the soups you like to make before investing. For most people there is no need for a battery of equipment. Always follow the manufacturer's instructions and recommendations for safe operation of electrical appliances.

Ingredients

Soups are only as good as the ingredients in them. While leftovers are traditionally used as a springboard for creativity in soup-making, and may certainly provide useful components, fresh ingredients at their peak provide optimum nutritional benefits and taste.

Water is the most basic ingredient for soup. Even stock is essentially flavoured water. Many soups taste best made with water, as the pure flavours are highlighted; this is especially true of vegetable soups.

Introduction

Be careful with your use of stock ingredients; it is easy to overdo strong-tasting vegetables or meats, which will drown the taste of the main flavour in your soup. Carrots and chicken form the basis of excellent stock.

Some soups make their own stock during the cooking process. Others call for stock as an ingredient. This can be homemade, bought ready-made, made up from stock cubes, powder or liquid stock base, or canned consommé or clear broth. It is useful to know how to make stock, as homemade is more economical and normally has a superior flavour.

Stock-making

Making stock is easy. After getting it under way, it requires little attention, just time. You can save stock ingredients in the freezer until you need them; chicken carcasses, giblets, necks, backs and trimmings; scraps and bones from meat roasts; vegetable trimmings such as leek greens, celery leaves and stems, mushroom stalks, pieces of carrot and unused onion halves.

Fresh ingredients are determined by the kind of stock you want. Chicken or turkey wings are inexpensive and provide excellent flavours for poultry stock. Veal bones give more flavour than beef and pork lends sweetness. Lamb or ham bones are not suitable for a general purpose meat stock, as flavours are too pronounced, but can make delicious stocks when their flavours are appropriate, such as ham stock for split pea or bean soup.

Aromatic vegetables –carrots, onions, leeks and garlic, for instance, are almost always included in stock. Strongly flavoured vegetables such as cabbage should be used sparingly as the stock produced would be unsuitable for delicate soups. Avoid dark greens as they make pale stock murky.

Brown the main ingredients first, either by roasting or frying, as this adds colour and flavour to the stock. Adding a roast chicken carcass is an easy way to do this.

Use cold water to make the stock; it helps extract the impurities. For a flavourful stock, keep the amount of water in proportion to the ingredients, which should be covered with about 5 cm/2 inches of water. Skim off the scum or foam that rises to the surface as

Introduction

stock is heated, as it contains impurities that can make stock cloudy. Cook stock uncovered and do not allow it to boil at any time or fat may be incorporated into the liquid, which will not be removable.

Stock needs slow cooking over a low heat. Beef or meat stock takes 4–6 hours to extract maximum flavour, chicken or other poultry stock 2–3 hours. Fish stock requires about half an hour.

Remove the fat from stock before using. The easiest way to do this is to refrigerate it, allowing the fat to congeal, and then lift it off. If time is short, use a fat separator (a jug or pitcher with the spout at the bottom) to remove the fat from warm stock, or spoon off the fat, although that is not always as effective as other methods.

For greater flavour, stock can be reduced – cooked slowly, uncovered, to reduce it and concentrate it. This procedure may also be useful to reduce the volume for storage. Stock keeps refrigerated for about three days, or frozen for up to three months.

Serving Soup

Soup is more flexible in terms of portions than many other foods. In this book, a range of servings may be indicated as a soup will provide more servings as a starter than as the main focus of a meal. Starter portions vary from 225 ml/8 fl oz/1 cup for very rich recipes to 350 ml/12 fl oz/1.5 cups; main courses from 400 ml/14 fl oz/1.75 cups to about 600 ml/1 pint/2 cups.

Soup is a perfect food for almost any occasion, from the most casual to the most formal. It can set the tone for the rest of the meal or be the meal itself. It brings satisfaction to those who make it as well as those who eat it and nourishes both the body and the soul.

Basic Recipes

Chinese Stock

This basic stock is used in Chinese cooking not only as the basis for soup-making, but also whenever liquid is required instead of plain water.

MAKES 2.5L/4½ PINTS/10 CUPS

750 g/1 lb 10 oz chicken pieces

750 g/1 lb 10 oz pork spare ribs

3.75 litres/6½ pints/15 cups cold water

3-4 pieces ginger root, crushed

3-4 spring onions (scallions), each tied into a knot

3-4 tbsp Chinese rice wine or dry sherry

1 Trim off any excess fat from the chicken and spare ribs; chop them into large pieces.

2 Place the chicken and pork in a large pan with the water; add the ginger and spring onion (scallion) knots.

3 Bring to the boil, and skim off the scum. Reduce the heat and simmer uncovered for at least 2-3 hours.

4 Strain the stock, discarding the chicken, pork, ginger and spring onions (scallions); add the wine and return to the boil, simmer for 2-3 minutes.

5 Refrigerate the stock when cool; it will keep for up to 4-5 days. Alternatively, it can be frozen in small containers and be defrosted as required.

Fresh Chicken Stock

MAKES 1.75 LITRES/3 PINTS/7½ CUPS

1 kg/2 lb 4 oz chicken, skinned

2 celery sticks

1 onion

2 carrots

1 garlic clove

few sprigs of fresh parsley

2 litres/3½ pints/9 cups water

salt and pepper

1 Put all the ingredients into a large saucepan.

2 Bring to the boil. Skim away surface scum using a large flat spoon. Reduce the heat to a gentle simmer, partially cover, and cook for 2 hours. Allow to cool.

3 Line a sieve (strainer) with clean muslin (cheesecloth) and place over a large jug or bowl. Pour the stock through the sieve (strainer). The cooked chicken can be used in another recipe. Discard the other solids. Cover the stock and chill.

4 Skim away any fat that forms before using. Store in the refrigerator for 3-4 days, until required, or freeze in small batches.

Fresh Vegetable Stock

This can be kept chilled for up to three days or frozen for up to three months. Salt is not added when cooking the stock: it is better to season it according to the dish in which it its to be used.

MAKES 1.5 LITRES/2¾ PINTS/6¼ CUPS

250 g/9 oz shallots

1 large carrot, diced

1 celery stalk, chopped

½ fennel bulb

1 garlic clove

1 bay leaf

a few fresh parsley and tarragon sprigs

2 litres/ 3½ pints/8¾ cups water

pepper

1 Put all the ingredients in a large saucepan and bring to the boil.

2 Skim off the surface scum with a flat spoon and reduce to a gentle simmer. Partially cover and cook for 45 minutes. Leave to cool.

3 Line a sieve (strainer) with clean muslin (cheesecloth) and put over a large jug or bowl. Pour the stock through the sieve (strainer). Discard the herbs and vegetables.

4 Cover and store in small quantities in the refrigerator for up to three days.

Fresh Lamb Stock

MAKES 1.75 LITRES/3 PINTS/7½ CUPS

about 1 kg/2 lb 4 oz bones from a cooked
    joint or raw chopped lamb bones

2 onions, studded with 6 cloves, or sliced or
chopped coarsely

2 carrots, sliced

1 leek, sliced

1-2 celery sticks, sliced

1 Bouquet Garni

about 2.25 litres/4 pints/2 quarts water

1 Chop or break up the bones and place in a large saucepan with the other ingredients.

2 Bring to the boil and remove any scum from the surface with a perforated spoon. Cover and simmer gently for 3-4 hours. Strain the stock and leave to cool.

3 Remove any fat from the surface and chill. If stored for more than 24 hours the stock must be boiled every day, cooled quickly and chilled again. The stock may be frozen for up to 2 months; place in a large plastic bag and seal, leaving at least 2.5 cm/1 inch of headspace to allow for expansion.

Fresh Fish Stock

MAKES 1.75 LITRES/3 PINTS/7½ CUPS

1 head of a cod or salmon, etc, plus the
    trimmings, skin and bones or just the
    trimmings, skin and bones

1-2 onions, sliced

1 carrot, sliced

1-2 celery sticks, sliced

good squeeze of lemon juice

1 Bouquet Garni or 2 fresh or dried bay
    leaves

1 Wash the fish head and trimmings and place in a saucepan. Cover with water and bring to the boil.

2 Remove any scum with a perforated spoon, then add the remaining ingredients. Cover and simmer for about 30 minutes.

3 Strain and cool. Store in ther refrigerator and use within 2 days.

Cornflour (cornstarch) Paste

Cornflour (cornstarch) paste is made by mixing 1 part cornflour (cornstarch) with about 1½ parts of cold water. Stir until smooth. The paste is used to thicken sauces.

How to Use This Book

Each recipe contains a wealth of useful information, including a breakdown of nutritional quantities, preparation and cooking times, and level of difficulty. All of this information is explained in detail below.

The nutritional information provided for each recipe is per serving or per portion. Optional ingredients, variations or serving suggestions have not been included in the calculations.

The number of chef's hats represents the difficulty of each recipe, ranging from easy (1 chef's hat) to difficult (5 chef's hats).

This amount of time represents the preparation of ingredients, including cooling, chilling and soaking times.

This represents the cooking time.

The ingredients for each recipe are listed in the order that they are used.

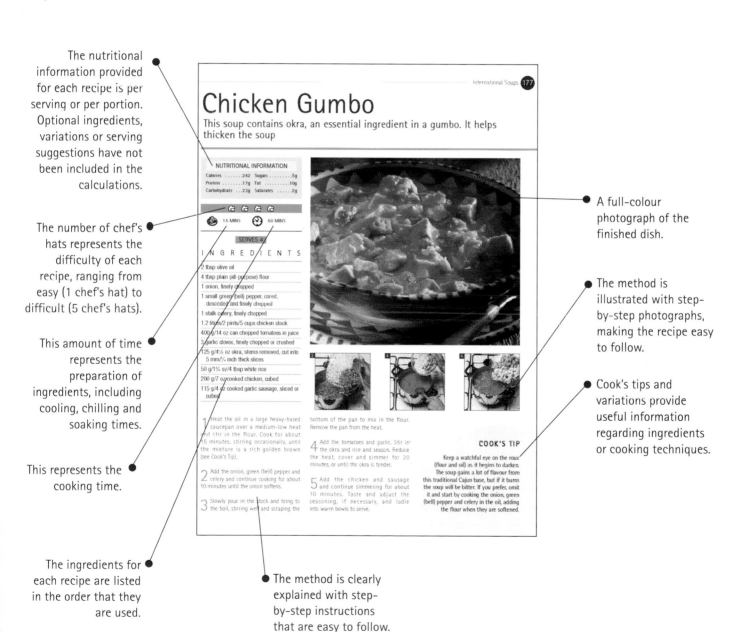

International Soups 177

Chicken Gumbo

This soup contains okra, an essential ingredient in a gumbo. It helps thicken the soup

NUTRITIONAL INFORMATION

Calories 242   Sugars 5g
Protein ....17g   Fat 10g
Carbohydrate ...23g   Saturates 2g

15 MINS   60 MINS

SERVES 4

INGREDIENTS

2 tbsp olive oil
4 tbsp plain (all-purpose) flour
1 onion, finely chopped
1 small green (bell) pepper, cored, deseeded and finely chopped
1 stalk celery, finely chopped
1.2 litres/2 pints/5 cups chicken stock
400 g/14 oz can chopped tomatoes in juice
3 garlic cloves, finely chopped or crushed
125 g/4½ oz okra, stems removed, cut into 5 mm/¼ inch thick slices
50 g/1¾ oz/4 tbsp white rice
200 g/7 oz cooked chicken, cubed
115 g/4 oz cooked garlic sausage, sliced or cubed

1 Heat the oil in a large heavy-based saucepan over a medium-low heat and stir in the flour. Cook for about 15 minutes, stirring occasionally, until the mixture is a rich golden brown (see Cook's Tip).

2 Add the onion, green (bell) pepper and celery and continue cooking for about 10 minutes until the onion softens.

3 Slowly pour in the stock and bring to the boil, stirring well and scraping the bottom of the pan to mix in the flour. Remove the pan from the heat.

4 Add the tomatoes and garlic. Stir in the okra and rice and season. Reduce the heat, cover and simmer for 20 minutes, or until the okra is tender.

5 Add the chicken and sausage and continue simmering for about 10 minutes. Taste and adjust the seasoning, if necessary, and ladle into warm bowls to serve.

COOK'S TIP

Keep a watchful eye on the roux (flour and oil) as it begins to darken. The soup gains a lot of flavour from this traditional Cajun base, but if it burns the soup will be bitter. If you prefer, omit it and start by cooking the onion, green (bell) pepper and celery in the oil, adding the flour when they are softened.

A full-colour photograph of the finished dish.

The method is illustrated with step-by-step photographs, making the recipe easy to follow.

Cook's tips and variations provide useful information regarding ingredients or cooking techniques.

The method is clearly explained with step-by-step instructions that are easy to follow.

Vegetable

Soups

Vegetables are endlessly variable and eminently enjoyable. Each vegetable can be used in many ways – in creamy soups, broths and thick, hearty ones. They provide a light

start to a meal or a satisfying main course, can be cooked quickly and last longer than other soups. Choose plump, fresh vegetables, as they have more flavour than tired ones, and use plenty to give a pleasing density. Use the recipes that follow freely and don't be afraid to experiment with them.

Beetroot Soup

Here are two variations using the same vegetable: a creamy soup made with puréed cooked beetroot and a traditional clear soup, Bortsch.

NUTRITIONAL INFORMATION

Calories 106	Sugars 11g
Protein 3g	Fat 5g
Carbohydrate . . .13g	Saturates 3g

25 MINS   35–55 MINS

SERVES 6

INGREDIENTS

BORTSCH

500 g/1 lb 2 oz raw beetroot (beet), peeled
   and grated

2 carrots, finely chopped

1 large onion, finely chopped

1 garlic clove, crushed

1 bouquet garni

1 litre/1¾ pints/5 cups vegetable stock

2–3 tsp lemon juice

salt and pepper

150 ml/¼ pint/⅔ cup soured cream, to serve

CREAMED BEETROOT (BEET) SOUP

60 g/2 oz/¼ cup butter or margarine

2 large onions, finely chopped

1–2 carrots, chopped

2 celery sticks, chopped

500 g/1 lb 2 oz cooked beetroot (beet), diced

1–2 tbsp lemon juice

900 ml/1½ pints/3½ cups vegetable stock

300 ml/½ pint/1¼ cups milk

salt and pepper

TO SERVE

grated cooked beetroot (beet) or 6 tbsp
   double (heavy) cream, lightly whipped

1 To make bortsch, place the beetroot (beet), carrots, onion, garlic, bouquet garni, stock and lemon juice in a saucepan and season to taste with salt and pepper. Bring to the boil, cover and simmer for 45 minutes.

2 Press the soup through a fine strainer or a strainer lined with muslin (cheesecloth), then pour into a clean pan. Taste and adjust the seasoning and add extra lemon juice, if necessary.

3 Bring to the boil and simmer for 1–2 minutes. Serve with a spoonful of soured cream swirled through.

4 To make creamed beetroot (beet) soup, melt the butter or margarine in a saucepan. Add the onions, carrots and celery and fry until just beginning to colour.

5 Add the beetroot (beet), 1 tablespoon of the lemon juice, the stock and seasoning and bring to the boil. Cover and simmer for 30 minutes, until tender.

6 Cool slightly, then press through a strainer or process in a food processor or blender. Pour into a clean pan. Add the milk and bring to the boil. Adjust the seasoning and add extra lemon juice, if necessary. Top with grated beetroot (beet) or double (heavy) cream.

Fresh Tomato Soup

Made with fresh tomatoes, the taste of this soup is subtle and complex. Basil is a proven partner for tomatoes, but you could also try tarragon.

NUTRITIONAL INFORMATION

Calories 222	Sugars 13g	
Protein 3g	Fat 17g	
Carbohydrate ...15g	Saturates 9g	

 10 MINS   60 MINS

SERVES 4

INGREDIENTS

1 kg/2 lb 4 oz ripe plum tomatoes, skinned

2 tsp olive oil

1 large sweet onion, finely chopped

1 carrot, finely chopped

1 stalk celery, finely chopped

2 garlic cloves, finely chopped or crushed

1 tsp fresh marjoram leaves, or ¼ tsp dried marjoram

450 ml/16 fl oz/ 2 cups water

4–5 tbsp double (heavy) cream, plus extra to garnish

2 tbsp chopped fresh basil leaves

salt and pepper

1 Cut the tomatoes in half and scrape the seeds into a sieve set over a bowl to catch the juice. Reserve the juice and discard the seeds. Chop the tomato flesh into large chunks.

COOK'S TIP

For the best flavour, this soup needs to be made with ripe tomatoes. If supermarket tomatoes are pale and hard, leave them to ripen at room temperature for several days. This is especially important in winter when most tomatoes are picked and shipped before they are ripe.

2 Heat the olive oil in a large saucepan. Add the onion, carrot and celery and cook over a medium-low heat for 3–4 minutes, stirring occasionally.

3 Add the tomatoes and their juice, with the garlic and marjoram. Cook for 2 minutes. Stir in the water, reduce the heat and simmer, covered, for about 45 minutes until the vegetables are very soft, stirring occasionally.

4 Allow the soup to cool slightly, then transfer to a blender or food processor and purée until smooth, working in batches, if necessary. (If using a food processor, strain off the cooking liquid and reserve. Purée the soup solids with enough cooking liquid to moisten them, then combine with the remaining liquid.)

5 Return the soup to the saucepan and place over a medium-low heat. Add the cream and stir in the basil. Season with salt and pepper and heat through; do not allow to boil.

6 Ladle the soup into warm bowls and swirl a little extra cream into each serving. Serve at once.

Speedy Beetroot Soup

Quick and easy to prepare in a microwave oven, this deep red soup of puréed beetroot and potatoes makes a stunning first course.

NUTRITIONAL INFORMATION

Calories . . . . . . .120 Sugars 11g
Protein . . . . .4g Fat 2g
Carbohydrate . . .22g Saturates 1g

 20 MINS   30 MINS

SERVES 6

INGREDIENTS

1 onion, chopped

350 g/12 oz potatoes, diced

1 small cooking apple, peeled,
   cored and grated

3 tbsp water

1 tsp cumin seeds

500 g/1 lb 2 oz cooked beetroot (beet),
   peeled and diced

1 bay leaf

pinch of dried thyme

1 tsp lemon juice

600 ml/1 pint/2½ cups hot vegetable stock

4 tbsp soured cream

salt and pepper

few dill sprigs, to garnish

1 Place the onion, potatoes, apple and water in a large bowl. Cover and cook on HIGH power for 10 minutes.

2 Stir in the cumin seeds and cook on HIGH power for 1 minute.

3 Stir in the beetroot (beet), bay leaf, thyme, lemon juice and hot vegetable stock. Cover and cook on HIGH power for 12 minutes, stirring halfway through the cooking time.

4 Leave to stand, uncovered, for 5 minutes. Remove and discard the bay leaf. Strain the vegetables and reserve the liquid. Process the vegetables with a little of the reserved liquid in a food processor or blender until they are smooth and creamy. Alternatively, either mash the vegetables with a potato masher or press them through a strainer with the back of a wooden spoon.

5 Pour the vegetable purée into a clean bowl with the reserved liquid and mix well. Season to taste. Cover and cook on HIGH power for 4–5 minutes, until the soup is piping hot.

6 Serve the soup in warmed bowls. Swirl 1 tablespoon of soured cream into each serving and garnish with a few sprigs of fresh dill.

Aubergine Soup

The parsnip and carrot bring a balancing sweetness to the aubergines in this delicious soup.

NUTRITIONAL INFORMATION

Calories	131	Sugar	. . . . .9g
Protein	. . . . .3g	Fats	. . . . .8g
Carbohydrates	. . .12g	Saturates	. . . . . .3g

🧊 20 MINS   🕐 1¼ HOURS

SERVES 4

I N G R E D I E N T S

1 tbsp olive oil, plus extra for brushing

750 g/1 lb 10 oz aubergines (eggplants), halved lengthways

1 carrot, halved

1 small parsnip, halved

2 onions, finely chopped

3 garlic cloves, finely chopped

1 litre/1¾ pints/4 cups chicken or vegetable stock

¼ tsp fresh thyme leaves, or a pinch of dried thyme

1 bay leaf

⅛ tsp ground coriander

1 tbsp tomato purée (paste)

150 ml/5 fl oz/⅔ cup single (light) cream

freshly squeezed lemon juice

salt and pepper

LEMON-GARLIC SEASONING:

grated rind of ½ lemon

1 garlic clove, finely chopped

3 tbsp chopped fresh parsley

1 Oil a shallow roasting tin (pan) and add the aubergine, cut sides down, and the carrot and parsnip. Brush the vegetables with oil. Roast in a preheated oven at 200oC/400oF/Gas Mark 6 for 30 minutes, turning once.

2 When cool enough to handle, scrape the aubergine (eggplant) flesh away from the skin, or scoop it out, then roughly chop. Cut the parsnip and carrot into chunks.

3 Heat the oil in a large saucepan over a medium-low heat. Add the onions and garlic and cook for about 5 minutes, stirring frequently, until softened. Add the aubergine (eggplant), parsnip, carrot, stock, thyme, bay leaf, coriander and tomato purée (paste), with a little salt. Stir to combine. Cover and simmer for 30 minutes, or until very tender.

4 Allow the soup to cool slightly, then transfer to a blender or food processor

and purée until smooth, working in batches if necessary. (If using a food processor, strain off the cooking liquid and reserve. Purée the soup solids with enough cooking liquid to moisten them, then combine with the remaining liquid.)

5 Return the puréed soup to the saucepan and stir in the cream. Reheat the soup over a low heat for about 10 minutes until hot. Adjust the seasoning, adding lemon juice to taste.

6 To make the lemon-garlic seasoning, chop together the lemon rind, garlic and parsley until very fine and well mixed. Ladle the soup into warm bowls, then garnish with some freshly chopped parsley.

Smoky Green Bean Soup

For the most robust flavour, use bacon that has been fairly heavily smoked and has a pronounced taste.

NUTRITIONAL INFORMATION

Calories 192	Sugars 7g	
Protein 9g	Fat 8g	
Carbohydrate ...22g	Saturates 2g	

 15 MINS   60 MINS

SERVES 4

INGREDIENTS

1 tbsp oil

100 g/3½ oz lean smoked back bacon, finely chopped

1 onion, finely chopped

1–2 garlic cloves, finely chopped or crushed

2 tbsp plain (all-purpose) flour

1.2 litres/2 pints/5 cups water

1 leek, thinly sliced

1 carrot, finely chopped

1 small potato, finely chopped

500 g/1 lb 2 oz green beans

1 bay leaf

freshly grated nutmeg

salt and pepper

garlic croûtons, to garnish

1 Heat the oil in a large wide saucepan over a medium heat. Add the bacon and cook for 8–10 minutes until golden. Remove the bacon from the pan with a

VARIATION

Use frozen green beans instead of fresh if you wish. There is no need to defrost them.

slotted spoon and drain on paper towels. Pour off all the fat from the pan.

2 Add the onion and garlic to the pan and cook for about 3 minutes, stirring frequently, until the onion begins to soften.

3 Stir in the flour and continue cooking for 2 minutes. Add half of the water and stir well, scraping the bottom of the pan to mix in the flour.

4 Add the leek, carrot, potato, beans and bay leaf. Stir in the remaining water and season with salt and pepper. Bring just to the boil, stirring occasionally, reduce the heat and simmer, partially covered, for 35–40 minutes, or until the beans are very tender.

5 Allow the soup to cool slightly, then transfer to a blender or food processor, and purée until smooth, working in batches if necessary. (If using a food processor, strain off the cooking liquid and reserve. Purée the soup solids with enough cooking liquid to moisten them, then combine with the remaining liquid.)

6 Return the soup to the saucepan, add the bacon and simmer over a low heat for a few minutes until heated through, stirring occasionally. Taste and adjust the seasoning, adding nutmeg, pepper and, if needed, more salt. Sprinkle with croûtons to serve.

Broad Bean Soup

Fresh broad beans are best for this scrumptious soup, but if they are unavailable, use frozen beans instead.

NUTRITIONAL INFORMATION

Calories 224	Sugars 4g	
Protein 12g	Fat 6g	
Carbohydrate ...31g	Saturates 1g	

 15 MINS   40 MINS

SERVES 4

INGREDIENTS

2 tbsp olive oil

1 red onion, chopped

2 garlic cloves, crushed

2 potatoes, diced

500 g/1 lb 2 oz/3 cups broad (fava) beans,
   thawed if frozen

850 ml/1½ pints/3¾ cups vegetable stock

2 tbsp freshly chopped mint

mint sprigs and natural
   (unsweetened) yogurt, to garnish

1 Heat the olive oil in a large saucepan. Add the onion and garlic and sauté for 2–3 minutes, until softened.

2 Add the potatoes and cook, stirring constantly, for 5 minutes.

3 Stir in the beans and the stock, cover and simmer for 30 minutes, or until the beans and potatoes are tender.

4 Remove a few vegetables with a slotted spoon and set aside until required. Place the remainder of the soup in a food processor or blender and process until smooth.

5 Return the soup to a clean saucepan and add the reserved vegetables and chopped mint. Stir thoroughly and heat through gently.

6 Transfer the soup to a warm tureen or individual serving bowls. Garnish with swirls of yogurt and sprigs of fresh mint and serve immediately.

VARIATION

Use fresh coriander (cilantro) and ½ tsp ground cumin as flavourings in the soup, if you prefer.

Green Soup

This fresh-tasting soup with green beans, cucumber and watercress can be served warm, or chilled on a hot summer day.

NUTRITIONAL INFORMATION

Calories 121   Sugars 2g
Protein . . . . .2g   Fat 8g
Carbohydrate . . .10g   Saturates 1g

 5 MINS   🕐 25–30 MINS

SERVES 4

I N G R E D I E N T S

1 tbsp olive oil

1 onion, chopped

1 garlic clove, chopped

200 g/7 oz potato, peeled and cut into
   2.5 cm/1 inch cubes

700 ml/1 ¼ pints/scant 3 cups vegetable or
   chicken stock

1 small cucumber or ½ large cucumber, cut
   into chunks

80 g/3 oz bunch watercress

125 g/4 ½ oz green (dwarf) beans, trimmed
   and halved lengthwise

salt and pepper

VARIATION

Try using 125 g/4 ½ oz
mange tout (snow peas)
instead of the beans, if
you prefer.

1 Heat the oil in a large pan and fry the onion and garlic for 3–4 minutes or until softened.

2 Add the cubed potato and fry for a further 2–3 minutes.

3 Stir in the stock, bring to the boil and leave to simmer for 5 minutes.

4 Add the cucumber to the pan and cook for a further 3 minutes or until the potatoes are tender. Test by inserting the tip of a knife into the potato cubes – it should pass through easily.

5 Add the watercress and allow to wilt. Then place the soup in a food processor and blend until smooth. Alternatively, before adding the watercress, mash the soup with a potato masher and push through a sieve, then chop the watercress finely and stir into the soup.

6 Bring a small pan of water to the boil and steam the beans for 3–4 minutes or until tender.

7 Add the beans to the soup, season and warm through.

Tarragon Pea Soup

This soup is simple and quick to make using frozen peas and stock made from a cube, ingredients you are likely to have on hand.

NUTRITIONAL INFORMATION

Calories 147   Sugars 6g
Protein ....9g   Fat 4g
Carbohydrate ...20g   Saturates 2g

 15 MINS   60 MINS

SERVES 4

INGREDIENTS

2 tsp butter

1 onion, finely chopped

2 leeks, finely chopped

1 ½ tbsp white rice

500 g/1 lb 2 oz frozen peas

1 litre/1¾ pints/4 cups water

1 chicken or vegetable stock cube

½ tsp dried tarragon

salt and pepper

chopped hard-boiled (hard-cooked) egg or croûtons, to garnish

1 Melt the butter in a large saucepan over a medium-low heat. Add the onion, leeks and rice. Cover and cook for about 10 minutes, stirring occasionally, until the vegetables are soft.

2 Add the peas, water, stock cube and tarragon and bring just to the boil. Season with a little pepper. Cover and simmer for about 35 minutes, stirring occasionally, until the vegetables are very tender.

3 Allow the soup to cool slightly, then transfer to a blender or food processor and purée until smooth, working in batches if necessary. (If using a food processor, strain off the cooking liquid and reserve. Purée the soup solids with enough cooking liquid to moisten them, then combine with the remaining liquid.)

4 Return the puréed soup to the saucepan. Taste and adjust the seasoning, adding plenty of pepper and, if needed, salt. Gently reheat the soup over a low heat for about 10 minutes until hot.

5 Ladle into warm bowls and garnish with egg or croûtons.

COOK'S TIP

The rice gives the soup a little extra body, but a small amount of raw or cooked potato would do the same job.

VARIATION

Substitute frozen green beans for the peas and omit the tarragon, replacing it with a little dried thyme and/or marjoram.

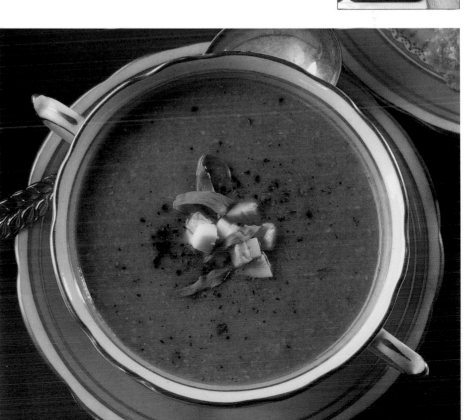

Broccoli Soup

This soup highlights the rich flavour of broccoli. It is a popular vegetable with almost everyone and particularly healthy.

NUTRITIONAL INFORMATION

Calories	208	Sugar	.........5g
Protein	.........6g	Fats	..........16g
Carbohydrates	...10g	Saturates	......9g

  15 MINS   40 MINS

SERVES 4

INGREDIENTS

400 g/14 oz broccoli (from 1 large head)

2 tsp butter

1 tsp oil

1 onion, finely chopped

1 leek, thinly sliced

1 small carrot, finely chopped

3 tbsp white rice

850 ml/1½ pints/3¾ cups water

1 bay leaf

4 tbsp double (heavy) cream

100 g/3½ oz soft (cream) cheese

freshly grated nutmeg

salt and pepper

croûtons, to serve (see Cook's Tip)

1 Divide the broccoli into small florets and cut off the stems. Peel the large stems and chop all the stems into small pieces.

2 Heat the butter and oil in a large saucepan over a medium heat and add the onion, leek and carrot. Cook for 3–4 minutes, stirring frequently, until the onion is soft.

3 Add the broccoli stems, rice, water, bay leaf and a pinch of salt. Bring just to the boil and reduce the heat to low.

Cover and simmer for 15 minutes. Add the broccoli florets and continue cooking, covered, for 15–20 minutes until the rice and vegetables are tender. Remove the bay leaf.

4 Season the soup with nutmeg, pepper and, if needed, more salt. Stir in the cram and soft cheese. Simmer over a low heat for a few minutes until heated through, stirring occasionally. Taste and adjust the seasoning, if needed. Ladle into warm bowls and serve sprinkled with croûtons.

COOK'S TIP

To make croûtons, remove the crusts from thick slices of bread, then cut the bread into dice. Fry in vegetable oil, stirring constantly, until evenly browned, then drain on paper towels.

Silky Spinach Soup

This soup has a rich brilliant colour and an intense pure flavour. You can taste the goodness!

NUTRITIONAL INFORMATION

Calories	69	Sugars	.........4g
Protein	.........4g	Fat	...........4g
Carbohydrate	....5g	Saturates	......1g

10 MINS   40 MINS

SERVES 4

INGREDIENTS

1 tbsp olive oil

1 onion, halved and thinly sliced

1 leek, split lengthways and thinly sliced

1 potato, finely diced

1 litre/1¾ pints/4 cups water

2 sprigs fresh marjoram or ¼ tsp dried

2 sprigs fresh thyme or ¼ tsp dried

1 bay leaf

400 g/14 oz young spinach, washed

freshly grated nutmeg

salt and pepper

4 tbsp single (light) cream, to serve

1 Heat the oil in a heavy-based saucepan over a medium heat. Add the onion and leek and cook for about 3 minutes, stirring occasionally, until they begin to soften.

2 Add the potato, water, marjoram, thyme and bay leaf, along with a large pinch of salt. Bring to the boil, reduce the heat, cover and cook gently for about 25 minutes until the vegetables are tender. Remove the bay leaf and the herb stems.

3 Add the spinach and continue cooking for 3–4 minutes, stirring frequently, just until it is completely wilted.

4 Allow the soup to cool slightly, then transfer to a blender or food processor and purée until smooth, working in batches if necessary. (If using a food processor, strain off the cooking liquid and reserve. Purée the soup solids with enough cooking liquid to moisten them, then combine with the remaining liquid.)

5 Return the soup to the saucepan and thin with a little more water, if wished. Season with salt, a good grinding of pepper and a generous grating of nutmeg. Place over a low heat and simmer until reheated.

6 Ladle the soup into warm bowls and swirl a table-spoonful of cream into each serving.

Cream Cheese & Herb Soup

Make the most of home-grown herbs to create this wonderfully creamy soup with its marvellous garden-fresh fragrance.

NUTRITIONAL INFORMATION

Calories ....275 Sugars 5g
Protein ....7g Fat 22g
Carbohydrate ...14g Saturates 11g

15 MINS   35 MINS

SERVES 4

I N G R E D I E N T S

25 g/1 oz/2 tbsp butter or margarine

2 onions, chopped

850 ml/1½ pints/3½ cups vegetable stock

25 g/1 oz coarsely chopped mixed
    herbs, such as parsley, chives, thyme,
    basil and oregano

200 g/7 oz/1 cup full-fat soft cheese

1 tbsp cornflour (cornstarch)

1 tbsp milk

chopped chives, to garnish

1 Melt the butter or margarine in a large, heavy-based saucepan. Add the onions and fry over a medium heat for 2 minutes, then cover and turn the heat to low. Continue to cook the onions for 5 minutes, then remove the lid.

2 Add the vegetable stock and herbs to the saucepan. Bring to the boil over a moderate heat. Lower the heat, cover and simmer gently for 20 minutes.

3 Remove the saucepan from the heat. Transfer the soup to a food processor or blender and process for about 15 seconds, until smooth. Alternatively, press it through a strainer with the back of a wooden spoon. Return the soup to the saucepan.

4 Reserve a little of the cheese for garnish. Spoon the remaining cheese into the soup and whisk until it has melted and is incorporated.

5 Mix the cornflour (cornstarch) with the milk to a paste, then stir the mixture into the soup. Heat, stirring constantly, until thickened and smooth.

6 Pour the soup into warmed individual bowls. Spoon some of the reserved cheese into each bowl and garnish with chives. Serve at once.

Onion & Broad Bean Soup

This soup has well-balanced vegetable flavours and a satisfying crunch from the crispy bacon. It makes a good lunch, served with crusty bread.

NUTRITIONAL INFORMATION

Calories	.213	Sugar	.8g
Protein	.10g	Fats	.9g
Carbohydrates	.24g	Saturates	.4g

 15 MINS   1 HOUR 10 MINS

SERVES 4

INGREDIENTS

1 tbsp butter

2 tsp oil

2 large onions, finely chopped

1 leek, thinly sliced

1 garlic clove, crushed

1.2 litres/2 pints/5 cups water

75 g/2 ¾ oz/6 tbsp white rice

1 bay leaf

½ tsp chopped fresh rosemary leaves

½ tsp chopped fresh thyme leaves

350 g/12 oz fresh or defrosted frozen broad (fava) beans

100 g/3½ oz rindless streaky bacon, finely chopped

350 ml/12 fl oz/1½ cups milk, plus extra if needed

freshly grated nutmeg

salt and pepper

1 Heat the butter and half the oil in a large saucepan over a medium heat. Add the onions, leek and garlic. Season with salt and pepper and cook for 10–15 minutes, stirring frequently, until the onion is soft.

2 Add the water, rice and herbs with a large pinch of salt. Bring just to the boil and reduce the heat to low. Cover and simmer for 15 minutes.

3 Add the broad (fava) beans, cover again and continue simmering for a further 15 minutes, or until the vegetables are tender.

4 Allow the soup to cool a bit, transfer to a blender or food processor and purée until smooth, working in batches if necessary. (If using a food processor, strain off the cooking liquid and reserve. Purée the soup solids with enough cooking liquid to moisten them, then combine with the remaining liquid.)

5 Heat the remaining oil in a small frying pan (skillet) over a medium-low heat. Add the bacon and cook until crispy, stirring occasionally. Drain on paper towels.

6 Return the soup to the sauce-pan and stir in the milk, adding a little extra for a thinner soup. Taste and adjust the seasoning, adding salt and pepper to taste and a good grating of nutmeg. Simmer over a low heat for about 10 minutes until heated through, stirring occasionally. Ladle the soup into warm bowls and sprinkle with bacon. Serve immediately.

Parsnip & Orange Soup

The exotic flavours give this simple soup a lift. If you wish, use bought ginger purée instead of grating it.

NUTRITIONAL INFORMATION

Calories 142   Sugars 16g
Protein ....4g   Fat 3g
Carbohydrate ...27g   Saturates 0g

15 MINS   60 MINS

SERVES 4

INGREDIENTS

2 tsp olive oil

1 large onion, chopped

1 large leek, sliced

2 carrots, thinly sliced

800 g/1 lb 12 oz parsnips, sliced

4 tbsp grated peeled fresh ginger root (about 60 g/2 oz)

2–3 garlic cloves, finely chopped

grated rind of ½ orange

1.4 litres/2½ pints/6 cups water

225 ml/8 fl oz/1 cup orange juice

salt and pepper

snipped chives or slivers of spring onion (scallion), to garnish

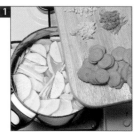

1 Heat the olive oil in a large saucepan over a medium heat. Add the onion and leek and cook for about 5 minutes, stirring occasionally, until softened,

2 Add the parsnips, carrots, ginger, garlic, grated orange rind, water and a large pinch of salt. Reduce the heat, cover and simmer for about 40 minutes, stirring occasionally, until the vegetables are very soft.

3 Allow the soup to cool slightly, then transfer to a blender or food processor and purée until smooth, working in batches if necessary. (If using a food processor, strain off the cooking liquid and reserve. Purée the soup solids with enough cooking liquid to moisten them, then combine with the remaining liquid.)

4 Return the soup to the saucepan and stir in the orange juice. Add a little water or more orange juice, if you prefer a thinner consistency. Taste and adjust the seasoning with salt and pepper

5 Then simmer for about 10 minutes to heat through. Ladle into warm bowls, garnish with chives or slivers of spring onion (scallion) and serve.

VARIATION

You could make the soup using equal amounts (450 g/1 lb each) of carrots and parsnips.

Wild Mushroom Soup

This soup has an intense, earthy flavour that brings to mind woodland aromas. It makes a memorable, rich tasting starter.

NUTRITIONAL INFORMATION

Calories 118	Sugars 5g	
Protein 4g	Fat 7g	
Carbohydrate 7g	Saturates 4g	

  15 MINS 1 HOUR 20 MINS

SERVES 4

I N G R E D I E N T S

25 g/1 oz dried porcini mushrooms

350 ml/12 fl oz/1 ½ cups boiling water

125 g/4 ½ oz fresh ceps or porcini mushrooms

2 tsp olive oil

1 stalk celery, chopped

1 carrot, chopped

1 onion, chopped

3 garlic cloves, crushed

1.2 litres/2 pints/5 cups vegetable stock or water

leaves from 2 thyme sprigs

1 tbsp butter

3 tbsp dry or medium sherry

2–3 tbsp soured cream

salt and pepper

chopped fresh parsley, to garnish

1 Put the dried mushrooms in a bowl and pour the boiling water over them. Allow to stand for 10–15 minutes.

2 Brush or wash the fresh mushrooms. Trim and reserve the stalks; slice large mushroom caps.

3 Heat the oil in a large sauce-pan over a medium heat. Add the celery, carrot, onion, and mushroom stems. Cook for

about 8 minutes, stirring frequently, until the onion begins to colour. Stir in the garlic and continue cooling for 1 minute.

4 Add the stock and thyme leaves with a large pinch of salt. Using a slotted spoon, transfer the soaked dried mushrooms to the saucepan. Strain the soaking liquid through a muslin-lined sieve into the pan. Bring to the boil, reduce the heat and simmer, partially covered, for 30–40 minutes, or until the carrots are tender.

5 Allow the soup to cool slightly, then transfer the soup solids with enough of the cooking liquid to moisten to a blender or food processor and purée until smooth. Return it to the saucepan, combine with the remaining cooking liquid and simmer gently, covered.

6 Melt the butter in a frying pan (skillet) over a medium heat. Add the fresh mushroom caps and season with salt and pepper. Cook for about 8 minutes until they start to colour, stirring occasionally at first, then stirring more often as the liquid evaporates. When the pan becomes dry, add the sherry and bubble briefly.

7 Add the mushrooms and sherry to the soup. Taste and adjust the seasoning, if necessary. Ladle into warm bowls, put a dollop of cream in each and garnish with parsley.

Beans & Greens Soup

Include some pungent greens in this soup, if you can. They add a wonderful flavour, and of course are very good for you!

NUTRITIONAL INFORMATION

Calories 257	Sugar 9g
Protein 16g	Fats 4g
Carbohydrates . . .41g	Saturates 1g

 15 MINS   2 HOURS

SERVES 4

I N G R E D I E N T S

250 g/9 oz dried haricot or cannellini beans

1 tbsp olive oil

2 onions, finely chopped

4 garlic cloves, finely chopped

1 stalk celery, thinly sliced

2 carrots, halved and thinly sliced

1.2 litres/2 pints/5 cups water

¼ tsp dried thyme

¼ tsp dried marjoram

1 bay leaf

125 g/4½ oz leafy greens, such as chard, mustard, spinach and kale, washed

salt and pepper

1 Pick over the beans, cover generously with cold water and leave to soak for 6 hours or overnight. Drain the beans, put in a saucepan and add enough cold water to cover by 5 cm/2 inches. Bring to the boil and boil for 10 minutes. Drain and rinse well.

2 Heat the oil in a large sauce-pan over a medium heat. Add the onion and cook, covered, for 3–4 minutes, stirring occasionally, until the onion is just softened. Add the garlic, celery and carrots, and continue cooking for 2 minutes.

3 Add the water, drained beans, thyme, marjoram and bay leaf. When the mixture begins to bubble, reduce the heat to low. Cover and simmer gently, stirring occasionally, for about 1¼ hours until the beans are tender; the cooking time will vary depending on the type of bean. Season with salt and pepper.

4 Allow the soup to cool slightly, then transfer 450 ml/16 fl oz/2 cups to a blender or food processor. Purée until smooth and recombine with the soup.

5 A handful at a time, cut the greens crossways into thin ribbons, keeping tender leaves like spinach separate. Add the thicker leaves and cook gently, uncovered, for 10 minutes. Stir in any remaining greens and continue cooking for 5–10 minutes, until all the greens are tender.

6 Taste and adjust the seasoning, if necessary. Ladle the soup into warm bowls and serve.

Split Pea & Ham Soup

A hearty and heartwarming soup, this is perfect for weekend lunches – or make it ahead for a nourishing mid-week supper, all ready to reheat.

NUTRITIONAL INFORMATION

Calories	275	Sugar	.........5g
Protein	........21g	Fats	...........7g
Carbohydrates	...36g	Saturates	......1g

 10 MINS   🕐 1¾ HOURS

SERVES 6

INGREDIENTS

500 g/1 lb 2 oz split green peas

1 tbsp olive oil

1 large onion, finely chopped

1 large carrot, finely chopped

1 stalk celery, finely chopped

1 litre/1¾ pints/4 cups chicken or vegetable stock

1 litre/1¾ pints/4 cups water

225 g/8 oz lean smoked ham, finely diced

¼ tsp dried thyme

¼ tsp dried marjoram

1 bay leaf

salt and pepper

1 Rinse the peas under cold running water. Put in a saucepan and cover generously with water. Bring to the boil and boil for 3 minutes, skimming off the foam from the surface. Drain the peas.

2 Heat the oil in a large saucepan over a medium heat. Add the onion and cook for 3–4 minutes, stirring occasionally, until just softened.

3 Add the carrot and celery and continue cooking for 2 minutes. Add the peas, pour over the stock and water and stir to combine.

4 Bring just to the boil and stir the ham into the soup. Add the thyme, marjoram and bay leaf. Reduce the heat, cover and cook gently for 1–1½ hours until the ingredients are very soft. Remove the bay leaf.

5 Taste and adjust the seasoning. Ladle into warm soup bowls and serve.

VARIATION

You could add sliced, cooked sausages instead of or in addition to the ham. If you have a ham bone, use in place of the diced ham. Trim off the fat and cook the bone in the soup. Before serving, remove the bone, cut off the meat and return the meat to the soup.

Split Pea & Parsnip Soup

This soup is surprisingly delicate. The yellow peas give it an appealing light colour, while the parsnips add an aromatic flavour.

NUTRITIONAL INFORMATION

Calories	293	Sugars	.........9g
Protein	........16g	Fat	...........7g
Carbohydrate	...44g	Saturates	......1g

 15 MINS   1 HOUR

SERVES 4

INGREDIENTS

250 g/9 oz split yellow peas

1 tbsp olive oil

1 onion, finely chopped

1 small leek, finely chopped

3 garlic cloves, finely chopped

2 parsnips, sliced (about 225 g/8 oz)

2 litres/3½ pints/8 cups water

10 sage leaves, or ¼ tsp dried sage

⅛ tsp dried thyme

¼ tsp ground coriander

1 bay leaf

salt and pepper

freshly grated nutmeg

chopped fresh coriander leaves (cilantro) or
    parsley, to garnish

2 Heat the oil in a large saucepan over a medium heat. Add the onion and leek and cook for about 3 minutes, stirring frequently, until just softened. Add the garlic and parsnips and continue cooking for 2 minutes, stirring occasionally.

3 Add the peas, water, sage, thyme, coriander and bay leaf. Bring almost to the boil, reduce the heat, cover and cook gently for about 40 minutes until the vegetables are very soft. Remove the bay leaf.

4 Allow the soup to cool slightly, then transfer to a blender or food processor and purée until smooth, working in batches if necessary. (If using a food processor, strain off the cooking liquid and reserve. Purée the soup solids with enough cooking liquid to moisten them, then combine with the remaining liquid.)

5 Return the soup to the saucepan and thin with a little more water, if wished. Season generously with salt, pepper and nutmeg. Place over a low heat and simmer until reheated. Ladle into warm soup plates and garnish with fresh coriander leaves (cilantro) or parsley.

1 Rinse the peas well under cold running water. Put in a saucepan and cover generously with water. Bring to the boil and boil for 3 minutes, skimming off the foam from the surface. Drain the peas.

Chickpea & Chorizo Soup

This soup is satisfying and colourful, with an appealing piquancy from the chorizo.

NUTRITIONAL INFORMATION

Calories	382	Sugar	.........11g
Protein	........23g	Fats	..........12g
Carbohydrates	...50g	Saturates	......3g

   15 MINS   1¾ HOURS

SERVES 4

INGREDIENTS

250 g/9 oz dried chick-peas (garbanzo beans), soaked overnight in cold water to cover generously

125 g/4½ oz lean chorizo, peeled and finely diced

1 onion, finely chopped

1 shallot, finely chopped

1 carrot, thinly sliced

2 garlic cloves, finely chopped

400 g/14 oz can chopped tomatoes in juice

1.2 litres/2 pints/5 cups water

1 bay leaf

¼ tsp dried thyme

¼ tsp dried oregano

225 g/8 oz pumpkin, diced

225 g/8 oz potato, diced

125 g/4½ oz curly kale leaves, finely chopped

salt and pepper

COOK'S TIP

You can easily chop the kale in a food processor; it should be like chopped parsley. Alternatively, slice crosswise into very thin ribbons.

1 Drain the chick-peas (garbanzo beans) and put in a saucepan with enough cold water to cover generously. Bring to the boil over a high heat and cook for 10 minutes. Drain.

2 Put the chorizo in a large saucepan over a medium-low heat. Cook for 5–10 minutes, stirring, frequently to render as much fat as possible. Remove with a slotted spoon and drain on paper towels.

3 Pour off the fat and add the onion, shallot, carrot and garlic. Cook for 3–4 minutes.

4 Add the chick-peas (garbanzo beans), tomatoes, water, herbs and chorizo. Bring almost to the boil, reduce the heat, cover and cook gently for 30 minutes.

5 Stir in the pumpkin and potato, cover and continue cooking for about 30 minutes until the chick-peas (garbanzo beans) are tender. Season with salt and pepper.

6 Stir in the kale and continue to cook, uncovered, for 15–20 minutes, or until it is tender. Taste and adjust the seasoning. Ladle into warm bowls and serve.

Potato & Split Pea Soup

Split green peas are sweeter than other varieties of split pea and reduce down to a purée when cooked, which acts as a thickener in soups.

NUTRITIONAL INFORMATION

Calories 260   Sugars 5g
Protein . . . . .11g   Fat 10g
Carbohydrate . . .32g   Saturates 3g

5–10 MINS   45 MINS

SERVES 4

INGREDIENTS

2 tbsp vegetable oil

2 unpeeled floury (mealy) potatoes, diced

2 onions, diced

75 g/2¾ oz split green peas

1 litre/1¾ pints/4½ cups vegetable stock

5 tbsp grated Gruyère cheese

salt and pepper

CROUTONS

40 g/1½ oz/3 tbsp butter

1 garlic clove, crushed

1 tbsp chopped parsley

1 thick slice white bread, cubed

1 Heat the vegetable oil in a large saucepan. Add the potatoes and onions and sauté over a low heat, stirring constantly, for about 5 minutes.

VARIATION

For a richly coloured soup, red lentils could be used instead of split green peas. Add a large pinch of brown sugar to the recipe for extra sweetness if red lentils are used.

2 Add the split green peas to the pan and stir to mix together well.

3 Pour the vegetable stock into the pan and bring to the boil. Reduce the heat to low and simmer for 35 minutes, until the potatoes are tender and the split peas cooked.

4 Meanwhile, make the croûtons. Melt the butter in a frying pan (skillet). Add the garlic, parsley and bread cubes and

cook, turning frequently, for about 2 minutes, until the bread cubes are golden brown on all sides.

5 Stir the grated cheese into the soup and season to taste with salt and pepper. Heat gently until the cheese is starting to melt.

6 Pour the soup into warmed individual bowls and sprinkle the croûtons on top. Serve at once.

Vegetable Chilli Soup

This is a hearty and flavourful soup that is good on its own or spooned over cooked rice or baked potatoes for a more substantial meal.

NUTRITIONAL INFORMATION

Calories .... .209   Sugar .... .10g
Protein ....12g   Fats .... .10g
Carbohydrates ...19g   Saturates 5g

 10 MINS   1 HOUR 15 MINS

SERVES 4

INGREDIENTS

1 medium auberglne (eggplant), peeled if wished, cut into 2.5 cm/1 inch slices

1 tbsp olive oil, plus extra for brushing

1 large red or yellow onion, finely chopped

2 (bell) peppers, finely chopped

3–4 garlic cloves, finely chopped or crushed

2 x 400 g/14 oz cans chopped tomatoes in juice

1 tbsp mild chilli powder, or to taste

½ lsp ground cumin

½ tsp dried oregano

2 small courgettes (zucchini), quartered lengthways and sliced

400 g/14 oz can kidney beans, drained and rinsed

450 ml/16 fl oz/2 cups water

1 tbsp tomato purée (paste)

6 spring onions (scallions), finely chopped

115 g/4 oz grated Cheddar cheese

salt and pepper

1 Brush the aubergine (eggplant) slices on one side with olive oil. Heat half the oil in a large frying pan (skillet) over a medium-high heat. Add the aubergine (eggplant), oiled side up, and cook for 5–6 minutes until browned on one side. Turn, brown the other side and transfer to a plate. Cut into bite-sized pieces.

2 Heat the remaining oil in a large saucepan over a medium heat. Add the onion and (bell) peppers, cover and cook for 3–4 minutes, stirring occasionally, until the onion is just softened. Add the garlic and continue cooking for 2–3 minutes, or until the onion begins to colour.

3 Add the tomatoes, chilli powder, cumin and oregano. Season with salt and pepper. Bring just to the boil, reduce the heat, cover and simmer for 15 minutes.

4 Add the courgettes, (zucchini), aubergine (eggplant) pieces and beans. Stir in the water and tomato purée (paste.) Cover again and continue simmering for about 45 minutes, or until the vegetables are tender. Taste and adjust the seasoning. If you prefer it hotter, stir in a little more chilli powder.

5 Season to taste. Ladle into bowls, and top with spring onions (scallions) and cheese.

Tomato & Lentil Soup

This soup is simple and satisfying, with subtle, slightly exotic flavours.

NUTRITIONAL INFORMATION

Calories	195	Sugar	.........9g
Protein	........12g	Fats	...........3g
Carbohydrates	...33g	Saturates	......0g

10 MINS   55 MINS

SERVES 6

INGREDIENTS

1 tbsp olive oil

1 leek, thinly sliced

1 large carrot, quartered and thinly sliced

1 large onion, finely chopped

2 garlic cloves, finely chopped

250 g/9 oz split red lentils

1.2 litres/2 pints/5 cups water

350 ml/12 fl oz/1½ cups tomato juice

400 g/14 oz can chopped tomatoes in juice

¼ tsp ground cumin

¼ tsp ground coriander

1 bay leaf

salt and pepper

chopped fresh dill or parsley, to garnish

1 Heat the oil in a large saucepan over a medium heat. Add the leek, carrot, onion and garlic. Cover and cook for 4–5 minutes, stirring frequently, until the leek and onion are slightly softened.

2 Rinse and drain the lentils (check for any small stones). Add the lentils to the pan and stir in the water, tomato juice and tomatoes. Add the cumin, coriander and bay leaf with a large pinch of salt. Bring to the boil, reduce the heat and simmer for about 45 minutes, or until the vegetables are tender.

3 If you prefer a smooth soup, allow it to cool slightly, then transfer to a blender or food processor and purée until smooth, working in batches if necessary. (If using a food processor, strain off the cooking liquid and reserve. Purée the soup solids with enough cooking liquid to moisten them, then combine with the remaining liquid.) Only purée about half of the soup, if you prefer a more chunky soup.

4 Return the puréed soup to the saucepan and stir to blend. Season with salt and pepper to taste. Simmer over a medium-low heat until reheated.

5 Ladle the soup into warm bowls, garnish with dill or parsley and serve.

Curried Lentil & Onion Soup

This soup is a typical Indian treatment of lentils, called dhal.

NUTRITIONAL INFORMATION

Calories 232	Sugars 6g	
Protein 11g	Fat 8g	
Carbohydrate ...31g	Saturates 1g	

  10 MINS   55 MINS

SERVES 4

INGREDIENTS

2 tsp olive oil

1 large onion, finely chopped

1 large leek, thinly sliced

1 large carrot, grated

1–2 garlic cloves, finely chopped

½ tsp chilli purée (paste)

½ tsp grated peeled fresh ginger root or
ginger purée (paste)

⅓ tsp garam masala or curry powder

¼ tsp ground cumin

⅛ tsp ground turmeric

1.2 litres/2 pints/5 cups water

250 g/9 oz split red lentils or yellow split
peas

salt and pepper

TO GARNISH

1 red onion, halved and thinly sliced into
half-rings

oil, for frying

1 Heat the olive oil in a large saucepan over a medium heat. Add the onion and cook for 4–5 minutes, stirring frequently, until it just begins to brown. Add the leek, carrot and garlic and continue cooking for 2 minutes, stirring occasionally.

2 Stir in the chilli purée (paste), ginger, garam masala or curry powder, cumin and turmeric. Add the water and stir to mix well.

3 Rinse and drain the lentils (check for any small stones). Add to the saucepan. Bring to the boil, reduce the heat, cover and simmer gently for 35 minutes, or until the lentils and vegetables are very soft, stirring occasionally.

4 Allow the soup to cool slightly, then transfer to a blender or food processor and purée until smooth, working in batches if necessary. (If using a food processor, strain off the cooking liquid and reserve. Purée the soup solids with enough cooking liquid to moisten them, then combine with the remaining liquid.)

5 Return the soup to the saucepan and simmer over a low heat. Season with salt and pepper to taste.

6 For the fried onion garnish, heat oil to a depth of about 1 cm/½ inch in a small frying pan (skillet) over a medium-high heat until it begins to smoke. Drop in about one-third of the onion slices and fry until deep golden brown. Using a slotted spoon, transfer to paper towels and drain. Cook the remainder of the onion slices in batches and drain.

7 Ladle the soup into warm bowls and scatter the fried onions over the top. Serve the soup immediately.

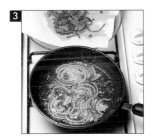

Lentil, Potato & Ham Soup

A comforting and satisfying cold-weather soup, this is good served with bread as a light main course,

NUTRITIONAL INFORMATION

Calories 254	Sugar 6g
Protein 19g	Fats 4g
Carbohydrates ...38g	Saturates 1g

 10 MINS   45 MINS

SERVES 5

I N G R E D I E N T S

300 g/10½ oz Puy lentils

2 tsp butter

1 large onion, finely chopped

2 carrots, finely chopped

1 garlic clove, finely chopped

450 ml/16 fl oz/2 cups water

1 bay leaf

¼ tsp dried sage or rosemary

225 g/8 oz potatoes, diced
  (see Cook's Tip)

1 litre/1¾ pints/4 cups chicken stock

1 tbsp tomato purée (paste)

125 g/4 oz smoked ham, finely diced

salt and pepper

chopped fresh parsley, to garnish

1 Rinse and drain the lentils and check for any small stones.

2 Melt the butter in a large saucepan or flameproof casserole over a medium heat. Add the onion, carrots and garlic, cover and cook for 4–5 minutes until the onion is slightly softened, stirring frequently.

3 Add the lentils to the vegetables with the water, bay leaf and sage or rosemary. Bring to the boil, reduce the heat, cover and simmer for 10 minutes.

4 Add the stock, potatoes, tomato purée (paste) and ham. Bring back to a simmer. Cover and continue simmering for 25–30 minutes, or until the vegetables are tender.

5 Season to taste with salt and pepper and remove the bay leaf. Ladle into warm bowls, garnish with parsley and serve.

COOK'S TIP

Cut the potatoes into small dice, about 5 mm/¼ inch, so they will be in proportion with the lentils.

Vegetable & Lentil Soup

In this simple-to-make soup, the flavours meld after blending to create a delicious taste. It is also very healthy and looks appealing.

NUTRITIONAL INFORMATION

Calories	165	Sugars	.........8g
Protein	........11g	Fat	...........3g
Carbohydrate	...25g	Saturates	......0g

15 MINS   50 MINS

SERVES 6

I N G R E D I E N T S

1 tbsp olive oil

1 onion, finely chopped

1 garlic clove, finely chopped

1 carrot, halved and thinly sliced

450 g/1 lb young green cabbage, cored, quartered and thinly sliced

400 g/14 oz can chopped tomatoes in juice

½ tsp dried thyme

2 bay leaves

1.5 litres/2¾ pints/6¼ cups chicken or vegetable stock

200 g/7 oz Puy lentils

450 ml/16 fl oz/2 cups water

salt and pepper

fresh coriander leaves (cilantro) or parsley, to garnish

1 Heat the oil in a large saucepan over a medium heat, add the onion, garlic and carrot and cook for 3–4 minutes, stirring frequently, until the onion starts to soften. Add the cabbage and cook for a further 2 minutes.

2 Add the tomatoes, thyme and 1 bay leaf, then pour in the stock. Bring to the boil, reduce the heat to low and cook gently, partially covered, for about 45 minutes until the vegetables are tender.

3 Meanwhile, put the lentils in another saucepan with the remaining bay leaf and the water. Bring just to the boil, reduce the heat and simmer for about 25 minutes until tender. Drain off any remaining water, and set aside.

4 When the vegetable soup is cooked, allow it to cool slightly, then transfer to a blender or food processor and purée until smooth, working in batches, if necessary. (If using a food processor, strain off the cooking liquid and reserve. Purée the soup solids with enough cooking liquid to moisten them, then combine with the remaining liquid.)

5 Return the soup to the saucepan and add the cooked lentils. Taste and adjust the seasoning, and cook for about 10 minutes to heat through. Ladle into warm bowls and garnish with coriander leaves (cilantro) or parsley.

Barley & Fennel Soup

This rustic vegetable soup is appealing in its simplicity. Serve it with ciabatta, focaccia or garlic bread.

NUTRITIONAL INFORMATION

Calories	...109	Sugar	...3g
Protein	...5g	Fats	...3g
Carbohydrates	...16g	Saturates	...0g

 15 MINS 1¼ HOURS

SERVES 4

INGREDIENTS

60 g/2 oz pearl barley

1.5 litres/2¾ pints/6¼ cups chicken or vegetable stock

1 bay leaf

½ tsp chopped fresh thyme leaves, or ⅛ tsp dried thyme

250 g/9 oz broccoli head

2 tsp olive oil

1 large leek, halved lengthways and finely chopped

2 garlic cloves, finely chopped

1 stalk celery, thinly sliced

1 large fennel bulb, thinly sliced
1 tbsp chopped fresh basil

freshly grated Parmesan cheese, to serve

2 Cut the florets off the broccoli head and peel the stem. Cut the stem into very thin matchsticks, about 2.5 cm/1 inch long, along with any large stems from the florets. Cut the florets into small slivers and reserve them seperately.

3 Heat the oil in a large pan over a medium-low heat and add the leek and garlic. Cover and cook for about 5 minutes, stirring frequently, until softened. Add the celery, fennel and broccoli stems and cook for 2 minutes.

4 Stir in the remaining stock and bring to the boil. Add the barley with its cooking liquid. Season with salt and pepper. Reduce the heat, cover and simmer gently for 10 minutes, stirring occasionally.

5 Uncover the pan and adjust the heat so the soup bubbles gently. Stir in the broccoli florets and continue cooking for 10–12 minutes, or until the broccoli is tender. Stir in the basil. Taste and adjust the seasoning, if necessary. Ladle into warm bowls and serve with plenty of Parmesan cheese to sprinkle over.

1 Rinse the barley and drain. Bring 450 ml/16 fl oz/2 cups of the stock to the boil in a small saucepan. Add the bay leaf and thyme. If the stock is unsalted, add a large pinch of salt. Stir in the barley, reduce the heat, partially cover and simmer for 30–40 minutes until tender.

Wild Rice & Spinach Soup

Although it is generally classed as a grain, wild rice is actually a native North American grass that grows in water.

NUTRITIONAL INFORMATION

Calories 602	Sugar 12g	
Protein 14g	Fats 39g	
Carbohydrates . . .51g	Saturates 20g	

 15 MINS   1¼ HOURS

SERVES 4

INGREDIENTS

2 tsp olive oil

80 g/3 oz smoked back (Canadian) bacon, finely chopped

1 large onion, finely chopped

120 g/4½ oz/ ⅔ cup wild rice, rinsed in cold water and drained

1.2 litres/2 pints/5 cups water

1–2 garlic cloves, finely chopped or crushed

1 bay leaf

70 g/2½ oz/ ½ cup plain (all-purpose) flour

450 ml/16 fl oz/2 cups milk

225 g/8 oz spinach leaves, finely chopped

225 ml/8 fl oz/1 cup double (heavy) cream

freshly grated nutmeg

salt and pepper

1 Heat the oil in a large saucepan over a medium heat. Add the bacon and cook for 6–7 minutes until lightly browned. Add the onion and wild rice and continue cooking for 3–4 minutes, stirring frequently, until the onion softens.

2 Add the water, garlic and bay leaf and season with a little salt and pepper. Bring to the boil, reduce the heat, cover and boil very gently for about 1 hour, or

until some of the grains of wild rice have split open.

3 Put the flour in a mixing bowl and very slowly whisk in enough of the milk to make a thick paste. Add the remainder of the milk, whisking to make a smooth liquid. Put the flour and milk mixture in a saucepan and ladle in as much of the rice cooking liquid as possible. Bring to the boil, stirring almost constantly. Reduce the heat so that the liquid just bubbles gently and cook for 10 minutes, stirring occasionally. Add the spinach and cook for 1–2 minutes until wilted.

4 Allow the soup to cool slightly, then transfer to a blender or food processor and purée, working in batches if necessary. (If using a food processor, strain off the cooking liquid and reserve. Purée the soup solids with enough cooking liquid to moisten them, then combine with the remaining liquid.)

5 Combine the puréed soup with the rice mixture in a saucepan and place over a medium-low heat. Stir in the cream and a grating of nutmeg. Simmer the soup until reheated. Taste and adjust the seasoning, if needed, and ladle into warm bowls.

Tomato & Rice Soup

This is a good soup for impromptu entertaining, especially if you have leftover rice to hand.

 15 MINS   1¼ HOURS

SERVES 4

INGREDIENTS

1 tbsp olive oil

1 large onion, finely chopped

2 garlic cloves, finely chopped or crushed

2 carrots, grated

1 stalk celery, thinly sliced

2 x 400 g/14 oz cans plum tomatoes in juice

1 tsp dark brown sugar, or to taste

850 ml/1½ pints/3¾ cups vegetable stock or water

1 bay leaf

175 g/6 oz/1 cup cooked white rice

2 tbsp chopped fresh dill

80 ml/ 2¾ fl oz/6 tbsp double (heavy) cream

salt and pepper

fresh dill sprigs, to garnish

1 Heat the olive oil in a large saucepan over a medium heat. Add the onion, cover and cook for 3–4 minutes, stirring occasionally, until the onion is just softened.

2 Add the garlic, carrots, celery, tomatoes, brown sugar and stock or water with the bay leaf to the saucepan. Reduce the heat, cover and simmer for 1 hour, stirring occasionally.

3 Allow the soup to cool slightly, then transfer to a blender or food processor and purée until smooth, working in batches if necessary. (If using a food processor, strain off the cooking liquid and reserve. Purée the soup solids with enough cooking liquid to moisten them, then combine with the remaining liquid.)

4 Return the soup to the saucepan and stir in the rice and dill. Season with salt, if needed, and pepper. Cook gently over a medium-low heat for about 5 minutes, or until hot.

5 Stir in the cream. Taste the soup and adjust the seasoning, if necessary. Ladle into warm soup bowls and garnish each serving with a swirl of cream and dill sprigs. Serve at once.

Vegetable Soup with Bulgur

This healthy and colourful soup makes good use of your herb garden.
The fresh herbs give it a vibrant flavour.

NUTRITIONAL INFORMATION

Calories 110	Sugars 7g	
Protein 5g	Fat 3g	
Carbohydrate . . .17g	Saturates 0g	

 15 MINS   50 MINS

SERVES 5

I N G R E D I E N T S

1 tbsp olive oil

2 onions, chopped

3 garlic cloves, finely chopped or crushed

50 g/1¾ oz/⅓ cup bulgur wheat

5 tomatoes, skinned and sliced, or 400 g/
    14 oz can plum tomatoes in juice

225 g/8 oz peeled pumpkin or acorn
    squash, diced

1 large courgette (zucchini), quartered
    lengthways and sliced

1 litre/1¾ pints/4 cups boiling water

2 tbsp tomato purée (paste)

¼ tsp chilli purée (paste)

40 g/1½ oz chopped mixed fresh oregano,
    basil and flat-leaf parsley

25 g/1 oz rocket (arugula) leaves, coarsely
    chopped

175 g/6 oz/1⅓ cups shelled fresh or
    frozen peas

salt and pepper

freshly grated Parmesan cheese, to serve

1 Heat the oil in a large saucepan over a medium-low heat and add the onions and garlic. Cover and cook for 5–8 minutes until the onions soften.

2 Stir in the bulgur wheat and continue cooking for 1 minute.

3 Layer the tomatoes, pumpkin or squash and courgette (zucchini) in the saucepan.

4 Combine half the water with the tomato purée (paste), chilli purée (paste) and a large pinch of salt. Pour over the vegetables. Cover and simmer for 15 minutes.

5 Uncover the saucepan and stir. Put all the herbs and the rocket (arugula) on top of the soup and layer the peas over them. Pour over the remaining water and gently bring to the boil. Reduce the heat and simmer for about 20–25 minutes, or until all the vegetables are tender.

6 Stir the soup. Taste and adjust the seasoning, adding salt and pepper if necessary, and a little more chilli purée (paste) if you wish. Ladle into warm bowls and serve with Parmesan cheese.

Hot &
Spicy Soups

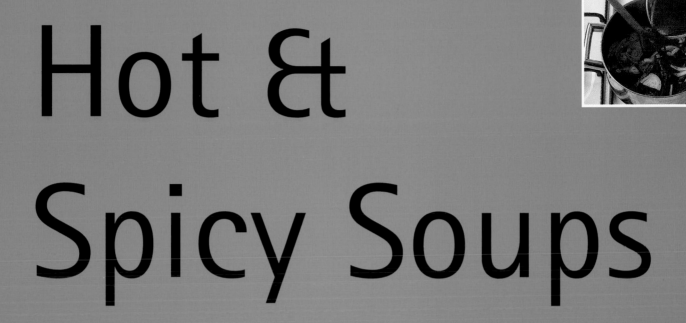

Soups are a part of nearly every meal in the Far East, and are usually served between courses to clear the palate. This chapter

provides a range of soups from all over the Far East, from thick Indian dhal soups to hot, sour Chinese vegetarian soups and combinations of seafood and noodles. All the ingredients are readily available from good stores, and although several recipes demand a little time, all are worth any extra effort in the making.

Curried Parsnip Soup

Parsnips make a delicious soup as they have a slightly sweet flavour. In this recipe, spices are added to complement this sweetness.

NUTRITIONAL INFORMATION

Calories 152	Sugars 7g
Protein 3g	Fat 8g
Carbohydrate ...18g	Saturates 3g

 10 MINS   35 MINS

SERVES 4

INGREDIENTS

1 tbsp vegetable oil

15 g/½ oz/1 tbsp butter

1 red onion, chopped

3 parsnips, chopped

2 garlic cloves, crushed

2 tsp garam masala

½ tsp chilli powder

1 tbsp plain (all-purpose) flour

850 ml/1½ pints/3¾ cups vegetable stock

grated rind and juice of 1 lemon

salt and pepper

lemon rind, to garnish

1 Heat the oil and butter in a large saucepan until the butter has melted. Add the onion, parsnips and garlic and sauté, stirring frequently, for about 5–7 minutes, until the vegetables have softened, but not coloured.

2 Add the garam masala and chilli powder and cook, stirring constantly, for 30 seconds. Sprinkle in the flour, mixing well and cook, stirring constantly, for a further 30 seconds.

3 Stir in the stock, lemon rind and juice and bring to the boil. Reduce the heat and simmer for 20 minutes.

4 Remove some of the vegetable pieces with a slotted spoon and reserve until required. Process the remaining soup and vegetables in a food processor or blender for about 1 minute, or until a smooth purée. Alternatively, press the vegetables through a strainer with the back of a wooden spoon.

5 Return the soup to a clean saucepan and stir in the reserved vegetables. Heat the soup through for 2 minutes until piping hot.

6 Season to taste with salt and pepper, then transfer to soup bowls, garnish with grated lemon rind and serve.

Curried Courgette Soup

This soup is lightly curried to allow the delicate flavour of the courgettes to come through.

NUTRITIONAL INFORMATION

Calories 147	Sugars 8g
Protein 6g	Fat 9g
Carbohydrate ...10g	Saturates 5g

 10 MINS 35 MINS

SERVES 4

I N G R E D I E N T S

2 tsp butter

1 large onion, finely chopped

900 g/2 lb courgettes (zucchini), sliced

450 ml/16 fl oz/2 cups chicken or vegetable stock

1 tsp curry powder

120 ml/4 fl oz/ ½ cup soured cream

salt and pepper

1 Melt the butter in a large saucepan over a medium heat. Add the onion and cook for about 3 minutes until it begins to soften.

2 Add the stock, courgettes (zucchini) and curry powder, along with a large pinch of salt if using unsalted stock. Bring the soup to the boil, reduce the heat, cover and cook gently for about 25 minutes until the vegetables are tender.

3 Allow the soup to cool slightly, then transfer to a blender or food processor, working in batches if necessary. Purée the soup until just smooth, but still with green flecks. (If using a food processor, strain off the cooking liquid and reserve. Purée the soup solids with enough cooking liquid to moisten them, then combine with the remaining liquid.)

4 Return the soup to the saucepan and stir in the soured cream. Reheat gently over a low heat just until hot. (Do not boil.)

5 Taste and adjust the seasoning, if needed. Ladle into warm bowls and serve.

COOK'S TIP

Stock made from a cube or liquid stock base is fine for this soup. In this case, you may wish to add a little more soured cream. The soup freezes well, but freeze it without the cream and add before serving.

Indian Potato & Pea Soup

A slightly hot and spicy Indian flavour is given to this soup with the use of garam masala, chilli, cumin and coriander.

NUTRITIONAL INFORMATION

Calories	153	Sugars	.........6g
Protein	.........6g	Fat	...........6g
Carbohydrate	...18g	Saturates	.......1g

10 MINS   35 MINS

SERVES 4

I N G R E D I E N T S

2 tbsp vegetable oil

225 g/8 oz floury (mealy) potatoes, diced

1 large onion, chopped

2 garlic cloves, crushed

1 tsp garam masala

1 tsp ground coriander

1 tsp ground cumin

850 ml/1½ pints/3¾ cups vegetable stock

1 red chilli, chopped

100 g/3½ oz/scant 1 cup frozen peas

4 tbsp natural (unsweetened) yogurt

salt and pepper

chopped coriander (cilantro),
    to garnish

warm bread, to serve

VARIATION

For slightly less heat, seed the chilli before adding it to the soup. Always wash your hands after handling chillies as they contain volatile oils that can irritate the skin and make your eyes burn if you touch your face.

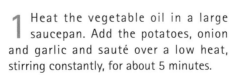

1 Heat the vegetable oil in a large saucepan. Add the potatoes, onion and garlic and sauté over a low heat, stirring constantly, for about 5 minutes.

2 Add the garam masala, ground coriander and cumin and cook, stirring constantly, for 1 minute.

3 Stir in the vegetable stock and chopped red chilli and bring the mixture to the boil. Reduce the heat, cover the pan and simmer for 20 minutes, until the potatoes begin to break down.

4 Add the peas and cook for a further 5 minutes. Stir in the yogurt and season to taste with salt and pepper.

5 Pour into warmed soup bowls, garnish with chopped fresh coriander (cilantro) and serve hot with warm bread.

Indian Bean Soup

A thick and hearty soup, nourishing and substantial enough to serve as a main meal with wholemeal bread.

NUTRITIONAL INFORMATION

Calories . . . . . . .237 Sugars 9g
Protein . . . . .9g Fat 9g
Carbohydrate . . .33g Saturates 1g

 20 MINS   50 MINS

SERVES 6

INGREDIENTS

4 tbsp vegetable ghee or vegetable oil

2 onions, peeled and chopped

225 g/8 oz/1½ cups potato, cut
   into chunks

225 g/8 oz/1½ cups parsnip, cut
   into chunks

225 g/8 oz/1½ cups turnip or swede
   (rutabaga), cut into chunks

2 celery sticks, sliced

2 courgettes (zucchini), sliced

1 green (bell) pepper, seeded and cut into
   1 cm/½ inch pieces

2 garlic cloves, crushed

2 tsp ground coriander

1 tbsp paprika

1 tbsp mild curry paste

1.2 litres/2 pints/5 cups vegetable stock

salt

400 g/14 oz can black-eye beans (peas),
   drained and rinsed

chopped coriander (cilantro),
   to garnish (optional)

1 Heat the ghee or oil in a saucepan, add all the prepared vegetables, except the courgettes (zucchini) and green (bell) pepper, and cook over a moderate heat, stirring frequently, for 5 minutes. Add the garlic, ground coriander, paprika and curry paste and cook, stirring constantly, for 1 minute.

2 Stir in the stock and season with salt to taste. Bring to the boil, cover and simmer over a low heat, stirring occasionally, for 25 minutes.

3 Stir in the black-eye beans (peas), sliced courgettes (zucchini) and green (bell) pepper, cover and continue cooking for a further 15 minutes, or until all the vegetables are tender.

4 Process 300 ml/½ pint/1¼ cups of the soup mixture (about 2 ladlefuls) in a food processor or blender. Return the puréed mixture to the soup in the saucepan and reheat until piping hot. Sprinkle with chopped coriander (cilantro), if using and serve hot.

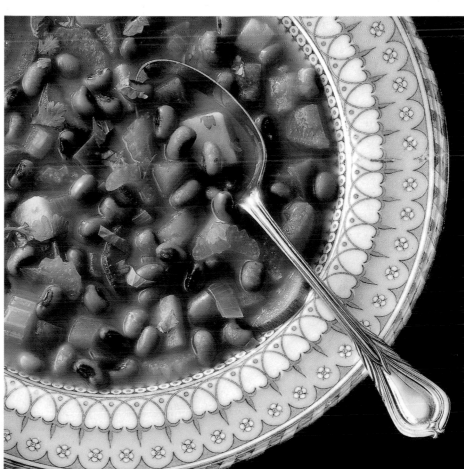

Dhal Soup

Dhal is the name given to a delicious Indian lentil dish. This soup is a variation of the theme – it is made with red lentils and curry powder.

NUTRITIONAL INFORMATION

Calories 284	Sugars 13g
Protein 16g	Fat 9g
Carbohydrate ...38g	Saturates 5g

 5 MINS   40 MINS

SERVES 4

I N G R E D I E N T S

25 g/1 oz/2 tbsp butter

2 garlic cloves, crushed

1 onion, chopped

½ tsp turmeric

1 tsp garam masala

¼ tsp chilli powder

1 tsp ground cumin

1 kg/2 lb 4 oz canned, chopped
    tomatoes, drained

175 g/6 oz/1 cup red lentils

2 tsp lemon juice

600 ml/1 pint/2½ cups vegetable stock

300 ml/½ pint/1¼ cups coconut milk

salt and pepper

chopped coriander (cilantro) and lemon
    slices, to garnish

naan bread, to serve

1 Melt the butter in a large saucepan. Add the garlic and onion and sauté, stirring, for 2–3 minutes. Add the turmeric, garam masala, chilli powder and cumin and cook for a further 30 seconds.

2 Stir in the tomatoes, red lentils, lemon juice, vegetable stock and coconut milk and bring to the boil.

3 Reduce the heat to low and simmer the soup, uncovered, for about 25–30 minutes, until the lentils are tender and cooked.

4 Season to taste with salt and pepper and ladle the soup into a warm tureen. Garnish with chopped coriander (cilantro) and lemon slices and serve immediately with warm naan bread.

COOK'S TIP

You can buy cans of coconut milk from supermarkets and delicatessens. It can also be made by grating creamed coconut, which comes in the form of a solid bar, and then mixing it with water.

Spicy Dhal & Carrot Soup

This delicious, warming and nutritious soup includes a selection of spices to give it a 'kick'. It is simple to make and extremely good to eat.

NUTRITIONAL INFORMATION

Calories	173	Sugars	........11g
Protein	.........9g	Fat	...........5g
Carbohydrate	...24g	Saturates	......1g

 10 MINS   50 MINS

SERVES 6

INGREDIENTS

125 g/4½ oz split red lentils

1.2 litres/2 pints/5 cups vegetable stock

350 g/12 oz carrots, peeled and sliced

2 onions, peeled and chopped

1 x 250 g/9 oz can chopped tomatoes

2 garlic cloves, peeled and chopped

2 tbsp vegetable ghee or oil

1 tsp ground cumin

1 tsp ground coriander

1 fresh green chilli, seeded and chopped, or use 1 tsp minced chilli (from a jar)

½ tsp ground turmeric

15 ml/1 tbsp lemon juice

salt

300 ml/½ pint/1¼ cups skimmed milk

30 ml/2 tbsp chopped fresh coriander (cilantro)

yogurt, to serve

1 Place the lentils in a sieve and wash well under cold running water. Drain and place in a large saucepan with 850 ml/1½ pints/3½ cups of the vegetable stock, the carrots, onions, tomatoes and garlic. Bring the mixture to the boil, reduce the heat, cover and simmer for 30 minutes.

2 Meanwhile, heat the ghee or oil in a small pan, add the cumin, coriander, chilli and turmeric and fry gently for 1 minute.

3 Remove from the heat and stir in the lemon juice and salt to taste.

4 Purée the soup in batches in a blender or food processor. Return the soup to the saucepan, add the spice mixture and the remaining 300 ml/½ pint/ 1¼ cups stock or water and simmer for 10 minutes.

5 Add the milk to the soup and adjust the seasoning according to taste.

6 Stir in the chopped coriander (cilantro) and reheat gently. Serve hot, with a swirl of yogurt.

Indian Potato & Pea Soup

A slightly hot and spicy Indian flavour is given to this soup with the use of garam masala, chilli, cumin and coriander.

NUTRITIONAL INFORMATION

Calories 153   Sugars 6g
Protein . . . . .6g   Fat 6g
Carbohydrate . . .18g   Saturates 1g

🥔 5 MINS   🕐 35 MINS

SERVES 4

INGREDIENTS

2 tbsp vegetable oil

225 g/8 oz floury (mealy) potatoes, diced

1 large onion, chopped

2 garlic cloves, crushed

1 tsp garam masala

1 tsp ground coriander

1 tsp ground cumin

900 ml/1½ pints/3¾ cups vegetable stock

1 red chilli, chopped

100 g/3½ oz frozen peas

4 tbsp low-fat natural yogurt

salt and pepper

chopped fresh coriander (cilantro), to garnish

1 Heat the vegetable oil in a large saucepan and add the diced potatoes, onion and garlic. Sauté gently for about 5 minutes, stirring constantly. Add the ground spices and cook for 1 minute, stirring all the time.

2 Stir in the vegetable stock and chopped red chilli and bring the mixture to the boil. Reduce the heat, cover the pan and simmer for 20 minutes.

3 Add the peas and cook for a further 5 minutes. Stir in the yogurt and season to taste.

4 Pour the soup into warmed bowls, garnish with the chopped fresh coriander (cilantro) and serve hot with warm bread.

COOK'S TIP

For slightly less heat, deseed the chilli before adding it to the soup. Always wash your hands after handling chillies as they contain volatile oils that can irritate the skin and make your eyes burn if you touch your face.

Sweetcorn & Lentil Soup

This pale-coloured soup is made with sweetcorn and green lentils, and is similar in style to the traditional crab and sweetcorn soup.

NUTRITIONAL INFORMATION

Calories	171	Sugars	9g
Protein	5g	Fat	2g
Carbohydrate	30g	Saturates	0.3g

🍲 5 MINS   🕐 30 MINS

SERVES 4

INGREDIENTS

25 g/1 oz/2 tbsp green lentils

1 litre/1¾ pints/4 cups vegetable stock

1 cm/½ inch piece ginger root, chopped finely

2 tsp soy sauce

1 tsp sugar

1 tbsp cornflour (cornstarch)

3 tbsp dry sherry

325 g/11½ oz can sweetcorn

1 egg white

1 tsp sesame oil

salt and pepper

TO GARNISH

spring onion (scallion), cut into strips

red chilli, cut into strips

 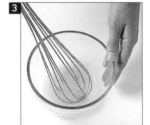 

1 Wash the lentils in a sieve (strainer). Place in a saucepan with the stock, ginger root, soy sauce and sugar. Bring to the boil and boil rapidly, uncovered, for 10 minutes. Skim off any froth on the surface. Reduce the heat, cover and simmer for 15 minutes.

2 Mix the cornflour (cornstarch) with the sherry in a small bowl. Add the sweetcorn with the liquid from the can and cornflour (cornstarch) mixture to the saucepan. Simmer for 2 minutes.

3 Whisk the egg white lightly with the sesame oil. Pour the egg mixture into the soup in a thin stream, remove from the heat and stir. The egg white will form white strands. Season with salt and pepper to taste.

4 Pour into 4 warmed soup bowls and garnish with strips of spring onion (scallion) and red chilli. Serve the soup immediately.

COOK'S TIP

To save time use a 425 g/15 oz can of green lentils instead of dried ones. Place the lentils and sweetcorn in a large saucepan with the stock and flavourings, bring to the boil and simmer for 2 minutes, then continue the recipe from step 2 as above.

Spinach & Tofu Soup

This is a very colourful and delicious soup. If spinach is not in season, watercress or lettuce can be used instead.

NUTRITIONAL INFORMATION

Calories	33	Sugar	.........1g
Protein	.........4g	Fat	..........2g
Carbohydrate	....1g	Saturates	.....0.2g

 3¹/₂ HOURS   10 MINS

SERVES 4

INGREDIENTS

1 cake tofu (bean curd)

125 g/4½ oz spinach leaves without stems

700 ml/1¼ pints/3 cups Chinese Stock (see page 14) or water

1 tbsp light soy sauce

salt and pepper

1 Using a sharp knife, cut the tofu into small pieces about 5 mm (¼ inch) thick.

2 Wash the spinach leaves thoroughly under cold, running water and drain thoroughly.

3 Cut the spinach leaves into small pieces or shreds, discarding any discoloured leaves and tough stalks. (If possible, use fresh young spinach leaves, which have not yet developed tough ribs. Otherwise, it is important to cut out all the ribs and stems for this soup.) Set the spinach aside until required.

4 In a preheated wok or large frying pan (skillet), bring the Chinese stock or water to a rolling boil.

5 Add the tofu (bean curd) cubes and light soy sauce, bring back to the boil and simmer for about 2 minutes over a medium heat.

6 Add the shredded spinach leaves and simmer for 1 more minute, stirring gently. Skim the surface of the soup to make it clear, adjust the seasoning to taste.

7 Transfer the spinach and tofu (bean curd) soup to a warm soup tureen or individual serving bowls and serve with chopsticks, to pick up the pieces of food and a broad, shallow spoon for drinking the soup.

COOK'S TIP

Soup is an integral part of a Chinese meal; it is usually presented in a large bowl placed in the centre of the table, and consumed as the meal progresses. It serves as a refresher between different dishes and as a beverage throughout the meal.

Vegetarian Hot & Sour Soup

This popular soup is easy to make and very filling. It can be eaten as a meal on its own or served as an appetizer before a light menu.

NUTRITIONAL INFORMATION

Calories 61   Sugars 1g
Protein . . . . .5g   Fat 2g
Carbohydrate . . . .8g   Saturates 0.2g

30 MINS   10 MINS

SERVES 4

I N G R E D I E N T S

4 Chinese dried mushrooms
   (if unavailable, use open-cup
   mushrooms)

125 g/4½ oz firm tofu (bean curd)

60 g/2 oz/1 cup canned bamboo
   shoots

600 ml/1 pint/2½ cups vegetable stock
   or water

60 g/2 oz/⅓ cup peas

1 tbsp dark soy sauce

2 tbsp white wine vinegar

2 tbsp cornflour (cornstarch)

salt and pepper

sesame oil, to serve

1 Place the Chinese dried mushrooms in a small bowl and cover with warm water. Leave to soak for about 20–25 minutes.

2 Drain the mushrooms and squeeze out the excess water, reserving this. Remove the tough centres and cut the mushrooms into thin shreds. Shred the tofu (bean curd) and bamboo shoots.

3 Bring the stock or water to the boil in a large saucepan. Add the mushrooms, tofu (bean curd), bamboo shoots and peas. Simmer for 2 minutes.

4 Mix together the soy sauce, vinegar and cornflour (cornstarch) with 2 tablespoons of the reserved mushroom liquid.

5 Stir the soy sauce and cornflour (cornstarch) mixture into the soup with the remaining mushroom liquid. Bring to the boil and season with salt and plenty of pepper. Simmer for 2 minutes.

6 Serve in warmed bowls with a few drops of sesame oil sprinkled over the top of each.

COOK'S TIP

If you use open-cup mushrooms instead of dried mushrooms, add an extra 150 ml/ ¼ pint/⅔ cup vegetable stock or water to the soup, as these mushrooms do not need soaking.

Noodle & Mushroom Soup

This soup is very quickly and easily put together, and is cooked so that each ingredient can still be tasted in the finished dish.

NUTRITIONAL INFORMATION

Calories	74	Sugars	.........1g
Protein	........13g	Fat	...........3g
Carbohydrate	....9g	Saturates	.....0.4g

4 HOURS   10 MINS

SERVES 4

I N G R E D I E N T S

15 g/½ oz/¼ cup dried Chinese mushrooms
    or 125 g/4½ oz/1⅓ cups field or chestnut
    (crimini) mushrooms

1 litre/1¾ pints/4 cups hot Fresh Vegetable
    Stock (page 30)

125 g/4½ oz thread egg noodles

2 tsp sunflower oil

3 garlic cloves, crushed

2.5 cm/1 inch piece ginger,
    shredded finely

½ tsp mushroom ketchup

1 tsp light soy sauce

125 g/4½ oz/2 cups bean sprouts

coriander (cilantro) leaves,
    to garnish

1 Soak the dried Chinese mushrooms, if using, for at least 30 minutes in 300 ml/½ pint/1¼ cups of the hot vegetable stock. Remove the stalks and discard, then slice the mushrooms. Reserve the stock.

2 Cook the noodles for 2–3 minutes in boiling water. Drain, rinse and set aside until required.

3 Heat the oil over a high heat in a wok or large, heavy frying pan (skillet). Add the garlic and ginger, stir and add the mushrooms. Stir over a high heat for 2 minutes.

4 Add the remaining vegetable stock with the reserved stock and bring to the boil. Add the mushroom ketchup and soy sauce and mix well.

5 Stir in the bean sprouts and cook until tender. Serve over the noodles, garnished with coriander (cilantro) leaves.

COOK'S TIP

Dried mushrooms are highly fragrant and add a special flavour to Chinese dishes. There are many different varieties but Shiitake are the best. Although not cheap, a small amount will go a long way and they will keep indefinitely in an airtight jar.

Sweet & Sour Cabbage Soup

This healthy soup is made with an unusual combination of fruits and vegetables, creating a tantalising flavour that will keep people guessing.

NUTRITIONAL INFORMATION

Calories ....138 Sugars 27g
Protein ....3g Fat 2g
Carbohydrate ...28g Saturates 0g

25 MINS   1¼ HOURS

SERVES 4

INGREDIENTS

½ cup sultanas (golden raisins)

120 ml/4 fl oz/1/2 cup orange juice

1 tbsp olive oil

1 large onion, chopped

250 g/9 oz/3 cups shredded cabbage

2 apples, peeled and diced

120 ml/4 fl oz/ ½ cup apple juice

400 g/14 oz can peeled tomatoes in juice

225 ml/8 fl oz/1 cup tomato or vegetable juice

100 g/3 ½ oz pineapple flesh, finely chopped

1.2 litres/2 pints/5 cups water

2 tsp wine vinegar

salt and pepper

fresh mint leaves, to garnish

1 Put the sultanas (golden raisins) in a bowl, pour the orange juice over and leave for 15 minutes.

2 Heat the oil in a large saucepan over a medium heat, add the onion, cover and cook for 3–4 minutes, stirring frequently, until it starts to soften. Add the cabbage and cook for a further 2 minutes; do not allow it to brown.

3 Add the apples and apple juice, cover and cook gently for 5 minutes.

4 Stir in the tomatoes, tomato juice, pineapple and water. Season with salt and pepper and add the vinegar.

5 Add the sultanas (golden raisins) together with the orange juice soaking liquid. Bring to the boil, reduce the heat and simmer, partially covered, for about 1 hour until the fruit and vegetables are tender.

6 Allow the soup to cool slightly, then transfer to a blender or food processor and purée until smooth, working in batches if necessary. (If using a food processor, strain off the cooking liquid and reserve. Purée the soup solids with enough cooking liquid to moisten them, then combine with the remaining liquid.)

7 Return the soup to the saucepan and simmer gently for about 10 minutes to reheat. Ladle into warm bowls. Garnish with mint leaves and serve immediately.

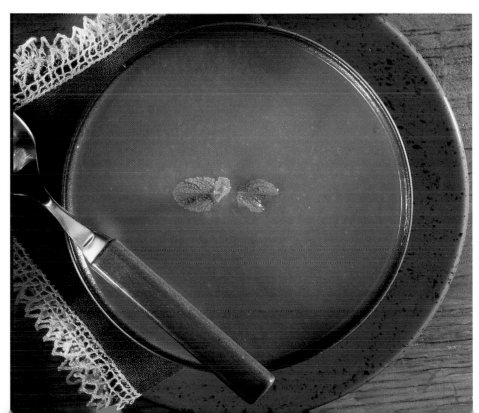

Pepper & Chilli Soup

This soup has a real Mediterranean flavour, using sweet red peppers, tomato, chilli and basil. It is great served with an olive bread.

NUTRITIONAL INFORMATION

Calories 55	Sugars 10g
Protein 2g	Fat 0.5g
Carbohydrate 11g	Saturates 0.1g

 10 MINS   25 MINS

SERVES 4

INGREDIENTS

225 g/8 oz red (bell) peppers,
   seeded and sliced

1 onion, sliced

2 garlic cloves, crushed

1 green chilli, chopped

300 ml/½ pint/1½ cups passata
   (sieved tomatoes)

600 ml/1 pint/2½ cups vegetable stock

2 tbsp chopped basil

basil sprigs, to garnish

1 Put the (bell) peppers in a large saucepan with the onion, garlic and chilli. Add the passata (sieved tomatoes) and vegetable stock and bring to the boil, stirring well.

VARIATION

This soup is also delicious served cold with 150 ml/¼ pint/⅔ cup of natural (unsweetened) yogurt swirled into it.

2 Reduce the heat to a simmer and cook for 20 minutes, or until the (bell) peppers have softened. Drain, reserving the liquid and vegetables separately.

3 Press the vegetables through a strainer with the back of a spoon. Alternatively, process in a food processor until smooth.

4 Return the vegetable purée to a clean saucepan with the reserved cooking liquid. Add the basil and heat through until hot. Garnish the soup with fresh basil sprigs and serve immediately.

Mixed Vegetable Soup

Select 3 or 4 vegetables for this soup: the Chinese like to blend different colours, flavours and textures to create harmony as well as contrast.

NUTRITIONAL INFORMATION

Calories 38   Sugars 3g
Protein . . . . .3g   Fat 2g
Carbohydrate . . . .4g   Saturates 0.2g

 3¹/₂ HOURS   5 MINS

SERVES 4

INGREDIENTS

about 30-60 g/1-2 oz each of
   mushrooms, carrots, asparagus,
   mangetout (snow peas), bamboo
   shoots, baby sweetcorn, cucumber,
   tomatoes, spinach, lettuce,
   Chinese leaves (cabbage),
   tofu (bean curd) etc.

600 ml/1 pint/2 ½ cups Chinese Stock
   (see page 14)

1 tbsp light soy sauce

a few drops sesame oil (optional)

salt and pepper

finely chopped spring onions (scallions),
   to garnish

1   Preheat a wok or large heavy-based frying pan (skillet).

2   Using a sharp knife or cleaver, cut your selection of vegetables into roughly uniform shapes and sizes (slices, shreds or cubes).

3   Pour the Chinese stock into the wok or frying pan (skillet) and bring to a rolling boil.

4   Add the vegetables, bearing in mind that some require a longer cooking time than others: add carrots and baby sweetcorn first, cook for 2 minutes, then add asparagus, mushrooms, Chinese leaves (cabbage), tofu (bean curd), and cook for another minute.

5   Spinach, lettuce, watercress, cucumber and tomato are added last. Stir, and bring the soup back to the boil.

6   Add the soy sauce and the sesame oil, if wished, and adjust the seasoning to taste.

7   Transfer the mixed vegetable soup to warm serving bowls and serve hot, garnished with spring onions (scallions).

COOK'S TIP

Sesame oil is a low-saturate oil widely used for its nutty, aromatic flavour. Made from toasted sesame seeds it is used as a seasoning, not as a cooking oil. Thick and dark, it burns easily, so it should be added at the last moment.

Chilli & Watercress Soup

This delicious soup is a wonderful blend of colours and flavours. It is very hot, so if you prefer a milder taste, omit the seeds from the chillies.

NUTRITIONAL INFORMATION

Calories	90	Sugars	.........1g
Protein	.........7g	Fat	...........6g
Carbohydrate	....2g	Saturates	.......1g

 10 MINS   15 MINS

SERVES 4

I N G R E D I E N T S

1 tbsp sunflower oil

250 g/9 oz smoked tofu
(bean curd), sliced

90 g/3 oz/1 cup shiitake
mushrooms, sliced

2 tbsp chopped fresh coriander (cilantro)

125 g/4½ oz/2 cups watercress

1 red chilli, sliced finely, to garnish

S T O C K

1 tbsp tamarind pulp

2 dried red chillies, chopped

2 kaffir lime leaves, torn in half

2.5 cm/1 inch piece ginger, chopped

5 cm/2 inch piece galangal, chopped

1 stalk lemon grass, chopped

1 onion, quartered

1 litre/1¾ pints/4 cups cold water

1 Put all the ingredients for the stock into a saucepan and bring to the boil.

2 Simmer the stock for 5 minutes. Remove from the heat and strain, reserving the stock.

3 Heat the sunflower oil in a wok or large, heavy frying pan (skillet) and cook the tofu (bean curd) over a high heat for about 2 minutes, stirring constantly so that the tofu (bean curd) cooks evenly on both sides. Add the strained stock.

4 Add the mushrooms and coriander (cilantro), and boil for 3 minutes.

5 Add the watercress and boil for 1 minute.

6 Serve immediately, garnished with red chilli slices.

VARIATION

You might like to try a mixture of different types of mushroom. Oyster, button and straw mushrooms are all suitable.

Chilli Fish Soup

Chinese mushrooms add an intense flavour to this soup which is unique. If they are unavailable, use open-cap mushrooms, sliced.

NUTRITIONAL INFORMATION

Calories ....166 Sugars 1g
Protein ....23g Fat 7g
Carbohydrate ....4g Saturates 1g

15 MINS   15 MINS

SERVES 4

INGREDIENTS

15 g/½ oz Chinese dried mushrooms

2 tbsp sunflower oil

1 onion, sliced

100 g/3½ oz/1½ cups mangetout (snow peas)

100 g/3½ oz/1½ cups bamboo shoots

3 tbsp sweet chilli sauce

1.2 litres/2 pints/5 cups fish or vegetable stock

3 tbsp light soy sauce

2 tbsp fresh coriander (cilantro), plus extra to garnish

450 g/1 lb cod fillet, skinned and cubed

COOK'S TIP

Cod is used in this recipe as it is a meaty white fish. For real luxury, use monkfish tail instead.

1 Place the mushrooms in a large bowl. Pour over enough boiling water to cover and leave to stand for 5 minutes. Drain the mushrooms thoroughly in a colander. Using a sharp knife, roughly chop the mushrooms.

2 Heat the sunflower oil in a preheated wok or large frying pan (skillet). Add the sliced onion to the wok and stir-fry for 5 minutes, or until softened.

3 Add the mangetout (snow peas), bamboo shoots, chilli sauce, stock and soy sauce to the wok and bring to the boil.

4 Add the coriander (cilantro) and cod and leave to simmer for 5 minutes or until the fish is cooked through.

5 Transfer the soup to warm bowls, garnish with extra coriander (cilantro), if wished, and serve hot.

Fish & Vegetable Soup

A chunky fish soup with strips of vegetables, all flavoured with ginger and lemon, makes a meal in itself.

NUTRITIONAL INFORMATION

Calories 88   Sugars 1g
Protein ....12g   Fat 3g
Carbohydrate ....3g   Saturates 0.5g

 40 MINS   20 MINS

SERVES 4

INGREDIENTS

250 g/9 oz white fish fillets (cod, halibut, haddock, sole etc)

½ tsp ground ginger

½ tsp salt

1 small leek, trimmed

2-4 crab sticks, defrosted if frozen (optional)

1 tbsp sunflower oil

1 large carrot, cut into julienne strips

8 canned water chestnuts, thinly sliced

1.2 litres/2 pints/5 cups fish or vegetable stock

1 tbsp lemon juice

1 tbsp light soy sauce

1 large courgette (zucchini), cut into julienne strips

black pepper

COOK'S TIP

To skin fish, place the fillet skin-side down and insert a sharp, flexible knife at one end between the flesh and the skin. Hold the skin tightly at the end and push the knife along, keeping the blade flat against the skin.

1 Remove any skin from the fish and cut into cubes, about 2.5 cm/1 inch. Combine the ground ginger and salt and use to rub into the pieces of fish. Leave to marinate for at least 30 minutes.

2 Meanwhile, divide the green and white parts of the leek. Cut each part into 2.5 cm/1 inch lengths and then into julienne strips down the length of each piece, keeping the two parts separate. Slice the crab sticks into 1 cm/½ inch pieces.

3 Heat the oil in the wok, swirling it around so it is really hot. Add the white part of the leek and stir-fry for a couple of minutes, then add the carrots and water chestnuts and continue to cook for 1-2 minutes, stirring thoroughly.

4 Add the stock and bring to the boil, then add the lemon juice and soy sauce and simmer for 2 minutes.

5 Add the fish and continue to cook for about 5 minutes until the fish begins to break up a little, then add the green part of the leek and the courgettes (zucchini) and simmer for about 1 minute. Add the sliced crab sticks, if using, and season to taste with black pepper. Simmer for a further minute or so and serve piping hot.

Oriental Fish Soup

This is a deliciously different fish soup which can be made quickly and easily in a microwave.

NUTRITIONAL INFORMATION

Calories 105	Sugars 1g
Protein 13g	Fat 5g
Carbohydrate 1g	Saturates 1g

 20 MINS   🕐 10 MINS

SERVES 4

I N G R E D I E N T S

1 egg

1 tsp sesame seeds, toasted

1 celery stick, chopped

1 carrot, cut into julienne strips

4 spring onions (scallions), sliced on the diagonal

1 tbsp oil

60 g/2 oz/1½ cups fresh spinach

850 ml/1½ pints/3½ cups hot vegetable stock

4 tsp light soy sauce

250 g/9 oz haddock, skinned and cut into small chunks

salt and pepper

VARIATION

Instead of topping the soup with omelette shreds, you could pour the beaten egg, without the sesame seeds, into the hot stock at the end of the cooking time. The egg will set in pretty strands to give a flowery look.

1 Beat the egg with the sesame seeds and seasoning. Lightly oil a plate and pour on the egg mixture. Cook on HIGH power for 1½ minutes until just setting in the centre. Leave to stand for a few minutes then remove from the plate. Roll up the egg and shred thinly.

2 Mix together the celery, carrot, spring onions (scallions) and oil. Cover and cook on HIGH power for 3 minutes.

3 Wash the spinach thoroughly under cold, running water. Cut off and discard any long stalks and drain well. Shred the spinach finely.

4 Add the hot stock, soy sauce, haddock and spinach to the vegetable mixture. Cover and cook on HIGH power for 5 minutes. Stir the soup and season to taste. Serve in warmed bowls with the shredded egg scattered over.

Saffron Fish Soup

This elegant soup makes a good dinner party starter. To make planning easier, the saffron-flavoured soup base can be made ahead.

NUTRITIONAL INFORMATION

Calories	364	Sugars	.........8g
Protein	........20g	Fat	..........18g
Carbohydrate	...25g	Saturates	.....11g

15 MINS   35 MINS

SERVES 4

INGREDIENTS

2 tsp butter

1 onion, finely chopped

1 leek, thinly sliced

1 carrot, thinly sliced

4 tbsp white rice

pinch of saffron threads

120 ml/4 fl oz/ ½ cup dry white wine

120 ml/4 fl oz/ ½ cup double (heavy) cream

350 g/12 oz skinless white fish fillet, such as cod, haddock or monkfish, cut into 1 cm/½ inch cubes

1 litre/1¾ pints/4 cups fish stock

4 tomatoes, skinned, deseeded and chopped

3 tbsp snipped fresh chives, to garnish

salt and pepper

2 Add the saffron, rice, wine and stock, bring just to the boil and reduce the heat to low. Season with salt and pepper. Cover and simmer for 20 minutes, or until the rice and vegetables are soft.

3 Allow the soup to cool slightly, then transfer to a blender or food processor and purée until smooth, working in batches if necessary. (If using a food processor, strain off the cooking liquid and reserve. Purée the soup solids with enough cooking liquid to moisten them, then combine with the remaining liquid.)

4 Return the soup to the saucepan, stir in the cream and simmer over a low heat for a few minutes until heated through, stirring occasionally.

5 Season the fish and add, with the tomatoes, to the simmering soup. Cook for 3–5 minutes, or until the fish is just tender.

6 Stir in most of the chives. Taste the soup and adjust the seasoning, if necessary. Ladle into warm shallow bowls, sprinkle the remaining chilies on top and serve.

1 Heat the butter in a saucepan over a medium heat and add the onion, leek and carrot. Cook for 3–4 minutes, stirring frequently, until the onion is soft.

Fish Soup with Wontons

This soup is topped with small wontons filled with prawns, making it both very tasty and satisfying.

NUTRITIONAL INFORMATION

Calories 115	Sugars 0g	
Protein 16g	Fat 5g	
Carbohydrate 1g	Saturates 1g	

🄖 🄖 🄖

🍲 10 MINS   🕐 15 MINS

SERVES 4

I N G R E D I E N T S

125 g/4½ oz large, cooked, peeled
  prawns (shrimp)

1 tsp chopped chives

1 small garlic clove, finely chopped

1 tbsp vegetable oil

12 wonton wrappers

1 small egg, beaten

850 ml/1½ pints/3¾ cups fish stock

175 g/6 oz white fish fillet, diced

dash of chilli sauce

sliced fresh red chilli and chives,
  to garnish

1 Roughly chop a quarter of the prawns (shrimp) and mix together with the chopped chives and garlic.

2 Heat the oil in a preheated wok or large frying pan (skillet) until it is really hot.

3 Stir-fry the prawn (shrimp) mixture for 1–2 minutes. Remove from the heat and set aside to cool completely.

4 Spread out the wonton wrappers on a work surface (counter). Spoon a little of the prawn (shrimp) filling into the centre of each wrapper. Brush the edges of the wrappers with beaten egg and press the edges together, scrunching them to form a 'moneybag' shape. Set aside while you are preparing the soup.

5 Pour the fish stock into a large saucepan and bring to the boil. Add the diced white fish and the remaining prawns (shrimp) and cook for 5 minutes.

6 Season to taste with the chilli sauce. Add the wontons and cook for a further 5 minutes.

7 Spoon into warmed serving bowls, garnish with sliced red chilli and chives and serve immediately.

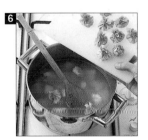

VARIATION

Replace the prawns (shrimp) with cooked crabmeat for an alternative flavour.

Three-Flavour Soup

Ideally, use raw prawns in this soup. If that is not possible, add ready-cooked ones at the very last stage.

NUTRITIONAL INFORMATION

Calories 117   Sugars 0g
Protein . . . . .20g   Fat 3g
Carbohydrate . . . .2g   Saturates 1g

 3½ HOURS   10 MINS

SERVES 4

I N G R E D I E N T S

125 g/4½ oz skinned, boned chicken breast

125 g/4½ oz raw peeled prawns (shrimp)

salt

½ egg white, lightly beaten

2 tsp cornflour (cornstarch) paste
  (see page 15)

125 g/4½ oz honey-roast ham

700 ml/1¼ pints/3 cups Chinese Stock
  (see page 14) or water

finely chopped spring onions (scallions), to
  garnish

1 Using a sharp knife or meat cleaver, thinly slice the chicken into small shreds. If the prawns (shrimp) are large, cut each in half lengthways, otherwise leave them whole.

2 Place the chicken and prawns (shrimps) in a bowl and mix with a pinch of salt, the egg white and cornflour (cornstarch) paste until well coated. Set aside until required.

3 Cut the honey-roast ham into small thin slices roughly the same size as the chicken pieces.

4 In a preheated wok or large, heavy frying pan (skillet), bring the Chinese stock or water to a rolling boil and add

the chicken, the raw prawns (shrimp) and the ham.

5 Bring the soup back to the boil, and simmer for 1 minute.

6 Adjust the seasoning to taste, then pour the soup into four warmed individual serving bowls, garnish with the spring onions (scallions) and serve immediately.

COOK'S TIP

Soups such as this are improved enormously in flavour if you use a well-flavoured stock. Either use a stock cube, or find time to make Chinese Stock – see the recipe on page 28. Better still, make double quantities and freeze some for future use.

Thai Seafood Soup

As taste and tolerance for chillies varies, using chilli purée offers more control of the heat.

NUTRITIONAL INFORMATION

Calories	92	Sugars	.........0g
Protein	........17g	Fat	...........2g
Carbohydrate	....3g	Saturates	......0g

  10 MINS 25 MINS

SERVES 4

I N G R E D I E N T S

1.2 litres/2 pints/5 cups fish stock

1 lemon grass stalk, split lengthways

pared rind of ½ lime, or 1 lime leaf

2.5 cm/1 inch piece fresh ginger root, peeled and sliced

¼ tsp chilli purée (paste), or to taste

4–6 spring onions (scallions), sliced

200 g/7 oz large of medium raw prawns (shrimp), peeled

250 g/9 oz scallops (16–20)

2 tbsp fresh coriander leaves (cilantro)

salt

finely chopped red (bell) pepper, or red chilli rings, to garnish

COOK'S TIP

If you have light chicken stock, but no fish stock, it will make an equally tasty though different version of this soup.

1 Put the stock in a saucepan with the lemon grass, lime rind or leaf, ginger and chilli purée (paste). Bring just to the boil, reduce the heat, cover and simmer for 10–15 minutes.

2 Cut the baby leek in half lengthways, then slice crossways very thinly. Cut the prawns (shrimp) almost in half lengthways, keeping the tail intact.

3 Strain the stock, return to the saucepan and bring to a simmer, with bubbles rising at the edges and the surface trembling. Add the leek and cook for 2–3 minutes. Taste and season with salt, if needed, and stir in a little more chilli purée (paste) if wished.

4 Add the scallops and prawns (shrimp) and poach for about 1 minute until they turn opaque and the prawns (shrimp) curl.

5 Drop in the fresh coriander leaves (cilantro), ladle the soup into warm bowls, dividing the shellfish evenly, and garnish with red (bell) pepper or chillies.

Seafood & Tofu Soup

Use prawn, squid or scallops, or a combination of all three in this healthy soup.

NUTRITIONAL INFORMATION

Calories 97	Sugars 0g
Protein 17g	Fat 2g
Carbohydrate 3g	Saturates 0.4g

3¹/₂ HOURS   10 MINS

SERVES 4

INGREDIENTS

250 g/9 oz seafood: peeled prawns (shrimp), squid, scallops, etc., defrosted if frozen

½ egg white, lightly beaten

1 tbsp cornflour (cornstarch) paste (see page 15)

1 cake tofu (bean curd)

700 ml/1¼ pints/3 cups Chinese Stock (see page 14)

1 tbsp light soy sauce

salt and pepper

fresh coriander (cilantro) leaves, to garnish (optional)

1 Small prawns (shrimp) can be left whole; larger ones should be cut into smaller pieces; cut the squid and scallops into small pieces.

2 If raw, mix the prawns (shrimp) and scallops with the egg white and cornflour (cornstarch) paste to prevent them from becoming tough when they are cooked. Cut the cake of tofu into about 24 small cubes.

3 Bring the stock to a rolling boil. Add the tofu and soy sauce, bring back to the boil and simmer for 1 minute.

4 Stir in the seafood, raw pieces first, pre-cooked ones last. Bring back to the boil and simmer for just 1 minute.

5 Adjust the seasoning to taste and serve, garnished with coriander (cilantro) leaves, if liked.

COOK'S TIP

Tofu, also known as bean curd, is made from puréed yellow soya beans, which are very high in protein. Although almost tasteless, tofu absorbs the flavours of other ingredients. It is widely available in supermarkets, and Oriental and health-food stores.

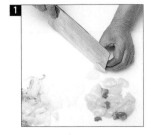

Prawn Soup

This soup is an interesting mix of colours and textures. The egg may be made into a flat omelette and added as thin strips if preferred.

NUTRITIONAL INFORMATION

Calories	123	Sugars	.......0.2g
Protein	........13g	Fat	..........8g
Carbohydrate	....1g	Saturates	.......1g

 5 MINS   20 MINS

SERVES 4

I N G R E D I E N T S

2 tbsp sunflower oil

2 spring onions (scallions), thinly sliced diagonally

1 carrot, coarsely grated

125 g/4½ oz large closed cup mushrooms, thinly sliced

1 litre/1¾ pints/4 cups fish or vegetable stock

½ tsp Chinese five-spice powder

1 tbsp light soy sauce

125 g/4½ oz large peeled prawns (shrimp) or peeled tiger prawns (shrimp), defrosted if frozen

½ bunch watercress, trimmed and roughly chopped

1 egg, well beaten

salt and pepper

4 large prawns (shrimp) in shells, to garnish (optional)

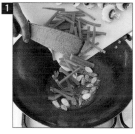  

1 Heat the oil in a wok, swirling it around until really hot. Add the spring onions (scallions) and stir-fry for a minute then add the carrots and mushrooms and continue to cook for about 2 minutes.

2 Add the stock and bring to the boil then season to taste with salt and pepper, five-spice powder and soy sauce and simmer for 5 minutes.

3 If the prawns (shrimp) are really large, cut them in half before adding to the wok and simmer for 3-4 minutes.

4 Add the watercress to the wok and mix well, then slowly pour in the beaten egg in a circular movement so that it cooks in threads in the soup. Adjust the seasoning and serve each portion topped with a whole prawn (shrimp).

COOK'S TIP

The large open mushrooms with black gills give the best flavour but they tend to spoil the colour of the soup, making it very dark. Oyster mushrooms can also be used.

Spicy Prawn Soup

Lime leaves are used as a flavouring in this soup to add tartness.

NUTRITIONAL INFORMATION

Calories	217	Sugars	........16g
Protein	........16g	Fat	...........4g
Carbohydrate	...31g	Saturates	.......1g

10 MINS   20 MINS

SERVES 4

INGREDIENTS

2 tbsp tamarind paste

4 red chilies, very finely chopped

2 cloves garlic, crushed

2.5 cm/1 inch piece Thai ginger, peeled and very finely chopped

4 tbsp fish sauce

2 tbsp palm sugar or caster (superfine) sugar

1.2 litres/2 pints/5 cups fish stock

8 lime leaves

100 g/3½ oz carrots, very thinly sliced

350 g/12 oz sweet potato, diced

100 g/3½ oz/1 cup baby corn cobs, halved

3 tbsp fresh coriander (cilantro), roughly chopped

100g/3½ oz cherry tomatoes, halved

225 g/8 oz fan-tail prawns (shrimp)

1 Place the tamarind paste, red chillies, garlic, ginger, fish sauce, sugar and fish stock in a preheated wok or large, heavy frying pan (skillet). Roughly tear the lime leaves and add to the wok. Bring to the boil, stirring constantly to blend the flavours.

2 Reduce the heat and add the carrot, sweet potato and baby corn cobs to the mixture in the wok.

3 Leave the soup to simmer, uncovered, for about 10 minutes, or until the vegetables are just tender.

4 Stir the coriander (cilantro), cherry tomatoes and prawns (shrimp) into the soup and heat through for 5 minutes.

5 Transfer the soup to a warm soup tureen or individual serving bowls and serve hot.

COOK'S TIP

Thai ginger or galangal is a member of the ginger family, but it is yellow in colour with pink sprouts. The flavour is aromatic and less pungent than ginger.

Crab & Ginger Soup

Two classic ingredients in Chinese cooking are blended together in this recipe for a special soup.

NUTRITIONAL INFORMATION

Calories ....32 Sugars 1g
Protein ....6g Fat 0.4g
Carbohydrate ....1g Saturates 0g

  10 MINS   25 MINS

SERVES 4

I N G R E D I E N T S

1 carrot

1 leek

1 bay leaf

850 ml/1½ pints/3¾ cups fish stock

2 medium-sized cooked crabs

2.5-cm/1-inch piece fresh root ginger (ginger root), grated

1 tsp light soy sauce

½ tsp ground star anise

salt and pepper

1 Using a sharp knife, chop the carrot and leek into small pieces and place in a large saucepan with the bay leaf and fish stock.

2 Bring the mixture in the saucepan to the boil.

3 Reduce the heat, cover and leave to simmer for about 10 minutes, or until the vegetables are nearly tender.

4 Remove all of the meat from the cooked crabs. Break off and reserve the claws, break the joints and remove the meat, using a fork or skewer.

5 Add the crabmeat to the pan of fish stock, together with the ginger, soy sauce and star anise and bring to the boil. Leave to simmer for about 10 minutes, or until the vegetables are tender and the crab is heated through.

6 Season the soup then ladle into a warmed soup tureen or individual serving bowls and garnish with crab claws. Serve immediately.

VARIATION

If fresh crabmeat is unavailable, use drained canned crabmeat or thawed frozen crabmeat instead.

Coconut & Crab Soup

Thai red curry paste is quite fiery, but adds a superb flavour to this dish. It is available in jars or packets from supermarkets.

NUTRITIONAL INFORMATION

Calories	122	Sugar	.........9g
Protein	........11g	Fats	...........4g
Carbohydrates	...11g	Saturates	......1g

5 MINS   10 MINS

SERVES 4

I N G R E D I E N T S

1 tbsp groundnut oil

2 tbsp Thai red curry paste

1 red (bell) pepper, deseeded and sliced

600 ml/1 pint/2½ cups coconut milk

600 ml/1 pint/2½ cups fish stock (see page 15)

2 tbsp fish sauce

225 g/8 oz canned or fresh white crab meat

225 g/8 oz fresh or frozen crab claws

2 tbsp chopped fresh coriander (cilantro)

3 spring onions (scallions), trimmed and sliced

COOK'S TIP

Clean the wok after use by washing it with water, using a mild detergent if necessary, and a soft cloth or brush. Do not scrub or use any abrasive cleaner as this will scratch the surface. Dry thoroughly then wipe the surface all over with a little oil to protect the surface.

1 Heat the oil in a large preheated wok.

2 Add the red curry paste and red (bell) pepper to the wok and stir-fry for 1 minute.

3 Add the coconut milk, fish stock and fish sauce and bring to the boil.

4 Add the crab meat, crab claws, coriander (cilantro) and spring onions (scallions) to the wok.

5 Stir the mixture well and heat thoroughly for 2–3 minutes or until everything is warmed through.

6 Transfer the soup to warm bowls and serve hot.

Crab & Sweetcorn Soup

Crab and sweetcorn are classic ingredients in Chinese cookery. Here egg noodles are added for a filling dish.

NUTRITIONAL INFORMATION

Calories 324	Sugars 6g
Protein 27g	Fat 8g
Carbohydrate ...39g	Saturates 2g

5 MINS   20 MINS

SERVES 4

INGREDIENTS

1 tbsp sunflower oil

1 tsp Chinese five-spice powder

225 g/8 oz carrots, cut into sticks

150 g/5½ oz/½ cup canned or frozen sweetcorn

75 g/2¾ oz/¼ cup peas

6 spring onions (scallions), trimmed and sliced

1 red chilli, deseeded and very thinly sliced

2 x 200 g/7 oz can white crab meat

175 g/6 oz egg noodles

1.7 litres/3 pints/7½ cups fish stock

3 tbsp soy sauce

1 Heat the sunflower oil in a large preheated wok or heavy-based frying pan (skillet).

2 Add the Chinese five-spice powder, carrots, sweetcorn, peas, spring onions (scallions) and red chilli to the wok and cook for about 5 minutes, stirring constantly.

3 Add the crab meat to the wok and stir-fry the mixture for 1 minute, distributing the crab meat evenly.

4 Roughly break up the egg noodles and add to the wok.

5 Pour the fish stock and soy sauce into the mixture in the wok and bring to the boil.

6 Cover the wok or frying pan (skillet) and leave the soup to simmer for 5 minutes.

7 Stir once more, then transfer the soup to a warm soup tureen or individual serving bowls and serve at once.

COOK'S TIP

Chinese five-spice powder is a mixture of star anise, fennel, cloves, cinnamon and Szechuan pepper. It has an unmistakeable flavour. Use it sparingly, as it is very pungent.

Beef & Vegetable Noodle Soup

Thin strips of beef are marinated in soy sauce and garlic to form the basis of this delicious soup. Served with noodles, it is both filling and delicious.

NUTRITIONAL INFORMATION

Calories	186	Sugars	.........1g
Protein	........17g	Fat	...........5g
Carbohydrate	...20g	Saturates	.......1g

🧤 35 MINS   🕐 20 MINS

SERVES 4

I N G R E D I E N T S

225 g/8 oz lean beef

1 garlic clove, crushed

2 spring onions (scallions), chopped

3 tbsp soy sauce

1 tsp sesame oil

225 g/8 oz egg noodles

850 ml/1½ pints/3¾ cups
    beef stock

3 baby corn cobs, sliced

½ leek, shredded

125 g/4½ oz broccoli, cut into florets
    (flowerets)

pinch of chilli powder

1 Using a sharp knife, cut the beef into thin strips and place in a bowl with the garlic, spring onions (scallions), soy sauce and sesame oil.

2 Mix together the ingredients in the bowl, turning the beef to coat. Cover and leave to marinate in the refrigerator for 30 minutes.

3 Cook the noodles in a saucepan of boiling water for 3–4 minutes. Drain the noodles thoroughly and set aside.

4 Put the beef stock in a large saucepan and bring to the boil. Add the beef, together with the marinade, the baby corn, leek and broccoli. Cover and leave to simmer over a low heat for 7–10 minutes, or until the beef and vegetables are tender and cooked through.

5 Stir in the noodles and chilli powder and cook for a further 2–3 minutes.

6 Transfer the soup to bowls and serve immediately.

VARIATION

Vary the vegetables used, or use those to hand.

If preferred, use a few drops of chilli sauce instead of chilli powder, but remember it is very hot!

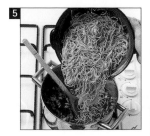

Chinese Potato & Pork Broth

In this recipe the pork is seasoned with traditional Chinese flavourings – soy sauce, rice wine vinegar and a dash of sesame oil.

NUTRITIONAL INFORMATION

Calories	166	Sugars	.........2g
Protein	........10g	Fat	...........5g
Carbohydrate	...26g	Saturates	.......1g

5 MINS   20 MINS

SERVES 4

I N G R E D I E N T S

1 litre/1¾ pints/4½ cups chicken stock

2 large potatoes, diced

2 tbsp rice wine vinegar

2 tbsp cornflour (cornstarch)

4 tbsp water

125 g/4½ oz pork fillet, sliced

1 tbsp light soy sauce

1 tsp sesame oil

1 carrot, cut into very thin strips

1 tsp ginger root, chopped

3 spring onions (scallions), sliced thinly

1 red (bell) pepper, sliced

225 g/8 oz can bamboo shoots, drained

VARIATION

For extra heat, add 1 chopped red chilli or 1 tsp of chilli powder to the soup in step 5.

1 Add the chicken stock, diced potatoes and 1 tbsp of the rice wine vinegar to a saucepan and bring to the boil. Reduce the heat until the stock is just simmering.

2 Mix the cornflour (cornstarch) with the water then stir into the hot stock.

3 Bring the stock back to the boil, stirring until thickened, then reduce the heat until it is just simmering again.

4 Place the pork slices in a dish and season with the remaining rice wine vinegar, the soy sauce and sesame oil.

5 Add the pork slices, carrot strips and ginger to the stock and cook for 10 minutes. Stir in the spring onions (scallions), red (bell) pepper and bamboo shoots. Cook for a further 5 minutes. Pour the soup into warmed bowls and serve immediately.

Pork & Vegetable Soup

Sold in cans, Szechuan preserved vegetable is pickled mustard root which is quite hot and salty, so rinse in water before use.

NUTRITIONAL INFORMATION

Calories	135	Sugars	.........1g
Protein	........14g	Fat	...........7g
Carbohydrate	....3g	Saturates	.......2g

 5 MINS   5 MINS

SERVES 4

INGREDIENTS

250 g/9 oz pork fillet

2 tsp cornflour (cornstarch) paste (see page 15)

125 g/4½ oz Szechuan preserved vegetable

700 ml/1¼ pints/3 cups Chinese stock (see page 14) or water

salt and pepper

a few drops sesame oil (optional)

2-3 spring onions (scallions), sliced, to garnish

1 Preheat a wok or large, heavy-based frying pan (skillet).

2 Using a sharp knife, cut the pork across the grain into thin shreds.

3 Mix the pork with the cornflour (cornstarch) paste until the pork is completely coated in the mixture.

4 Thoroughly wash and rinse the Szechuan preserved vegetable, then pat dry on absorbent kitchen paper (paper towels). Cut the Szechuan preserved vegetable into thin shreds the same size as the pork.

5 Pour the Chinese stock or water into the wok or frying pan (skillet) and

bring to a rolling boil. Add the pork to the wok and stir to separate the shreds. Return to the boil.

6 Add the shredded Szechuan preserved vegetable and bring back to the boil once more.

7 Adjust the seasoning to taste and sprinkle with sesame oil. Serve hot, garnished with spring onions (scallions).

COOK'S TIP

Szechuan preserved vegetable is actually mustard green root, pickled in salt and chillies. Available in cans from specialist Chinese supermarkets, it gives a crunchy, spicy taste to dishes. Rinse in cold water before use and store in the refrigerator.

Pork Chilli Soup

This meaty chilli tastes lighter than one made with beef. Good for informal entertaining, the recipe is easily doubled.

NUTRITIONAL INFORMATION

Calories	292	Sugar	.........11g
Protein	........41g	Fats	...........9g
Carbohydrates	...13g	Saturates	......0g

 10 MINS   50 MINS

SERVES 4

I N G R E D I E N T S

2 tsp olive oil

500 g/1 lb 2 oz lean minced (ground) pork

1 onion, finely chopped

1 stalk celery, finely chopped

1 (bell) pepper, cored, deseeded and finely chopped

2–3 garlic cloves, finely chopped

3 tbsp tomato purée (paste)

400 g/14 oz can chopped tomatoes in juice

450 ml/16 fl oz/2 cups chicken or meat stock

1/8 tsp ground coriander

1/8 tsp ground cumin

1/4 tsp dried oregano

1 tsp mild chilli powder, or to taste

salt and pepper

chopped fresh coriander leaves (cilantro) or parsley, to garnish

soured cream, to serve

COOK'S TIP

For a festive presentation, pass additional accompaniments, such as grated cheese, chopped spring onion (scallion) and guacamole.

1 Heat the oil in a large saucepan over a medium-high heat. Add the pork, season with salt and pepper, and cook until no longer pink, stirring frequently. Reduce the heat to medium and add the onion, celery, (bell) pepper and garlic. Cover and continue cooking for 5 minutes, stirring occasionally, until the onion is softened.

2 Add the tomatoes, tomato purée (paste) and the stock. Add the coriander, cumin, oregano and chilli powder. Stir the ingredients in to combine well.

3 Bring just to the boil, reduce the heat to low, cover and simmer for 30–40 minutes until all the vegetables are very tender. Taste and adjust the seasoning, adding more chilli powder if you like it hotter.

4 Ladle the chilli into warm bowls and sprinkle with coriander (cilantro) or parsley. Pass the soured cream separately, or top each serving with a spoonful.

Pork Balls & Greens in Broth

Steaming the meatballs over the soup gives added flavour to the broth.

NUTRITIONAL INFORMATION

Calories 98   Sugars 1g
Protein ....14g   Fat 3g
Carbohydrate ....4g   Saturates 0g

 15 MINS   20 MINS

SERVES 6

I N G R E D I E N T S

2 litres/3½ pints/8 cups chicken stock

80 g/3 oz shiitake mushrooms, thinly sliced

175 g/6 oz pak choy or other Oriental greens, sliced into thin ribbons

6 spring onions (scallions), finely sliced

salt and pepper

P O R K   B A L L S

225 g/8 oz lean minced (ground) pork

25 g/1 oz fresh spinach leaves, finely chopped

2 spring onions (scallions), finely chopped

1 garlic clove, very finely chopped

pinch of Oriental 5-spice powder

1 tsp soy sauce

1 To make the pork balls, put the pork, spinach, spring onions (scallions) and garlic in a bowl. Add the 5-spice powder and soy sauce and mix until combined.

2 Shape the pork mixture into 24 balls. Place them in one layer in a steamer that will fit over the top of a saucepan.

3 Bring the stock just to the boil in a saucepan that will accommodate the steamer. Regulate the heat so that the liquid bubbles gently. Add the mushrooms to the stock and place the steamer, covered, on top of the pan. Steam for 10 minutes. Remove the steamer and set aside on a plate.

4 Add the pak choy and spring onions (scallions) to the pan and cook gently in the stock for 3-4 minutes, or until the leaves are wilted. Taste the soup and adjust the seasoning, if necessary.

5 Divide the pork balls evenly among 6 warm bowls and ladle the soup over them. Serve at once.

Lamb & Rice Soup

This is a very filling soup, as it contains rice and tender pieces of lamb.
Serve before a light main course.

NUTRITIONAL INFORMATION

Calories 116	Sugars 0.2g
Protein 9g	Fat 4g
Carbohydrate . . .12g	Saturates 2g

5 MINS   35 MINS

SERVES 4

INGREDIENTS

150 g/5½ oz lean lamb

50 g/1¾ oz/¼ cup rice

850 ml/1½ pints/3¾ cups
  lamb stock

1 leek, sliced

1 garlic clove, thinly sliced

2 tsp light soy sauce

1 tsp rice wine vinegar

1 medium open-cap mushroom,
  thinly sliced

salt

1 Using a sharp knife, trim any fat from the lamb and cut the meat into thin strips. Set aside until required.

2 Bring a large pan of lightly salted water to the boil and add the rice. Bring back to the boil, stir once, reduce the heat and cook for 10–15 minutes, until tender.

3 Drain the rice, rinse under cold running water, drain again and set aside until required.

4 Meanwhile, put the lamb stock in a large saucepan and bring to the boil.

5 Add the lamb strips, leek, garlic, soy sauce and rice wine vinegar to the stock in the pan. Reduce the heat, cover and leave to simmer for 10 minutes, or until the lamb is tender and cooked through.

6 Add the mushroom slices and the rice to the pan and cook for a further 2–3 minutes, or until the mushroom is completely cooked through.

7 Ladle the soup into 4 individual warmed soup bowls and serve immediately.

VARIATION

Use a few dried Chinese mushrooms, rehydrated according to the packet instructions and chopped, as an alternative to the open-cap mushroom. Add the Chinese mushrooms with the lamb in step 4.

Asian Lamb Soup

This soup needs a light stock. If using a stock cube, make it up to half strength, as it will gain flavour from the vegetables and herbs.

NUTRITIONAL INFORMATION

Calories	96	Sugar	. . . . .2g
Protein	. . . . .10g	Fats	. . . . .5g
Carbohydrates	. . . .4g	Saturates	. . . . . .2g

15 MINS   30 MINS

SERVES 4

INGREDIENTS

150 g/5½ oz lean tender lamb, such as neck fillet or leg steak

2 garlic cloves, very finely chopped

2 tbsp soy sauce

1.2 litres/2 pints/5 cups chicken stock

1 tbsp grated peeled fresh ginger root

5 cm/2 inch piece lemon grass, sliced into very thin rounds

¼ tsp chilli purée (paste), or to taste

6-8 cherry tomatoes, quartered

4 spring onions (scallions), sliced finely

50 g/1 ¾ oz bean-sprouts, snapped in half

2 tbsp fresh coriander (cilantro) leaves

1 tsp olive oil

1 Trim all visible fat from the lamb and slice the meat thinly. Cut the slices into bite-sized pieces. Spread the meat in one layer on a plate and sprinkle over the garlic and 1 tbsp of the soy sauce. Leave to marinate, covered, for at least 10 minutes or up to 1 hour.

2 Put the stock in a saucepan with the ginger, lemon grass, remaining soy sauce and the chilli purée (paste). Bring just to the boil, reduce the heat, cover and simmer for 10-15 minutes. Warm 4 ovenproof bowls in a low oven.

3 When ready to serve the soup, drop the tomatoes, spring onions (scallions), bean-sprouts and fresh coriander (cilantro) leaves into the simmering stock.

4 Heat the oil in a frying pan (skillet) and add the lamb with its marinade. Stir-fry the lamb just until it is no longer red and divide among the warm bowls.

5 Ladle over the hot stock and serve immediately.

COOK'S TIP

Substitute lean, tender pork or beef instead of lamb. If preferred, use spinach or Chinese basil, sliced into thin ribbons, in place of fresh coriander (cilantro) leaves.

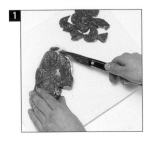

Spicy Lamb Soup

This thick and hearty main course soup is bursting with exotic flavours and aromas.

NUTRITIONAL INFORMATION

Calories	...... .306	Sugars	.... .6g
Protein	........26g	Fat	.... .12g
Carbohydrate	...25g	Saturates	...... .1g

🥘 15 MINS   🕐 2 HOURS

SERVES 4

I N G R E D I E N T S

1-2 tbsp olive oil

450 g/1 lb lean boneless lamb, such as shoulder or neck fillet, trimmed of fat and cut into 1 cm/½ inch cubes

1 onion, finely chopped

2-3 garlic cloves, crushed

1.2 litres/2 pints/5 cups water

400 g/14 oz can chopped tomatoes in juice

1 bay leaf

½ tsp dried thyme

½ tsp dried oregano

⅛ tsp ground cinnamon

¼ tsp ground cumin

¼ tsp ground turmeric

1 tsp harissa, or more to taste

400 g/14 oz can chick-peas (garbanzo beans), rinsed and drained

1 carrot, diced

1 potato, diced

1 courgette (zucchini), quartered lengthways and sliced

100 g/3½ oz fresh or defrosted frozen green peas

chopped fresh mint or coriander leaves (cilantro), to garnish

1 Heat the oil in a large saucepan or cast-iron casserole over a medium-high heat. Add the lamb, in batches if necessary to avoid crowding the pan, and cook until evenly browned on all sides, adding a little more oil if needed. Remove the meat, with a slotted spoon, when browned.

2 Reduce the heat and add the onion and garlic to the pan. Cook, stirring frequently, for 1–2 minutes.

3 Add the water and return all the meat to the pan. Bring just to the boil and skim off any foam that rises to the surface. Reduce the heat and stir in the tomatoes, bay leaf, thyme, oregano, cinnamon, cumin, turmeric and harissa. Simmer for about 1 hour, or until the meat is very tender. Discard the bay leaf.

4 Stir in the chick-peas (garbanzo beans), carrot and potato and simmer for 15 minutes. Add the courgette (zucchini) and peas and continue simmering for 15–20 minutes, or until all the vegetables are tender.

5 Adjust the seasoning, adding more harissa, if desired. Ladle the soup into warm bowls, garnish with mint or coriander (cilantro)

Wonton Soup

The recipe for the wonton skins makes 24 but the soup requires only half this quantity. The other half can be frozen ready for another time.

NUTRITIONAL INFORMATION

Calories 278	Sugars 2g	
Protein 10g	Fat 5g	
Carbohydrate ...50g	Saturates 1g	

45 MINS   5 MINS

SERVES 4

I N G R E D I E N T S

WONTON SKINS

1 egg

6 tbsp water

250 g/9 oz/2 cups plain (all-purpose) flour, plus extra for dusting

FILLING

125 g/4½ oz/½ cup frozen chopped spinach, defrosted

15 g/½ oz/1 tbsp pine kernels (nuts), toasted and chopped

25 g/1 oz/¼ cup minced quorn (TVP)

salt

SOUP

600 ml/1 pint/2½ cups vegetable stock

1 tbsp dry sherry

1 tbsp light soy sauce

2 spring onions (scallions), chopped

 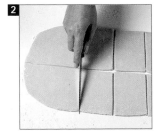 

1 To make the wonton skins, beat the egg lightly in a bowl and mix with the water. Stir in the flour to form a stiff dough. Knead lightly, then cover with a damp cloth and leave to rest for 30 minutes.

2 Roll the dough out into a large sheet about 1.5 mm/¼ inch thick. Cut out 24 x 7 cm/3 inch squares. Dust each one lightly with flour. Only 12 squares are required for the soup so freeze the remainder to use on another occasion.

3 To make the filling, squeeze out the excess water from the spinach. Mix the spinach with the pine kernels (nuts) and quorn (TVP) until thoroughly combined. Season with salt.

4 Divide the mixture into 12 equal portions. Using a teaspoon, place one portion in the centre of each square. Seal the wontons by bringing the opposite corners of each square together and squeezing well.

5 To make the soup, bring the vegetable stock, sherry and soy sauce to the boil, add the wontons and boil rapidly for 2–3 minutes. Add the spring onions (scallions) and serve in warmed bowls immediately.

Chicken, Noodle & Corn Soup

The vermicelli gives this Chinese-style soup an Italian twist, but you can use egg noodles if you prefer.

NUTRITIONAL INFORMATION

Calories 401   Sugars 6g
Protein . . . . .31g   Fat 24g
Carbohydrate . . .17g   Saturates 13g

 5 MINS   25 MINS

SERVES 4

I N G R E D I E N T S

450 g/1 lb boned chicken breasts, cut into strips

1.2 litres/2 pints/5 cups chicken stock

150 ml/¼ pint/⅝ cup double (heavy) cream

100 g/3½ oz/¾ cup dried vermicelli

1 tbsp cornflour (cornstarch)

3 tbsp milk

175 g/6 oz sweetcorn (corn-on-the-cob) kernels

salt and pepper

finely chopped spring onion (scallions), to garnish (optional)

1 Put the chicken strips, chicken stock and double (heavy) cream into a large saucepan and bring to the boil over a low heat.

2 Reduce the heat slightly and simmer for about 20 minutes. Season the soup with salt and black pepper to taste.

3 Meanwhile, cook the vermicelli in lightly salted boiling water for 10-12 minutes, until just tender. Drain the pasta and keep warm.

4 In a small bowl, mix together the cornflour (cornstarch) and milk to make a smooth paste. Stir the

cornflour (cornstarch) paste into the soup until thickened.

5 Add the sweetcorn (corn-on-the-cob) and vermicelli to the pan and heat through.

6 Transfer the soup to a warm tureen or individual soup bowls, garnish with spring onions (scallions), if desired, and serve immediately.

VARIATION

For crab and sweetcorn soup, substitute 450 g/1 lb cooked crabmeat for the chicken breasts. Flake the crabmeat well before adding it to the saucepan and reduce the cooking time by 10 minutes.

Curried Chicken & Corn Soup

Tender cooked chicken strips and baby corn cobs are the main flavours in this delicious clear soup, with just a hint of ginger.

NUTRITIONAL INFORMATION

Calories 206   Sugars 5g
Protein ....29g   Fat 5g
Carbohydrate ...13g   Saturates 1g

5 MINS   30 MINS

SERVES 4

INGREDIENTS

175 g/6 oz can sweetcorn
   (corn), drained

850 ml/1½ pints/3¾ cups
   chicken stock

350 g/12 oz cooked, lean chicken,
   cut into strips

16 baby corn cobs

1 tsp Chinese curry powder

1-cm/½-inch piece fresh root ginger
   (ginger root), grated

3 tbsp light soy sauce

2 tbsp chopped chives

1 Place the canned sweetcorn (corn) in a food processor, together with 150 ml/¼ pint/⅔ cup of the chicken stock and process until the mixture forms a smooth purée.

2 Pass the sweetcorn purée through a fine sieve (strainer), pressing with the back of a spoon to remove any husks.

3 Pour the remaining chicken stock into a large saucepan and add the strips of cooked chicken. Stir in the sweetcorn (corn) purée.

4 Add the baby corn cobs and bring the soup to the boil. Boil the soup for 10 minutes.

5 Add the Chinese curry powder, grated fresh root ginger and light soy sauce and stir well to combine. Cook for a further 10–15 minutes.

6 Stir the chopped chives into the soup.

7 Transfer the curried chicken and corn soup to warm soup bowls and serve immediately.

COOK'S TIP

Prepare the soup up to 24 hours in advance without adding the chicken, cool, cover and store in the refrigerator. Add the chicken and heat the soup through thoroughly before serving.

Chicken Soup with Almonds

This soup can also be made using pheasant breasts. For a really gamy flavour, make game stock from the carcass and use in the soup.

NUTRITIONAL INFORMATION

Calories 219	Sugars 2g	
Protein 18g	Fat 15g	
Carbohydrate 2g	Saturates 2g	

🍲 10 MINS   🕐 20 MINS

SERVES 4

I N G R E D I E N T S

1 large or 2 small boneless skinned chicken breasts

1 tbsp sunflower oil

4 spring onions (scallions), thinly sliced diagonally

1 carrot, cut into julienne strips

700 ml/1¼ pints/3 cups chicken stock

finely grated rind of ¼ lemon

40 g/1½ oz/⅓ cup ground almonds

1 tbsp light soy sauce

1 tbsp lemon juice

25 g/1 oz/¼ cup flaked almonds, toasted

salt and pepper

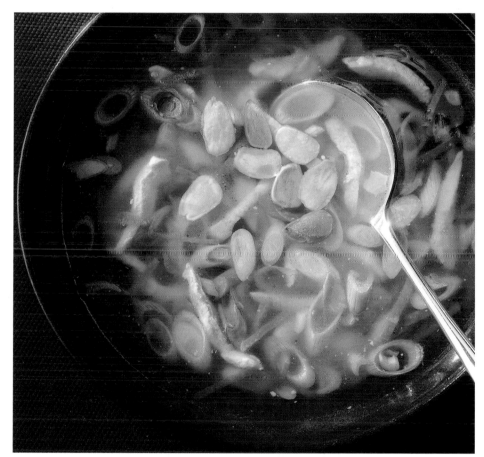

1 Cut each breast into 4 strips lengthways, then slice very thinly across the grain to give shreds of chicken.

2 Heat the oil in a wok, swirling it around until really hot.

3 Add the spring onions (scallions) and cook for 2 minutes, then add the chicken and toss it for 3-4 minutes until sealed and almost cooked through, stirring all the time. Add the carrot strips and stir.

4 Add the stock to the wok and bring to the boil. Add the lemon rind, ground almonds, soy sauce, lemon juice and plenty of seasoning. Bring back to the boil and simmer, uncovered, for 5 minutes, stirring from time to time.

5 Adjust the seasoning, add most of the toasted flaked almonds and continue to cook for a further 1-2 minutes.

6 Serve the soup very hot, in individual bowls, sprinkled with the remaining flaked almonds.

COOK'S TIP

To make game stock, break up a pheasant carcass and place in a pan with 2 litres/3½ pints/8 cups water. Bring to the boil slowly, skimming off any scum. Add 1 bouquet garni, 1 peeled onion and seasoning. Cover and simmer gently for 1½ hours. Strain, and skim any surface fat.

Chicken Wonton Soup

This Chinese-style soup is fiddly to make but is delicious as a starter to an Oriental meal or as a light meal.

NUTRITIONAL INFORMATION

Calories 101	Sugars 0.3g	
Protein 14g	Fat 4g	
Carbohydrate 3g	Saturates 1g	

 15 MINS 10 MINS

SERVES 4-6

I N G R E D I E N T S

FILLING

350 g/12 oz minced (ground) chicken

1 tbsp soy sauce

1 tsp grated, fresh ginger root

1 garlic clove, crushed

2 tsp sherry

2 spring onions (scallions), chopped

1 tsp sesame oil

1 egg white

½ tsp cornflour (cornstarch)

½ tsp sugar

about 35 wonton wrappers

SOUP

1.5 litres/2¾ pints/6 cups chicken stock

1 tbsp light soy sauce

1 spring onion (scallion), shredded

1 small carrot, cut into very thin slices

1 Place all the ingredients for the filling in a large bowl and mix until thoroughly combined.

2 Place a small spoonful of the filling in the centre of each wonton wrapper.

3 Dampen the edges and gather up the wonton wrapper to form a small pouch enclosing the filling.

4 Cook the filled wontons in boiling water for 1 minute or until they float to the top. Remove with a slotted spoon and set aside.

5 Bring the chicken stock to the boil. Add the soy sauce, spring onion (scallion) and carrot.

6 Add the wontons to the soup and simmer gently for 2 minutes. Serve.

COOK'S TIP

Make double quantities of wonton skins and freeze the remainder. Place small squares of baking parchment in between each skin, then place in a freezer bag and freeze. Defrost thoroughly before using.

Clear Chicken & Egg Soup

This tasty chicken soup has the addition of poached eggs, making it both delicious and filling. Use fresh, home-made stock for a better flavour.

NUTRITIONAL INFORMATION

Calories 138	Sugars 1g
Protein 16g	Fat 7g
Carbohydrate 1g	Saturates 2g

5 MINS   35 MINS

SERVES 4

INGREDIENTS

1 tsp salt

1 tbsp rice wine vinegar

4 eggs

850 ml/1½ pints/3¾ cups
   chicken stock

1 leek, sliced

125 g/4½ oz broccoli florets

125 g/4½ oz/1 cup shredded
   cooked chicken

2 open-cap mushrooms, sliced

1 tbsp dry sherry

dash of chilli sauce

chilli powder, to garnish

VARIATION

You could use 4 dried Chinese mushrooms, rehydrated according to the packet instructions, instead of the open-cap mushrooms, if you prefer.

1 Bring a large saucepan of water to the boil and add the salt and rice wine vinegar.

2 Reduce the heat so that it is just simmering and carefully break the eggs into the water, one at a time. Poach the eggs for 1 minute.

3 Remove the poached eggs with a slotted spoon and set aside.

4 Bring the chicken stock to the boil in a separate pan and add the leek, broccoli, chicken, mushrooms and sherry and season with chilli sauce to taste. Cook for 10–15 minutes.

5 Add the poached eggs to the soup and cook for a further 2 minutes. Carefully transfer the soup and poached eggs to 4 soup bowls. Dust with a little chilli powder and serve immediately.

Chicken & Sweetcorn Soup

A hint of chilli and sherry flavour this soup while red pepper and tomato add colour.

NUTRITIONAL INFORMATION

Calories	199	Sugars	.........8g
Protein	........12g	Fat	...........8g
Carbohydrate	...19g	Saturates	.......1g

5 MINS   20 MINS

SERVES 4

INGREDIENTS

1 skinless, boneless chicken breast, about 175 g/6 oz

2 tbsp sunflower oil

2–3 spring onions (scallions), thinly sliced diagonally

1 small or ½ large red (bell) pepper, thinly sliced

1 garlic clove, crushed

125 g/4½ oz baby sweetcorn (corn-on-the-cob), thinly sliced

1 litre/1¾ pints/4 cups chicken stock

200 g/7 oz can of sweetcorn niblets, well drained

2 tbsp sherry

2–3 tsp bottled sweet chilli sauce

2–3 tsp cornflour (cornstarch)

2 tomatoes, quartered and deseeded, then sliced

salt and pepper

chopped fresh coriander (cilantro) or parsley, to garnish

1 Cut the chicken breast into 4 strips lengthways, then cut each strip into narrow slices across the grain.

2 Heat the oil in a wok or frying pan (skillet), swirling it around until it is really hot.

3 Add the chicken and stir-fry for 3–4 minutes, moving it around the wok until it is well sealed all over and almost cooked through.

4 Add the spring onions (scallions), (bell) pepper and garlic, and stir-fry for 2–3 minutes. Add the sweetcorn and stock and bring to the boil.

5 Add the sweetcorn niblets, sherry, sweet chilli sauce and salt to taste, and simmer for 5 minutes, stirring from time to time.

6 Blend the cornflour (cornstarch) with a little cold water. Add to the soup and bring to the boil, stirring until the sauce is thickened. Add the tomato slices, season to taste and simmer for 1–2 minutes.

7 Serve the chicken and sweetcorn soup hot, sprinkled with chopped coriander (cilantro) or parsley.

Chicken Noodle Soup

Quick to make, this hot and spicy soup is hearty and warming. If you like your food really fiery, add a chopped dried or fresh chilli with its seeds.

NUTRITIONAL INFORMATION

Calories 196	Sugars 4g	
Protein 16g	Fat 11g	
Carbohydrate 8g	Saturates 2g	

  10 MINS   25 MINS

SERVES 4-6

INGREDIENTS

1 sheet of dried egg noodles
from a 250 g/9 oz pack

1 tbsp oil

4 skinless, boneless
chicken thighs, diced

1 bunch spring onions (scallions), sliced

2 garlic cloves, chopped

2 cm/¾ inch piece fresh
ginger root, finely chopped

850 ml/1½ pints/3¾ cups chicken stock

200 ml/7 fl oz/scant 1 cup coconut milk

3 tsp red curry paste

3 tbsp peanut butter

2 tbsp light soy sauce

1 small red (bell) pepper, chopped

60 g/2 oz/½ cup frozen peas

salt and pepper

1 Put the noodles in a shallow dish and soak in boiling water as the packet directs.

2 Heat the oil in a large preheated saucepan or wok.

3 Add the diced chicken to the pan or wok and fry for 5 minutes, stirring until lightly browned.

4 Add the white part of the spring onions (scallions), the garlic and ginger and fry for 2 minutes, stirring.

5 Stir in the chicken stock, coconut milk, red curry paste, peanut butter and soy sauce.

6 Season with salt and pepper to taste. Bring to the boil, stirring, then simmer for 8 minutes, stirring occasionally.

7 Add the red (bell) pepper, peas and green spring onion (scallion) tops and cook for 2 minutes.

8 Add the drained noodles and heat through. Spoon the chicken noodle soup into warmed bowls and serve with a spoon and fork.

VARIATION

Green curry paste can be used instead of red curry paste for a less fiery flavour.

Spicy Chicken Noodle Soup

This filling soup is filled with spicy flavours and bright colours for a really attractive and hearty dish.

NUTRITIONAL INFORMATION

Calories . . . . . . .286 Sugars 21g
Protein . . . . .22g Fat 6g
Carbohydrate . . .37g Saturates 1g

15 MINS   20 MINS

SERVES 4

INGREDIENTS

2 tbsp tamarind paste

4 red chillies, finely chopped

2 cloves garlic, crushed

2.5 cm/1-inch piece Thai ginger, peeled and very finely chopped

4 tbsp fish sauce

2 tbsp palm sugar or caster (superfine) sugar

8 lime leaves, roughly torn

1.2 litres/2 pints/5 cups chicken stock

350 g/12 oz boneless chicken breast

100 g/3½ oz carrots, very thinly sliced

350 g/12 oz sweet potato, diced

100 g/3½ oz baby corn cobs, halved

3 tbsp fresh coriander (cilantro), roughly chopped

100 g/3½ oz cherry tomatoes, halved

150 g/5½ oz flat rice noodles

fresh coriander (cilantro), chopped, to garnish

1 Preheat a large wok or frying pan (skillet). Place the tamarind paste, chillies, garlic, ginger, fish sauce, sugar, lime leaves and chicken stock in the wok and bring to the boil, stirring constantly. Reduce the heat and cook for about 5 minutes.

2 Using a sharp knife, thinly slice the chicken. Add the chicken to the wok and cook for a further 5 minutes, stirring the mixture well.

3 Reduce the heat and add the carrots, sweet potato and baby corn cobs to the wok. Leave to simmer, uncovered, for 5 minutes, or until the vegetables are just tender and the chicken is completely cooked through.

4 Stir in the chopped fresh coriander (cilantro), cherry tomatoes and flat rice noodles.

5 Leave the soup to simmer for about 5 minutes, or until the noodles are tender.

6 Garnish the spicy chicken noodle soup with chopped fresh coriander (cilantro) and serve hot.

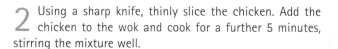

Peking Duck Soup

This is a hearty and robustly flavoured soup, containing pieces of duck and vegetables cooked in a rich stock.

🕒 5 MINS   🕐 35 MINS

SERVES 4

I N G R E D I E N T S

125 g/4½ oz lean duck breast meat

225 g/8 oz Chinese leaves (cabbage)

850 ml/1½ pints/3¾ cups chicken or duck stock

1 tbsp dry sherry or rice wine

1 tbsp light soy sauce

2 garlic cloves, crushed

pinch of ground star anise

1 tbsp sesame seeds

1 tsp sesame oil

1 tbsp chopped fresh parsley

1 Remove the skin from the duck breast and finely dice the flesh.

2 Using a sharp knife, shred the Chinese leaves (cabbage).

3 Put the stock in a large saucepan and bring to the boil. Add the sherry or rice wine, soy sauce, diced duck meat and shredded Chinese leaves and stir to mix thoroughly. Reduce the heat and leave to simmer gently for 15 minutes.

4 Stir in the garlic and star anise and cook over a low heat for a further 10–15 minutes, or until the duck is tender.

5 Meanwhile, dry-fry the sesame seeds in a preheated, heavy-based frying pan (skillet) or wok, stirring constantly.

6 Remove the sesame seeds from the pan and stir them into the soup, together with the sesame oil and chopped fresh parsley.

7 Spoon the soup into warm bowls and serve immediately.

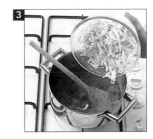

VARIATION

If Chinese leaves (cabbage) are unavailable, use leafy green cabbage instead. You may wish to adjust the quantity to taste, as Western cabbage has a stronger flavour and odour than Chinese leaves (cabbage).

Chicken & Coconut Soup

This fragrant soup combines citrus flavours with coconut and a hint of piquancy from chillies.

NUTRITIONAL INFORMATION

Calories 345	Sugars 2g	
Protein 28g	Fat 24g	
Carbohydrate 5g	Saturates 18g	

2¼ HOURS   15 MINS

SERVES 4

INGREDIENTS

350 g/12 oz/1¾ cups cooked, skinned chicken breast

125 g/4½ oz/1⅛ cups unsweetened desiccated coconut

500 ml/16 fl oz/2 cups boiling water

500 ml/18 fl oz/2 cups Fresh Chicken Stock (see page 14)

4 spring onions (scallions), white and green parts, sliced thinly

2 stalks lemon grass

1 lime

1 tsp grated ginger root

1 tbsp light soy sauce

2 tsp ground coriander

2 large fresh red chillies

1 tbsp chopped fresh coriander (cilantro)

1 tbsp cornflour (cornstarch), mixed with 2 tbsp cold water

salt and white pepper

chopped red chilli, to garnish

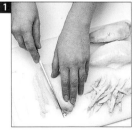  

1 Using a sharp knife, slice the chicken into thin strips.

2 Place the coconut in a heatproof bowl and pour over the boiling water. Work the coconut mixture through a sieve (strainer). Pour the coconut water into a large saucepan and add the stock.

3 Add the spring onions (scallions) to the saucepan. Slice the base of each lemon grass and discard damaged leaves. Bruise the stalks and add to the saucepan.

4 Peel the rind from the lime in large strips. Extract the juice and add to the pan with the lime strips, ginger, soy sauce and coriander. Bruise the chillies with a fork then add to the pan. Heat the pan to just below boiling point.

5 Add the chicken and fresh coriander (cilantro) to the saucepan, bring to the boil, then simmer for 10 minutes.

6 Discard the lemon grass, lime rind and red chillies. Pour the blended cornflour (cornstarch) mixture into the saucepan and stir until slightly thickened. Season with salt and white pepper to taste and serve immediately, garnished with chopped red chilli.

Thai-Style Chicken Soup

Make this soup when you want a change from traditional chicken soup.
Use a generous amount of fresh coriander leaves (cilantro) to garnish.

 10 MINS   40 MINS

SERVES 4

INGREDIENTS

1.2 litres/2 pints/5 cups chicken stock

200 g/7 oz skinless boned chicken

1 fresh chilli, split lengthways and deseeded

7.5 cm/3 inch piece lemon grass, split lengthways

3-4 lime leaves

2.5 cm/1 inch piece fresh ginger root, peeled and sliced

120 ml/4 fl oz/½ cup coconut milk

6-8 spring onions (scallions), sliced diagonally

¼ tsp chilli purée (paste), or to taste

salt

fresh coriander leaves (cilantro), to garnish

1 Put the stock in a pan with the chicken, chilli, lemon grass, lime leaves and ginger. Bring almost to the boil, reduce the heat, cover and simmer for 20–25 minutes, or until the chicken is cooked through and firm to the touch.

2 Remove the chicken and strain the stock. When the chicken is cool, slice thinly or shred into bite-sized pieces.

3 Return the stock to the saucepan and heat to simmering. Stir in the coconut milk and spring onions (scallions). Add the chicken and continue simmering for about 10 minutes, until the soup is heated through and the flavours have mingled.

4 Stir in the chilli purée (paste). Season to taste with salt and, if wished, add a little more chilli purée (paste).

5 Ladle into warm bowls and float fresh coriander leaves (cilantro) on top to serve.

COOK'S TIP

Once the stock is flavoured and the chicken cooked, this soup is very quick to finish. If you wish, poach the chicken and strain the stock ahead of time. Store in the refrigerator separately.

Hot & Sour Soup

This well-known soup from Peking is unusual in that it is thickened. The 'hot' flavour is achieved by the addition of plenty of black pepper.

NUTRITIONAL INFORMATION

Calories	124	Sugars	.........1g
Protein	.........5g	Fat	...........8g
Carbohydrate	....8g	Saturates	.......1g

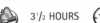

3½ HOURS   25 MINS

SERVES 4

I N G R E D I E N T S

2 tbsp cornflour (cornstarch)

4 tbsp water

2 tbsp light soy sauce

3 tbsp rice wine vinegar

½ tsp ground black pepper

1 small fresh red chilli, finely chopped

1 egg

2 tbsp vegetable oil

1 onion, chopped

850 ml/1½ pints/3¾ cups chicken or beef consommé

1 open-cap mushroom, sliced

50 g/1¾ oz skinless chicken breast, cut into very thin strips

1 tsp sesame oil

1 In a mixing bowl, blend the cornflour (cornstarch) with the water to form a smooth paste.

2 Add the soy sauce, rice wine vinegar and black pepper.

3 Finely chop the red chilli and add to the ingredients in the bowl. Mix well.

4 Break the egg into a separate bowl and beat well. Set aside while you cook the other ingredients.

5 Heat the oil in a preheated wok and fry the onion for 1–2 minutes until softened.

6 Stir in the consommé, mushroom and chicken and bring to the boil. Cook for about 15 minutes or until the chicken is tender.

7 Gradually pour the cornflour (cornstarch) mixture into the soup and cook, stirring constantly, until it thickens.

8 As you are stirring, gradually drizzle the egg into the soup, to create threads of egg.

9 Pour the hot and sour soup into a warm tureen or individual serving bowls, sprinkle with the sesame oil and serve immediately.

Chicken Soup with Stars

How delicious a simple, fresh soup can be. Chicken wings are good to use for making the stock, as the meat is very sweet and doesn't dry out.

NUTRITIONAL INFORMATION

Calories 551	Sugar 5g	
Protein 45g	Fats 35g	
Carbohydrates . . .15g	Saturates 9g	

  15 MINS   3 HOURS

SERVES 4

I N G R E D I E N T S

75 g/2¾ oz small pasta stars, or other very small shapes

chopped fresh parsley

C H I C K E N   S T O C K

1.2 kg/2 lb 8 oz chicken pieces, such as wings or legs

2.5 litres/4⅓ pints/10 cups water

1 celery stalk, sliced

1 large carrot, sliced

1 onion, sliced

1 leek, sliced

2 garlic cloves, crushed

8 peppercorns

4 allspice berries

3–4 parsley stems

2–3 fresh thyme sprigs

1 bay leaf

½ tsp salt

pepper

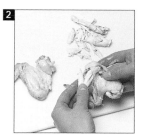

1 Put the chicken in a large 4 litre/7 pint/16 cup pot with the water, celery, carrot, onion, leek, garlic, peppercorns, allspice, herbs and salt. Bring just to the boil and skim off the foam that rises to the surface. Reduce the heat and simmer, partially covered, for 2 hours.

2 Remove the chicken from the stock and set aside to cool. Continue simmering the stock, uncovered, for about 30 minutes. When the chicken is cool enough to handle, remove the meat from the bones and, if necessary, cut into bite-sized pieces.

3 Strain the stock and remove as much fat as possible. Discard the vegetables and flavourings. (There should be about 1.8 litres/3 pints/7½ cups of chicken stock.)

4 Bring the stock to the boil in a clean saucepan. Add the pasta and regulate the heat so that the stock boils very gently. Cook for about 10 minutes, or until the pasta is tender.

5 Stir in the chicken meat. Taste the soup and adjust the seasoning. Ladle into warm bowls and serve sprinkled with parsley.

Chicken & Rice Soup

Any kind of rice is suitable for this soup – white or brown long-grain rice, or even wild rice. Leftover cooked rice is a handy addition for soups.

NUTRITIONAL INFORMATION

Calories	.100	Sugar	.4g
Protein	.4g	Fats	.2g
Carbohydrates	.19g	Saturates	.0g

 10 MINS   25 MINS

SERVES 4

I N G R E D I E N T S

1.5 litres/2¾ pints/6¼ cups chicken stock (see Cook's Tip)

2 small carrots, very thinly sliced

1 stalk celery, finely diced

1 baby leek, halved lengthways and thinly sliced

115 g/4 oz tiny peas, defrosted if frozen

175 g/6 oz/1 cup cooked rice

150 g/5½ oz cooked chicken meat, sliced

2 tsp chopped fresh tarragon

1 tbsp chopped fresh parsley

salt and pepper

fresh parsley sprigs, to garnish

1 Put the stock in a large saucepan and add the carrots, celery and leek. Bring to the boil, reduce the heat to low and simmer gently, partially covered, for 10 minutes.

2 Stir in the peas, rice and chicken meat and continue cooking for a further 10–15 minutes, or until the vegetables are tender.

3 Add the chopped tarragon and parsley, then taste and adjust the seasoning, adding salt and pepper as needed.

4 Ladle the soup into warm bowls, garnish with parsley and serve.

COOK'S TIP

If the stock you are using is a little weak, or if you have used a stock cube, add the herbs at the beginning, so that they can flavour the stock for a longer time.

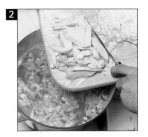

Oriental Duck Broth

This soup combines delicate flavours with a satisfying meaty taste.

NUTRITIONAL INFORMATION

Calories 76   Sugar 5g
Protein ....6g   Fats 2g
Carbohydrates ....9g   Saturates 1g

15 MINS   1¾ HOURS

SERVES 4

INGREDIENTS

2 duck leg quarters, skinned

1 litre/1¾ pints/4 cups water

600 ml/1 pint/2½ cups chicken stock

2.5 cm/1 inch piece fresh ginger root, peeled and sliced

1 large carrot, sliced

1 onion, sliced

1 leek, sliced

3 garlic cloves, crushed

I tsp black peppercorns

2 tbsp soy sauce, or to taste

I small carrot, cut into thin strips or slivers

I small leek, cut into thin strips or slivers

100 g/3½ oz shiitake mushrooms, thinly sliced

25 g/1 oz watercress leaves

salt and pepper

1 Put the duck in a large saucepan with the water. Bring just to the boil and skim off the foam that rises to the surface. Add the stock, ginger, carrot, onion, leek, garlic, peppercorns and soy sauce. Reduce the heat and simmer, partially covered, for 1½ hours.

2 Remove the duck from the stock and set aside. When the duck is cool enough to handle, remove the meat from the bones and slice thinly or shred into bite-sized pieces, discarding any fat.

3 Strain the stock and press with the back of a spoon to extract all the liquid. Remove as much fat as possible. Discard the vegetables and herbs.

4 Bring the stock just to the boil in a clean saucepan and add the strips of carrot and leek and the mushrooms together with the duck meat. Reduce the heat and cook gently for 5 minutes, or until the carrot is just tender.

5 Stir in the watercress and continue simmering for 1–2 minutes until it is wilted. Taste the soup and adjust the seasoning if needed, adding a little more soy sauce if wished. Ladle the soup into warm bowls and serve at once.

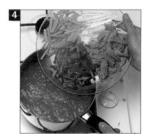

European
Soups

Soups are an important part of Mediterranean cuisine and vary in content from hearty bean concoctions suitable for the coldest winter's day to creamy Vichyssoise and meaty

stews. In this chapter there are nourishing lentil soup recipes, variations on Minestrone soup and thick fish soups. Dishes are also included from France, including Provence and Brittany, Hungary, and a delicious lemony-flavoured Greek bean soup. Many of these soups are suitable for a main-course meal when combined with delicious freshly baked bread.

Tomato & Pasta Soup

Plum tomatoes are ideal for making soups and sauces
as they have denser, less watery flesh than rounder varieties.

NUTRITIONAL INFORMATION

Calories 503	Sugars 16g	
Protein 9g	Fat 28g	
Carbohydrate ...59g	Saturates 17g	

5 MINS   50–55 MINS

SERVES 4

INGREDIENTS

60 g/2 oz/4 tbsp unsalted butter

1 large onion, chopped

600 ml/1 pint/2 ½ cups vegetable stock

900 g/2 lb Italian plum tomatoes, skinned
 and roughly chopped

pinch of bicarbonate of soda (baking soda)

225 g/8 oz/2 cups dried fusilli

1 tbsp caster (superfine) sugar

150 ml/ ¼ pint/ ⅔ cup double (heavy) cream

salt and pepper

fresh basil leaves, to garnish

1 Melt the butter in a large pan, add the
onion and fry for 3 minutes, stirring.
Add 300 ml/ ½ pint/1 ¼ cups of vegetable
stock to the pan, with the chopped
tomatoes and bicarbonate of soda (baking

soda). Bring the soup to the boil and
simmer for 20 minutes.

2 Remove the pan from the heat and
set aside to cool. Purée the soup in
a blender or food processor and pour
through a fine strainer back into
the saucepan.

3 Add the remaining vegetable stock
and the fusilli to the pan, and season
to taste with salt and pepper.

4 Add the sugar to the pan, bring to the
boil, then lower the heat and simmer
for about 15 minutes.

5 Pour the soup into a warm tureen,
swirl the double (heavy) cream around
the surface of the soup and garnish with
fresh basil leaves. Serve immediately.

VARIATION

To make orange and tomato
soup, simply use half the
quantity of vegetable stock,
topped up with the same amount
of fresh orange juice and garnish
the soup with orange rind.

Gazpacho

This Spanish soup is full of chopped and grated vegetables with a puréed tomato base. It requires chilling, so prepare well in advance.

NUTRITIONAL INFORMATION

Calories 140	Sugars 12g
Protein 3g	Fat 9g
Carbohydrate ...13g	Saturates 1g

6½ HOURS   0 MINS

SERVES 4

INGREDIENTS

½ small cucumber

½ small green (bell) pepper, seeded and
　　very finely chopped

500 g/1 lb 2 oz ripe tomatoes, peeled or
　　400 g/14 oz can chopped tomatoes

½ onion, coarsely chopped

2–3 garlic cloves, crushed

3 tbsp olive oil

2 tbsp white wine vinegar

1–2 tbsp lemon or lime juice

2 tbsp tomato purée (paste)

450 ml/16 fl oz/scant 2 cups tomato juice

salt and pepper

TO SERVE

chopped green (bell) pepper

thinly sliced onion rings

garlic croûtons

1 Coarsely grate the cucumber into a large bowl and add the chopped green (bell) pepper.

2 Process the tomatoes, onion and garlic in a food processor or blender, then add the oil, vinegar, lemon or lime juice and tomato purée (paste) and process until smooth. Alternatively, finely chop the tomatoes and finely grate the onion, then mix both with the garlic, oil, vinegar, lemon or lime juice and tomato purée (paste).

3 Add the tomato mixture to the bowl and mix well, then add the tomato juice and mix again.

4 Season to taste, cover the bowl with clear film (plastic wrap) and chill thoroughly – for at least 6 hours and preferably longer so that the flavours have time to meld together.

5 Prepare the side dishes of green (bell) pepper, onion rings and garlic croûtons, and arrange in individual serving bowls.

6 Ladle the soup into bowls, preferably from a soup tureen set on the table with the side dishes placed around it. Hand the dishes around to allow the guests to help themselves.

Thick Onion Soup

A delicious creamy soup with grated carrot and parsley for texture and colour. Serve with crusty cheese scones for a hearty lunch.

NUTRITIONAL INFORMATION

Calories 277	Sugars 12g
Protein 6g	Fat 20g
Carbohydrate ...19g	Saturates 8g

 20 MINS   1HR 10 MINS

SERVES 6

I N G R E D I E N T S

75 g/2¾ oz/5 tbsp butter

500 g/1 lb 2 oz onions, finely chopped

1 garlic clove, crushed

40 g/1½ oz/6 tbsp plain (all-purpose) flour

600 ml/1 pint/2½ cups vegetable stock

600 ml/1 pint/2½ cups milk

2–3 tsp lemon or lime juice

good pinch of ground allspice

1 bay leaf

1 carrot, coarsely grated

4–6 tbsp double (heavy) cream

2 tbsp chopped parsley

salt and pepper

C H E E S E S C O N E S (B I S C U I T S)

225 g/8 oz/2 cups malted wheat or
    wholemeal (whole wheat) flour

2 tsp baking powder

60 g/2 oz/¼ cup butter

4 tbsp grated Parmesan cheese

1 egg, beaten

about 75 ml/3 fl oz/⅓ cup milk

1 Melt the butter in a saucepan and fry the onions and garlic over a low heat, stirring frequently, for 10–15 minutes, until soft, but not coloured. Stir in the flour and cook, stirring, for 1 minute, then gradually stir in the stock and bring to the boil, stirring frequently. Add the milk, then bring back to the boil.

2 Season to taste with salt and pepper and add 2 teaspoons of the lemon or lime juice, the allspice and bay leaf. Cover and simmer for about 25 minutes until the vegetables are tender. Discard the bay leaf.

3 Meanwhile, make the scones (biscuits). Combine the flour, baking powder and seasoning and rub in the butter until the mixture resembles fine breadcrumbs. Stir in 3 tablespoons of the cheese, the egg and enough milk to mix to a soft dough.

4 Shape into a bar about 2 cm/¾ inch thick. Place on a floured baking tray (cookie sheet) and mark into slices. Sprinkle with the remaining cheese and bake in a preheated oven, 220°C/425°F/Gas Mark 7, for about 20 minutes, until risen and golden brown.

5 Stir the carrot into the soup and simmer for 2–3 minutes. Add more lemon or lime juice, if necessary. Stir in the cream and reheat. Garnish and serve with the warm scones (biscuits).

Potato & Pesto Soup

Fresh pesto is a treat to the taste buds and very different in flavour from that available from supermarkets. Store fresh pesto in the refrigerator.

NUTRITIONAL INFORMATION

Calories 548   Sugars 0g
Protein ....11g   Fat 52g
Carbohydrate ...10g   Saturates 18g

5–10 MINS   50 MINS

SERVES 4

INGREDIENTS

3 slices rindless, smoked, fatty bacon

450 g/1 lb floury potatoes

450 g/ 1 lb onions

2 tbsp olive oil

25 g/1 oz/2 tbsp butter

600 ml/1 pint/2 ½ cups chicken stock

600 ml/1 pint/2 ½ cups milk

100 g/3 ½ oz/ ¾ cup dried conchigliette

150 ml/ ¼ pint/ ⅝ cup double (heavy) cream

chopped fresh parsley

salt and pepper

freshly grated Parmesan cheese and garlic
    bread, to serve

PESTO SAUCE

60 g/2 oz/1 cup finely chopped fresh
    parsley

2 garlic cloves, crushed

60 g/2 oz/ ⅔ cup pine nuts (kernels),
    crushed

2 tbsp chopped fresh basil leaves

60 g/2 oz/ ⅔ cup freshly grated Parmesan
    cheese

white pepper

150 ml/ ¼ pint/ ⅝ cup olive oil

1 To make the pesto sauce, put all of the ingredients in a blender or food processor and process for 2 minutes, or blend by hand using a pestle and mortar.

2 Finely chop the bacon, potatoes and onions. Fry the bacon in a large pan over a medium heat for 4 minutes. Add the butter, potatoes and onions and cook for 12 minutes, stirring constantly.

3 Add the stock and milk to the pan, bring to the boil and simmer for 10 minutes. Add the conchigliette and simmer for a further 10-12 minutes.

4 Blend in the cream and simmer for 5 minutes. Add the parsley, salt and pepper and 2 tbsp pesto sauce. Transfer the soup to serving bowls and serve with Parmesan cheese and fresh garlic bread.

Broccoli & Potato Soup

This creamy soup has a delightful pale green colouring and rich flavour from the blend of tender broccoli and blue cheese.

NUTRITIONAL INFORMATION

Calories	452	Sugars	.........4g
Protein	........14g	Fat	..........35g
Carbohydrate	...20g	Saturates	......19g

 5-10 MINS   40 MINS

SERVES 4

INGREDIENTS

2 tbsp olive oil

2 potatoes, diced

1 onion, diced

225 g/8 oz broccoli florets

125 g/4½ oz blue cheese, crumbled

1 litre/1¾ pints/4½ cups vegetable stock

150 ml/¼ pint/⅔ cup double (heavy) cream

pinch of paprika

salt and pepper

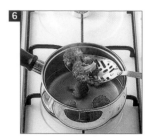

1 Heat the oil in a large saucepan. Add the potatoes and onion. Sauté, stirring constantly, for 5 minutes.

2 Reserve a few broccoli florets for the garnish and add the remaining broccoli to the pan. Add the cheese and vegetable stock.

COOK'S TIP

This soup freezes very successfully. Follow the method described here up to step 4, and freeze the soup after it has been puréed. Add the cream and paprika just before serving. Garnish and serve.

3 Bring to the boil, then reduce the heat, cover the pan and simmer for 25 minutes, until the potatoes are tender.

4 Transfer the soup to a food processor or blender in batches and process until the mixture is smooth. Alternatively, press the vegetables through a strainer with the back of a wooden spoon.

5 Return the purée to a clean saucepan and stir in the double (heavy) cream

and a pinch of paprika. Season to taste with salt and pepper.

6 Blanch the reserved broccoli florets in a little boiling water for about 2 minutes, then lift them out of the pan with a slotted spoon.

7 Pour the soup into warmed individual bowls and garnish with the broccoli florets and a sprinkling of paprika. Serve immediately.

Artichoke Soup

This refreshing chilled soup is ideal for *al fresco* dining. Bear in mind that this soup needs to be chilled for 3-4 hours, so allow plenty of time.

NUTRITIONAL INFORMATION

Calories 159	Sugars 2g
Protein 2g	Fat 15
Carbohydrate 5g	Saturates 6g

5 MINS   15 MINS

SERVES 4

I N G R E D I E N T S

1 tbsp olive oil

1 onion, chopped

1 garlic clove, crushed

2 x 400 g/14 oz can artichoke hearts,
    drained

600 ml/1 pint/2 ½ cups hot vegetable stock

150 ml/¼ pint/⅔ cup single (light) cream

2 tbsp fresh thyme, stalks removed

2 sun-dried tomatoes, cut into strips

fresh, crusty bread, to serve

1 Heat the oil in a large saucepan and fry the chopped onion and crushed garlic, stirring, for 2–3 minutes or until just softened.

2 Using a sharp knife, roughly chop the artichoke hearts. Add the artichoke pieces to the onion and garlic mixture in the pan. Pour in the hot vegetable stock, stirring well.

3 Bring the mixture to the boil, then reduce the heat and leave to simmer, covered, for about 3 minutes.

4 Place the mixture into a food processor and blend until smooth. Alternatively, push the mixture through a sieve to remove any lumps.

5 Return the soup to the saucepan. Stir the single (light) cream and fresh thyme into the soup.

6 Transfer the soup to a large bowl, cover, and leave to chill in the refrigerator for about 3–4 hours.

7 Transfer the chilled soup to individual soup bowls and garnish with strips of sun-dried tomato. Serve with crusty bread.

VARIATION

Try adding 2 tablespoons of dry vermouth, such as Martini, to the soup in step 5, if you wish.

Cream of Artichoke Soup

A creamy soup with the unique, subtle flavouring of Jerusalem artichokes and a garnish of grated carrots for extra crunch.

NUTRITIONAL INFORMATION

Calories 19   Sugars 0g
Protein ....0.4g   Fat 2g
Carbohydrate ...0.7g   Saturates 0.7g

 10–15 MINS   55–60 MINS

SERVES 6

INGREDIENTS

750 g/1 lb 10 oz Jerusalem artichokes

1 lemon, sliced thickly

60 g/2 oz/¼ cup butter or margarine

2 onions, chopped

1 garlic clove, crushed

1.25 litres/2¼ pints/5½ cups chicken or
    vegetable stock

2 bay leaves

¼ tsp ground mace or ground nutmeg

1 tbsp lemon juice

150 ml/¼ pint/⅔ cup single (light) cream or
    natural fromage frais

salt and pepper

TO GARNISH

coarsely grated carrot

chopped fresh parsley or coriander
    (cilantro)

1 Peel and slice the artichokes. Put into a bowl of water with the lemon slices.

2 Melt the butter or margarine in a large saucepan. Add the onions and garlic and fry gently for 3–4 minutes until soft but not coloured.

3 Drain the artichokes (discarding the lemon) and add to the pan. Mix well and cook gently for 2–3 minutes without allowing to colour.

4 Add the stock, seasoning, bay leaves, mace or nutmeg and lemon juice. Bring slowly to the boil, then cover and simmer gently for about 30 minutes until the vegetables are very tender.

5 Discard the bay leaves. Cool the soup slightly then press through a sieve (strainer) or blend in a food processor until smooth. If liked, a little of the soup may be only partially puréed and added to the rest of the puréed soup, to give extra texture.

6 Pour into a clean pan and bring to the boil. Adjust the seasoning and stir in the cream or fromage frais. Reheat gently without boiling. Garnish with grated carrot and chopped parsley or coriander (cilantro).

Roasted Vegetable Soup

Roasting the vegetables gives this soup its intense, rich flavour, reminiscent of ratatouille.

NUTRITIONAL INFORMATION

Calories 153   Sugar 13g
Protein ....5g   Fats 9g
Carbohydrates ...15g   Saturates 3g

15 MINS   1¼ HOURS

SERVES 6

I N G R E D I E N T S

2–3 tbsp olive oil

700 g/1 lb 9 oz ripe tomatoes, skinned, cored and halved

3 large yellow (bell) peppers, halved, cored and deseeded

3 courgettes (zucchini), halved lengthways

1 small aubergine (eggplant), halved lengthways

4 garlic cloves, halved

2 onions, cut into eighths

pinch of dried thyme

1 litre/1 ¾ pints/4 cups chicken, vegetable or meat stock

120 ml/4 fl oz/ ½ cup single (light) cream

salt and pepper

shredded basil leaves, to garnish

1 Brush a large shallow baking dish with olive oil. Laying them cut-side down, arrange the tomatoes, (bell) peppers, courgettes (zucchini) and aubergine (eggplant) in one layer (use two dishes, if necessary). Tuck the garlic cloves and onion pieces into the gaps and drizzle the vegetables with olive oil. Season lightly with salt and pepper and sprinkle with the thyme.

2 Place in a preheated oven at 190°C/375°C/Gas Mark 5 and bake, uncovered, for 30–35 minutes, or until soft and browned around the edges. Leave to cool, then scrape out the aubergine (eggplant) flesh and remove the skin from the (bell) peppers.

3 Working in batches, put the aubergine (eggplant) and (bell) pepper flesh, together with the courgettes (zucchini), into a food processor and chop to the consistency of salsa or pickle; do not purée. Alternatively, place in a bowl and chop together with a knife.

4 Combine the stock and chopped vegetable mixture in a saucepan and simmer over a medium heat for between 20–30 minutes until all the vegetables are tender and the flavours have completely blended.

5 Stir in the cream and simmer over a low heat for about 5 minutes, stirring occasionally until hot. Taste and adjust the seasoning, if necessary. Ladle the soup into warm bowls, garnish with basil and serve.

Vegetable with Pesto Soup

This soup takes advantage of summer vegetables bursting with flavour.

NUTRITIONAL INFORMATION

Calories	262	Sugar	.........6g
Protein	........14g	Fats	..........15g
Carbohydrates	...20g	Saturates	......4g

15 MINS   55 MINS

SERVES 6

INGREDIENTS

1 tbsp olive oil

1 onion, finely chopped

1 large leek, split and thinly sliced

1 stalk celery, thinly sliced

1 carrot, quartered and thinly sliced

1 garlic clove, finely chopped

1.4 litres/2½ pints/6 cups water

1 potato, diced

1 parsnip, finely diced

1 small kohlrabi or turnip, diced

150 g/5½ oz green beans, cut in small pieces

150 g/5½ oz fresh or frozen peas

2 small courgettes (zucchini), quartered lengthways and sliced

400 g/14 oz can flageolet beans, drained and rinsed

100 g/3½ oz spinach leaves, cut into thin ribbons

salt and pepper

PESTO:

1 large garlic clove, very finely chopped

15 g/½ oz basil leaves

75 g/2¾ oz Parmesan cheese, grated

4 tbsp extra-virgin olive oil

1 Heat the olive oil in a large saucepan over a medium-low heat. Add the onion and leek and cook for 5 minutes, stirring occasionally, until the onion softens. Add the celery, carrot and garlic and cook, covered, for a further 5 minutes, stirring frequently.

2 Add the water, potato, parsnip, kohlrabi or turnip and green beans. Bring to the boil, reduce the heat to low and simmer, covered, for 5 minutes.

3 Add the peas, courgettes (zucchini) and flageolet beans, and season generously with salt and pepper. Cover again and simmer for about 25 minutes until all the vegetables are tender.

4 Meanwhile, make the pesto. Put the garlic, basil and cheese in a food processor with the olive oil and process until smooth, scraping down the sides as necessary. Alternatively, pound together using a pestle and mortar.

5 Add the spinach to the soup and simmer for a further 5 minutes. Taste and adjust the seasoning and stir about a table-spoon of the pesto into the soup. Ladle into warm bowls and pass the remaining pesto separately.

Vichyssoise

This is a classic creamy soup made from potatoes and leeks. To achieve the delicate pale colour, be sure to use only the white parts of the leeks.

NUTRITIONAL INFORMATION

Calories 208	Sugars 5g	
Protein 5g	Fat 12g	
Carbohydrate ...20g	Saturates 6g	

 10 MINS   40 MINS

SERVES 6

INGREDIENTS

3 large leeks

40 g/1½ oz/3 tbsp butter or margarine

1 onion, thinly sliced

500 g/1 lb 2 oz potatoes, chopped

850 ml/1½ pints/3½ cups vegetable stock

2 tsp lemon juice

pinch of ground nutmeg

¼ tsp ground coriander

1 bay leaf

1 egg yolk

150 ml/¼ pint/⅔ cup single (light) cream

salt and white pepper

TO GARNISH

freshly snipped chives

1 Trim the leeks and remove most of the green part. Slice the white part of the leeks very finely.

2 Melt the butter or margarine in a saucepan. Add the leeks and onion and fry, stirring occasionally, for about 5 minutes without browning.

3 Add the potatoes, vegetable stock, lemon juice, nutmeg, coriander and

bay leaf to the pan, season to taste with salt and pepper and bring to the boil. Cover and simmer for about 30 minutes, until all the vegetables are very soft.

4 Cool the soup a little, remove and discard the bay leaf and then press through a strainer or process in a food processor or blender until smooth. Pour into a clean pan.

5 Blend the egg yolk into the cream, add a little of the soup to the mixture and then whisk it all back into the soup and reheat gently, without boiling. Adjust the seasoning to taste. Cool and then chill thoroughly in the refrigerator.

6 Serve the soup sprinkled with freshly snipped chives.

Tuscan Onion Soup

This soup is best made with white onions, which have a mild flavour. If you cannot get hold of them, try using large Spanish onions instead.

NUTRITIONAL INFORMATION

Calories 390   Sugars 0g
Protein ....9g   Fat 33g
Carbohydrate ...15g   Saturates 14g

  5–10 MINS   40–45 MINS

SERVES 4

I N G R E D I E N T S

50 g/1¾ oz pancetta ham, diced

1 tbsp olive oil

4 large white onions, sliced thinly into rings

3 garlic cloves, chopped

850 ml/1½ pints/3½ cups hot chicken or
  ham stock

4 slices ciabatta or other Italian bread

50 g/1¾ oz/3 tbsp butter

75 g/2¾ oz Gruyère or Cheddar

salt and pepper

1 Dry fry the pancetta in a large saucepan for 3–4 minutes until it begins to brown. Remove the pancetta from the pan and set aside until required.

2 Add the oil to the pan and cook the onions and garlic over a high heat for 4 minutes. Reduce the heat, cover and cook for 15 minutes or until the onions are lightly caramelized.

3 Add the stock to the saucepan and bring to the boil. Reduce the heat and leave the mixture to simmer, covered, for about 10 minutes.

4 Toast the slices of ciabatta on both sides, under a preheated grill (broiler), for 2–3 minutes or until golden. Spread the ciabatta with butter and top with the Gruyère or Cheddar cheese. Cut the bread into bite-size pieces.

5 Add the reserved pancetta to the soup and season with salt and pepper to taste.

6 Pour into 4 soup bowls and top with the toasted bread.

COOK'S TIP

Pancetta is similar to bacon, but it is air- and salt-cured for about 6 months. Pancetta is available from most delicatessens and some large supermarkets. If you cannot obtain pancetta use unsmoked bacon instead.

Fish Soup

There are many varieties of fish soup in Italy, some including shellfish. This one, from Tuscany, is more like a chowder.

 5–10 MINS   1 HOUR

SERVES 6

INGREDIENTS

1 kg/2 lb 4 oz assorted prepared fish

(including mixed fish fillets, squid, etc.)

2 onions, sliced thinly

2 celery stalks, sliced thinly

a few sprigs of parsley

2 bay leaves

150 ml/¼ pint/⅔ cup white wine

1 litre/1 ¾ pints/4 cups water

2 tbsp olive oil

1 garlic clove, crushed

1 carrot, chopped finely

400 g/14 oz can peeled tomatoes, puréed

2 potatoes, chopped

1 tbsp tomato purée (paste)

1 tsp chopped fresh oregano or ½ tsp

dried oregano

350 g/12 oz fresh mussels

175 g/6 oz peeled prawns (shrimp)

2 tbsp chopped fresh parsley

salt and pepper

crusty bread, to serve

1 Cut the fish into slices and put into a pan with half the onion and celery, the parsley, bay leaves, wine and water. Bring to the boil, cover and simmer for 25 minutes.

2 Strain the fish stock and discard the vegetables. Skin the fish, remove any bones and reserve.

3 Heat the oil in a pan. Fry the remaining onion and celery with the garlic and carrot until soft but not coloured, stirring occasionally. Add the puréed canned tomatoes, potatoes, tomato purée (paste), oregano, reserved stock and seasoning. Bring to the boil and simmer for about 15 minutes or until the potato is almost tender.

4 Meanwhile, thoroughly scrub the mussels. Add the mussels to the pan with the prawns (shrimp) and leave to simmer for about 5 minutes or until the mussels have opened (discard any that remain closed).

5 Return the fish to the soup with the chopped parsley, bring back to the boil and simmer for 5 minutes. Adjust the seasoning.

6 Serve the soup in warmed bowls with chunks of fresh crusty bread, or put a toasted slice of crusty bread in the bottom of each bowl before adding the soup. If possible, remove a few half shells from the mussels before serving.

Italian Fish Stew

This robust stew is full of Mediterranean flavours. If you do not want to prepare the fish yourself, ask your local fishmonger to do it for you.

NUTRITIONAL INFORMATION

Calories	236	Sugars	.........4g
Protein	........20g	Fat	...........7g
Carbohydrate	...25g	Saturates	.......1g

5–10 MINS   25 MINS

SERVES 4

I N G R E D I E N T S

2 tbsp olive oil

2 red onions, finely chopped

1 garlic clove, crushed

2 courgettes (zucchini), sliced

400 g/14 oz can chopped tomatoes

850 ml/1 ½ pints/3 ½ cups fish or vegetable
   stock

90 g/3 oz dried pasta shapes

350 g/12 oz firm white fish, such as cod,
   haddock or hake

1 tbsp chopped fresh basil or oregano or
   1 tsp dried oregano

1 tsp grated lemon rind

1 tbsp cornflour (cornstarch)

1 tbsp water

salt and pepper

sprigs of fresh basil or oregano, to garnish

  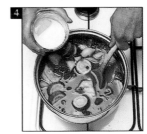

1 Heat the oil in a large saucepan and fry the onions and garlic for 5 minutes. Add the courgettes (zucchini) and cook for 2–3 minutes, stirring often.

2 Add the tomatoes and stock to the saucepan and bring to the boil. Add the pasta, cover and reduce the heat. Simmer for 5 minutes.

3 Skin and bone the fish, then cut it into chunks. Add to the saucepan with the basil or oregano and lemon rind and cook gently for 5 minutes until the fish is opaque and flakes easily (take care not to overcook it).

4 Blend the cornflour (cornstarch) with the water and stir into the stew. Cook gently for 2 minutes, stirring, until thickened. Season with salt and pepper to taste and ladle into 4 warmed soup bowls. Garnish with basil or oregano sprigs and serve at once.

Provençal Fish Soup

For the best results, you need to use flavourful fish, such as cod or haddock, for this recipe.

NUTRITIONAL INFORMATION

Calories 109   Sugars 3g
Protein . . . . .12g   Fat 3g
Carbohydrate . . . .4g   Saturates 0g

15 MINS   1 HOUR 20 MINS

SERVES 4

I N G R E D I E N T S

1 tbsp olive oil

2 onions, finely chopped

1 small leek, thinly sliced

1 small carrot, finely chopped

1 stalk celery, finely chopped

1 small fennel bulb, finely chopped
(optional)

3 garlic cloves, finely chopped

225 ml/8 fl oz/1 cup dry white wine

1.2 litres/2 pints/5 cups water

400 g/14 oz can tomatoes in juice

1 bay leaf

pinch of fennel seeds

2 strips orange rind

¼ tsp saffron threads

350 g/12 oz skinless white fish fillets

salt and pepper

garlic croûtons, to serve

1 Heat the oil in a large saucepan over a medium heat. Add the onions and cook for about 5 minutes, stirring frequently, until softened. Add the leek, carrot, celery, fennel and garlic and continue cooking for 4–5 minutes until the leek is wilted.

2 Add the wine and let it bubble for a minute. Add the tomatoes, bay leaf, fennel seeds, orange rind, saffron and water. Bring just to the boil, reduce the heat, cover and cook gently, stirring occasionally, for 30 minutes.

3 Add the fish and cook for a further 20–30 minutes until it is very soft and flaky. Remove the bay leaf and orange rind if possible.

4 Allow the soup to cool slightly, then transfer to a blender or food processor and purée until smooth, working in batches if necessary. (If using a food processor, strain off the cooking liquid and reserve. Purée the soup solids with enough cooking liquid to moisten them, then combine with the remaining liquid.)

5 Return the soup to the saucepan. Taste and adjust the seasoning, if necessary, and simmer for 5–10 minutes until heated through. Ladle the soup into warm bowls and sprinkle with croûtons.

Garlic Fish Soup

The delicate colour of this soup belies its heady flavours. The recipe has been adapted from a classic French recipe.

NUTRITIONAL INFORMATION

Calories	200	Sugars	.........4g
Protein	........19g	Fat	...........7g
Carbohydrate	...14g	Saturates	......3g

 15 MINS   40 MINS

SERVES 4

INGREDIENTS

2 tsp olive oil

1 large onion, chopped

1 small fennel bulb, chopped

1 leek, sliced

3–4 large garlic cloves, thinly sliced

120 ml/4 fl oz/½ cup dry white wine

1.2 litres/2 pints/5 cups fish stock

4 tbsp white rice

1 strip pared lemon rind

1 bay leaf

450 g/1 lb skinless white fish fillets, cut into 4 cm/1½ inch pieces

50 ml/2 fl oz/¼ cup double (heavy) cream

2 tbsp chopped fresh parsley

salt and pepper

1 Heat the oil in a large saucepan over a medium-low heat. Add the onion, fennel, leek and garlic and cook for 4–5 minutes, stirring frequently, until the onion is softened.

2 Add the wine and bubble briefly. Add the stock, rice, lemon rind and bay leaf. Bring to the boil, reduce the heat to medium-low and simmer for 20–25 minutes, or until the rice and vegetables are soft. Remove the lemon rind and bay leaf.

3 Allow the soup to cool slightly, then transfer to a blender or food processor and purée until smooth, working in batches if necessary. (If using a food processor, strain off the cooking liquid and reserve. Purée the soup solids with enough cooking liquid to moisten them, then combine with the remaining liquid.)

4 Return the soup to the saucepan and bring to a simmer. Add the fish to the soup, cover and continue simmering gently, stirring occasionally, for 4–5 minutes, or until the fish is cooked and begins to flake.

5 Stir in the cream. Taste and adjust the seasoning, adding salt, if needed, and pepper. Ladle into warm bowls and serve sprinkled with parsley.

Breton Fish Soup

Fishermen's soups are inevitably variable, depending on the season and the catch.

NUTRITIONAL INFORMATION

Calories 436   Sugars 8g
Protein . . . . .19g   Fat 28g
Carbohydrate . . .27g   Saturates 17g

  15 MINS   35 MINS

SERVES 4

INGREDIENTS

2 tsp butter

1 large leek, thinly sliced

2 shallots, finely chopped

120 ml/4 fl oz/ ½ cup dry (hard) cider

300 ml/10 fl oz/1¼ cups fish stock

250 g/9 oz potatoes, diced

1 bay leaf

4 tbsp plain (all-purpose) flour

200 ml/7 fl oz/ ¾ cup milk

200 ml/7 fl oz/ ¾ cup double (heavy) cream

60 g/2 oz fresh sorrel leaves

350 g/12 oz skinless monkfish or cod fillet, cut into 2.5 cm/1 inch pieces

salt and pepper

1 Melt the butter in a large saucepan over a medium-low heat. Add the leek and shallots and cook for about 5 minutes, stirring frequently, until they start to soften. Add the cider and bring to the boil.

2 Stir in the stock, potatoes and bay leaf with a larege pinch of salt (unless stock is salty) and bring back to the boil. Reduce the heat, cover and cook gently for 10 minutes.

3 Put the flour in a small bowl and very slowly whisk in a few tablespoons of the milk to make a thick paste. Stir in a little more to make a smooth liquid.

4 Adjust the heat so the soup bubbles gently. Stir in the flour mixture and cook, stirring frequently, for 5 minutes. Add the remaining milk and half the cream. Continue cooking for about 10 minutes until the potatoes are tender.

5 Chop the sorrel finely and combine with the remaining cream. (If using a food processor, add the sorrel and chop, then add the cream and process briefly.)

6 Stir the sorrel cream into the soup and add the fish. Continue cooking, stirring occasionally, for about 3 minutes, until the monkfish stiffens or the cod just begins to flake. Taste the soup and adjust the seasoning, if needed. Ladle into warm bowls and serve.

COOK'S TIP

Be careful not to overcook the fish, otherwise tender fish, such as cod, break up into smaller and smaller flakes and firm fish, like monkfish, can become tough.

Mussel, Potato & Parsley

This soup can be made in stages, so is suitable for entertaining.

NUTRITIONAL INFORMATION

Calories	538	Sugars	........11g
Protein	........22g	Fat	..........34g
Carbohydrate	...38g	Saturates	.....20g

15 MINS   50 MINS

SERVES 4

INGREDIENTS

1 kg/2 lb 4 oz mussels

300 g/10½ oz potatoes

3 tbsp plain (all-purpose) flour

600 ml/1 pint/2½ cups milk

300 ml/10 fl oz/1¼ cups whipping cream

1–2 garlic cloves, finely chopped

125 g/4 oz/6 cups curly parsley leaves (1 large bunch)

salt and pepper

1 Discard any broken mussels and those with open shells that do not close when tapped. Rinse under cold running water, pull off any 'beards' and scrape off barnacles with a knife. Put the mussels in a large heavy-based saucepan. Cover tightly and cook over a high heat for about 4 minutes, or until the mussels open.

2 When cool enough to handle, remove the mussels from the shells, adding any additional juices to the cooking liquid. Strain the cooking liquid into a bowl through a muslin-lined sieve and put aside.

3 Boil the potatoes, in their skins, in salted water for about 15 minutes until tender. When cool enough to handle, peel and cut into small dice.

4 Put the flour in a mixing bowl and very slowly whisk in a few tablespoons of the milk to make a thick paste. Stir in a little more to make a smooth liquid.

5 Put the remaining milk, cream and garlic in a saucepan and bring to the boil. Whisk in the flour mixture. Reduce the heat to medium-low and simmer for about 15 minutes until the garlic is tender and the liquid has thickened slightly. Drop in the parsley leaves and cook for about 2–3 minutes until bright green and wilted.

6 Allow the soup base to cool slightly, then transfer to a blender or food processor and purée until smooth, working in batches if necessary. (If using a food processor, strain off the cooking liquid and reserve. Purée the soup solids with enough cooking liquid to moisten, then combine with the remaining liquid.)

7 Return the purée to the saucepan and stir in the mussel cooking liquid and the potatoes. Season to taste with salt, if needed, and pepper. Simmer the soup gently for 5–7 minutes until reheated. Add the mussels and continue cooking for about 2 minutes until the soup is steaming and the mussels are hot. Ladle the soup into warm bowls and serve.

Italian Seafood Soup

This colourful mixed seafood soup would be superbly complemented by a dry white wine.

NUTRITIONAL INFORMATION

Calories 668	Sugars 3g	
Protein 48g	Fat 43g	
Carbohydrate ...21g	Saturates 25g	

 5 MINS   55 MINS

SERVES 4

INGREDIENTS

60 g/2 oz/4 tbsp butter

450 g/1 lb assorted fish fillets, such as red
 mullet and snapper

450 g/1 lb prepared seafood, such as squid
 and prawns (shrimp)

225 g/8 oz fresh crabmeat

1 large onion, sliced

25 g/1 oz/¼ cup plain (all-purpose) flour

1.2 litres/2 pints/5 cups fish stock

100 g/3½ oz/¾ cup dried pasta shapes,
 such as ditalini or elbow macaroni

1 tbsp anchovy essence (extract)

grated rind and juice of 1 orange

50 ml/2 fl oz/¼ cup dry sherry

300 ml/½ pint/1¼ cups double (heavy)
 cream

salt and pepper

crusty brown bread, to serve

1 Melt the butter in a large saucepan, add the fish fillets, seafood, crabmeat and onion and cook gently over a low heat for 6 minutes.

2 Add the flour to the seafood mixture, stirring thoroughly to avoid any lumps from forming.

3 Gradually add the stock, stirring, until the soup comes to the boil. Reduce the heat and simmer for 30 minutes.

4 Add the pasta to the pan and cook for a further 10 minutes.

5 Stir in the anchovy essence, orange rind, orange juice, sherry and double (heavy) cream. Season to taste with salt and pepper.

6 Heat the soup until completely warmed through.

7 Transfer the soup to a tureen or to warm soup bowls and serve with crusty brown bread.

Tuscan Veal Broth

Veal plays an important role in Italian cuisine and there are dozens of recipes for all cuts of this meat.

NUTRITIONAL INFORMATION

Calories	420	Sugars	.........5g
Protein	........54g	Fat	...........7g
Carbohydrate	...37g	Saturates	.......2g

 2¼ HOURS   4¾ HOURS

SERVES 4

INGREDIENTS

60 g/2 oz/⅓ cup dried peas, soaked for
    2 hours and drained

900 g/2 lb boned neck of veal, diced

1.2 litres/2 pints/5 cups beef or brown
    stock (see Cook's Tip)

600 ml/1 pint/2 ½ cups water

60 g/2 oz/⅓ cup barley, washed

1 large carrot, diced

1 small turnip (about 175 g/6 oz), diced

1 large leek, thinly sliced

1 red onion, finely chopped

100 g/3 ½ oz chopped tomatoes

1 fresh basil sprig

100 g/3 ½ oz/¾ cup dried vermicelli

salt and white pepper

1 Put the peas, veal, stock and water into a large pan and bring to the boil over a low heat. Using a slotted spoon, skim off any scum that rises to the surface.

2 When all of the scum has been removed, add the barley and a pinch of salt to the mixture. Simmer gently over a low heat for 25 minutes.

3 Add the carrot, turnip, leek, onion, tomatoes and basil to the pan, and

season with salt and pepper to taste. Leave to simmer for about 2 hours, skimming the surface from time to time to remove any scum. Remove the pan from the heat and set aside for 2 hours.

4 Set the pan over a medium heat and bring to the boil. Add the vermicelli and cook for 12 minutes. Season with salt and pepper to taste; remove and discard the basil. Ladle into soup bowls and serve immediately.

COOK'S TIP

The best brown stock is made with veal bones and shin of beef roasted with dripping (drippings) in the oven for 40 minutes. Transfer the bones to a pan and add sliced leeks, onion, celery and carrots, a bouquet garni, white wine vinegar and a thyme sprig and cover with cold water. Simmer over a very low heat for 3 hours; strain before use.

Veal & Mushroom Soup

Delicately scented with lemon, this luscious soup features the classic combination of tender veal with mushrooms and cream.

NUTRITIONAL INFORMATION

Calories 383	Sugars 6g	
Protein 23g	Fat 19g	
Carbohydrate ...31g	Saturates 11g	

15 MINS 1½ HOURS

SERVES 4

I N G R E D I E N T S

350 g/12 oz boneless veal, cut into
   1 cm/½ inch pieces

1 litre/1¾ pints/4 cups chicken stock

l onion, quartered

2 carrots, thinly sliced

2 garlic cloves, halved

1 pared strip lemon rind

1 bay leaf

1 tbsp butter

350 g /12 oz small button mushrooms,
   quartered

4 tbsp cornflour (cornstarch)

120 ml/4 fl oz/½ cup double (heavy) cream

freshly grated nutmeg

fresh lemon juice, to taste (optional)

1-2 tbsp chopped fresh parsley

salt and pepper

2 Add the onion, carrots, garlic, lemon rind and bay leaf. Season with salt and pepper. Reduce the heat and simmer, partially covered, for about 45 minutes, stirring occasionally, until the veal is very tender.

3 Remove the veal and carrots with a slotted spoon and reserve, covered. Strain the stock into a clean saucepan. Discard the onion and garlic, lemon rind and bay leaf.

4 Melt the butter in a frying pan (skillet) over a medium-high heat. Add the mushrooms, season, and fry gently until lightly golden. Reserve with the veal and carrots.

5 Mix together the cornflour (cornstarch) and cream. Bring the cooking liquid just to the boil and whisk in the cream mixture. Boil very gently for 2-3 minutes until it thickens, whisking almost constantly.

6 Add the reserved meat and vegetables to the soup and simmer over a low heat for about 5 minutes until heated through. Taste and adjust the seasoning, adding nutmeg and a squeeze of lemon juice, if wished. Stir in the parsley, then ladle into warm bowls and serve.

1 Put the veal in a large saucepan and add the stock. Bring just to the boil and skim off any foam that rises to the surface.

Veal & Wild Mushroom

Wild mushrooms are available commercially and an increasing range of cultivated varieties is now to be found in many supermarkets.

NUTRITIONAL INFORMATION

Calories 413	Sugars 3g	
Protein 28g	Fat 22g	
Carbohydrate . . .28g	Saturates 12g	

 5 MINS   3¼ HOURS

SERVES 4

I N G R E D I E N T S

450 g/1 lb veal, thinly sliced

450 g/1 lb veal bones

1.2 litres/2 pints/5 cups water

1 small onion

6 peppercorns

1 tsp cloves

pinch of mace

140 g/5 oz oyster and shiitake mushrooms, roughly chopped

150 ml/¼ pint/⅔ cup double (heavy) cream

100 g/3½ oz/¾ cup dried vermicelli

1 tbsp cornflour (cornstarch)

3 tbsp milk

salt and pepper

1 Put the veal, bones and water into a large saucepan. Bring to the boil and lower the heat. Add the onion, peppercorns, cloves and mace and simmer for about 3 hours, until the veal stock is reduced by one-third.

2 Strain the stock, skim off any fat on the surface with a slotted spoon, and pour the stock into a clean saucepan. Add the veal meat to the pan.

3 Add the mushrooms and cream, bring to the boil over a low heat and then leave to simmer for 12 minutes, stirring occasionally.

4 Meanwhile, cook the vermicelli in lightly salted boiling water for 10 minutes or until tender, but still firm to the bite. Drain and keep warm.

5 Mix the cornflour (cornstarch) and milk to form a smooth paste. Stir into the soup to thicken. Season to taste with salt and pepper and just before serving, add the vermicelli. Transfer the soup to a warm tureen and serve immediately.

COOK'S TIP

You can make this soup with the more inexpensive cuts of veal, such as breast or neck slices. These are lean and the long cooking time ensures that the meat is really tender.

Veal & Ham Soup

Veal and ham is a classic combination, complemented here with the addition of sherry to create a richly-flavoured Italian soup.

NUTRITIONAL INFORMATION

Calories 501   Sugars 10g
Protein . . . . .38g   Fat 18g
Carbohydrate . . .28g   Saturates 10g

  5 MINS   3¼ HOURS

SERVES 4

INGREDIENTS

60 g/2 oz/4 tbsp butter

1 onion, diced

1 carrot, diced

1 celery stick (stalk), diced

450 g/1 lb veal, very thinly sliced

450 g/1 lb ham, thinly sliced

60 g/2 oz/½ cup plain (all-purpose) flour

1 litre/1 ¾ pints/4 ⅜ cups beef stock

1 bay leaf

8 black peppercorns

pinch of salt

3 tbsp redcurrant jelly

150 ml/¼ pint/⅝ cup cream sherry

100 g/3 ½ oz/¾ cup dried vermicelli

garlic croûtons (see Cook's Tip), to serve

1 Melt the butter in a large pan. Add the onions, carrot, celery, veal and ham and cook over a low heat for 6 minutes.

2 Sprinkle over the flour and cook, stirring constantly, for a further 2 minutes. Gradually stir in the stock, then add the bay leaf, peppercorns and salt. Bring to the boil and simmer for 1 hour.

3 Remove the pan from the heat and add the redcurrant jelly and cream

sherry, stirring to combine. Set aside for about 4 hours.

4 Remove the bay leaf from the pan and discard. Reheat the soup over a very low heat until warmed through.

5 Meanwhile, cook the vermicelli in a saucepan of lightly salted boiling water for 10–12 minutes. Stir the vermicelli into the soup and transfer to soup bowls. Serve with garlic croûtons.

COOK'S TIP

To make garlic croûtons, remove the crusts from 3 slices of day-old white bread. Cut the bread into 5 mm/¼ inch cubes. Heat 3 tbsp oil over a low heat and stir-fry 1–2 chopped garlic cloves for 1–2 minutes. Remove the garlic and add the bread. Cook, stirring frequently, until golden. Remove with a slotted spoon and drain.

Chicken & Bean Soup

This hearty and nourishing soup, combining chickpeas and chicken, is an ideal starter for a family supper.

NUTRITIONAL INFORMATION

Calories 347	Sugars 2g	
Protein 28g	Fat 11g	
Carbohydrate ...37g	Saturates 4g	

5 MINS   1¾ HOURS

SERVES 4

INGREDIENTS

25 g/1 oz/2 tbsp butter

3 spring onions (scallions), chopped

2 garlic cloves, crushed

1 fresh marjoram sprig, finely chopped

350 g/12 oz boned chicken breasts, diced

1.2 litres/2 pints/5 cups chicken stock

350 g/12 oz can chick-peas (garbanzo
    beans), drained

1 bouquet garni

1 red (bell) pepper, diced

1 green (bell) pepper, diced

115 g/4 oz/1 cup small dried pasta shapes,
    such as elbow macaroni

salt and white pepper

croûtons, to serve

COOK'S TIP

If you prefer, you can use dried chick-peas (garbanzo beans). Cover with cold water and set aside to soak for 5–8 hours. Drain and add the beans to the soup, according to the recipe, and allow an additional 30 minutes–1 hour cooking time.

1 Melt the butter in a large saucepan. Add the spring onions (scallions), garlic, sprig of fresh marjoram and the diced chicken and cook, stirring frequently, over a medium heat for 5 minutes.

2 Add the chicken stock, chick-peas (garbanzo beans) and bouquet garni and season with salt and white pepper.

3 Bring the soup to the boil, lower the heat and simmer for about 2 hours.

4 Add the diced (bell) peppers and pasta to the pan, then simmer for a further 20 minutes.

5 Transfer the soup to a warm tureen. To serve, ladle the soup into individual serving bowls and serve immediately, garnished with the croûtons.

Chicken & Pasta Broth

This satisfying soup makes a good lunch or supper dish and you can use any vegetables you like. Children will love the tiny pasta shapes.

NUTRITIONAL INFORMATION

Calories 185   Sugars 5g
Protein ....17g   Fat 5g
Carbohydrate ...20g   Saturates 1g

  5 MINS   15–20 MINS

SERVES 6

INGREDIENTS

350 g/12 oz boneless chicken breasts

2 tbsp sunflower oil

1 medium onion, diced

250 g/9 oz/1 ½ cups carrots, diced

250 g/9 oz cauliflower florets

850 ml/1 ½ pints/3 ¾ cups chicken stock

2 tsp dried mixed herbs

125 g/4 ½ oz small pasta shapes

salt and pepper

Parmesan cheese (optional) and crusty
    bread, to serve

1 Using a sharp knife, finely dice the chicken, discarding any skin.

2 Heat the oil in a large saucepan and quickly sauté the chicken, onion, carrots and cauliflower until they are lightly coloured.

3 Stir in the chicken stock and dried mixed herbs and bring to the boil.

4 Add the pasta shapes to the pan and return to the boil. Cover the pan and leave the broth to simmer for 10 minutes, stirring occasionally to prevent the pasta shapes from sticking together.

5 Season the broth with salt and pepper to taste and sprinkle with Parmesan cheese, if using. Serve the broth with fresh crusty bread.

COOK'S TIP

You can use any small pasta shapes for this soup – try conchigliette or ditalini or even spaghetti broken up into small pieces. To make a fun soup for children you could add animal-shaped or alphabet pasta.

Lemon & Chicken Soup

This delicately flavoured summer soup is surprisingly easy to make, and tastes delicious.

NUTRITIONAL INFORMATION

Calories 506   Sugars 4g
Protein . . . . .19g   Fat 31g
Carbohydrate . . .41g   Saturates 19g

  5-10 MINS   1¼ HOURS

SERVES 4

I N G R E D I E N T S

60 g/2 oz/4 tbsp butter

8 shallots, thinly sliced

2 carrots, thinly sliced

2 celery sticks (stalks), thinly sliced

225 g/8 oz boned chicken breasts,
    finely chopped

3 lemons

1.2 litres/2 pints/5 cups chicken stock

225 g/8 oz dried spaghetti, broken into
    small pieces

150 ml/¼ pint/⅝ cup double (heavy) cream

salt and white pepper

TO GARNISH

fresh parsley sprig

3 lemon slices, halved

COOK'S TIP

You can prepare this soup up to the end of step 3 in advance, so that all you need do before serving is heat it through before adding the pasta and the finishing touches.

1 Melt the butter in a large saucepan. Add the shallots, carrots, celery and chicken and cook over a low heat, stirring occasionally, for 8 minutes.

2 Thinly pare the lemons and blanch the lemon rind in boiling water for 3 minutes. Squeeze the juice from the lemons.

3 Add the lemon rind and juice to the pan, together with the chicken stock. Bring slowly to the boil over a low heat and simmer for 40 minutes, stirring occasionally.

4 Add the spaghetti to the pan and cook for 15 minutes. Season to taste with salt and white pepper and add the cream. Heat through, but do not allow the soup to boil or it will curdle.

5 Pour the soup into a tureen or individual bowls, garnish with the parsley and half slices of lemon and serve immediately.

Ravioli in Tarragon Broth

Making filled pasta requires a bit of time and effort but the results are worth it. Homemade stock is essential.

NUTRITIONAL INFORMATION

Calories 278   Sugar 1g
Protein . . . . .14g   Fats 17g
Carbohydrates . . .17g   Saturates 9g

20 MINS   35 MINS

SERVES 6

I N G R E D I E N T S

2 litres/3½ pints/8 cups chicken stock

2 tbsp finely chopped fresh tarragon leaves

HOMEMADE PASTA

125 g/4½ oz/1 cup plain (all-purpose) flour, plus extra if needed

2 tbsp fresh tarragon leaves, with stems removed

1 egg

1 egg, separated

1 tsp extra-virgin olive oil

2–3 tbsp water

FILLING:

200 g/7 oz cooked chicken, coarsely chopped

½ tsp grated lemon rind

2 tbsp chopped mixed fresh tarragon, chives and parsley

4 tbsp whipping cream

salt and pepper

1 To make the pasta, combine the flour, tarragon and salt in a food processor. Beat together the egg, egg yolk, oil and 2 tablespoons of the water. With the machine running, pour in the egg mixture and process until it forms a ball, leaving the sides of the bowl virtually clean. If the dough is crumbly, add the remaining water; if the dough is sticky, add 1–2 tablespoons flour and continue kneading in the food processor until a ball forms. Wrap and chill for at least 30 minutes. Reserve the egg white.

2 To make the filling, put the chicken, lemon rind and mixed herbs in a food processor and season with salt and pepper. Chop finely, by pulsing; do not overprocess. Scrape into a bowl and stir in the cream. Taste and adjust the seasoning, if necessary.

3 Divide the pasta dough in half. Cover one half and roll the other half on a floured surface as thinly as possible, less than 1.5 mm/ ¹⁄₁₆ inch. Cut out rectangles about 10 x 5 cm/4 x 2 inches.

4 Place rounded teaspoons of filling on one half of the dough pieces. Brush around the edges with egg white and fold in half. Press the edges gently but firmly to seal. Arrange the ravioli in one layer on a baking (cookie) sheet, dusted generously with flour. Repeat with the remaining dough. Allow the ravioli to dry in a cool place for about 15 minutes or chill for 1–2 hours.

5 Bring a large quantity of salted water to the boil. Drop in half the ravioli and cook for 12–15 minutes until just tender. Drain on a clean tea towel (dish cloth) while cooking the remainder.

6 Meanwhile, put the stock and tarragon in a large saucepan. Bring to the boil and reduce the heat to bubble very gently. Cover and simmer for about 15 minutes, to infuse. Add the cooked ravioli to the stock and simmer for about 5 minutes until reheated. Ladle into warm soup plates to serve.

Provençal Turkey Soup

Pre-packed turkey, such as boneless breast or stir-fry meat, makes this a year-round favourite.

NUTRITIONAL INFORMATION

Calories	175	Sugars	........12g
Protein	........16g	Fat	..........5g
Carbohydrate	...13g	Saturates	......1g

 10 MINS   50 MINS

SERVES 4

I N G R E D I E N T S

1 tbsp olive oil

2 red, yellow or green (bell) peppers, cored, deseeded and finely chopped

1 stalk celery, thinly sliced

1 large onion, finely chopped

120 ml/4 fl oz/½ cup dry white wine

400 g/14 oz can plum tomatoes in juice

3-4 garlic cloves, finely chopped

1 litre/1¾ pints/4 cups turkey or chicken stock

¼ tsp dried thyme

1 bay leaf

2 courgettes (zucchini), finely diced

350 g/12 oz cooked cubed turkey

salt and pepper

fresh basil leaves, to garnish

COOK'S TIP

A large turkey leg can be used to make this soup. Put in a pan, add water to cover generously, and add 1 each carrot, celery stalk, leek and onion, coarsely chopped, and a little salt; poach for 3 hours. Reserve the meat, discard the skin, bone and vegetables and remove the fat from the stock before making the soup.

1 Heat the oil in a large saucepan over a medium heat. Add the (bell) peppers, celery and onion and cook for about 8 minutes until softened and just beginning to colour.

2 Add the wine and bubble for 1 minute. Add the tomatoes and garlic.

3 Stir in the stock. Add the thyme and bay leaf, season with salt and pepper and bring to the boil. Reduce the heat,

cover and simmer for about 25 minutes until the vegetables are tender.

4 Add the courgettes (zucchini) and turkey. Continue cooking for another 10 15 minutes until the courgettes (zucchini) are completely tender.

5 Taste the soup and adjust the seasoning. Ladle into warm bowls, garnish with basil leaves and serve.

Beef Goulash Soup

This aromatic dish originates from Hungary, where goulash soups are often served with dumplings. Noodles are a tasty and quick alternative.

NUTRITIONAL INFORMATION

Calories 320	Sugars 10g	
Protein 27g	Fat 13g	
Carbohydrate ...27g	Saturates 5g	

15 MINS   2.15 HOURS

SERVES 6

I N G R E D I E N T S

1 tbsp oil

500 g/1 lb 2 oz lean minced (ground) beef

2 onions, finely chopped

2 garlic cloves, finely chopped

2 tbsp plain (all-purpose) flour

225 ml/8 fl oz/1 cup water

400 g/14 oz can chopped tomatoes in juice

1 carrot, finely chopped

225 g/8 oz red (bell) pepper, roasted, peeled, de-seeded and chopped

1 tsp Hungarian paprika

¼ tsp caraway seeds

pinch of dried oregano

1 litre/1¾ pints/4 cups beef stock

60 g/2 oz tagliatelle, broken into small pieces

salt and pepper

soured cream and coriander (cilantro) to garnish

1 Heat the oil in a large wide saucepan over a medium-high heat. Add the beef and sprinkle with salt and pepper. Fry until lightly browned.

2 Reduce the heat and add the onions and garlic. Cook for about 3 minutes, stirring frequently, until the onions are softened. Stir in the flour and continue cooking for 1 minute.

3 Add the water and stir to combine well, scraping the bottom of the pan to mix in the flour. Stir in the tomatoes, carrot, pepper, paprika, caraway seeds, oregano and stock.

4 Bring just to the boil. Reduce the heat, cover and simmer gently for about 40 minutes, stirring occasionally, until all the vegetables are tender.

5 Add the noodles to the soup and simmer for a further 20 minutes, or until the noodles are cooked.

6 Taste the soup and adjust the seasoning, if necessary. Ladle into warm bowls and top each with a tablespoonful of soured cream. Garnish with coriander (cilantro).

Squid & Tomato Soup

This soup is full of interesting flavours. The chorizo gives it appealing spicy undertones that marry well with the meaty squid.

NUTRITIONAL INFORMATION

Calories	165	Sugar	.........5g
Protein	........18g	Fats	...........8g
Carbohydrates	....7g	Saturates	......3g

 15 MINS   1 HOUR

SERVES 6

INGREDIENTS

450 g/1 lb cleaned squid

150 g/5 ½ oz lean chorizo, peeled and very finely diced

1 onion, finely chopped

1 stalk celery, thinly sliced

1 carrot, thinly sliced

2 garlic cloves, finely chopped or crushed

400 g/14 oz can chopped tomatoes in juice

1.2 litres/2 pints/5 cups fish stock

½ tsp ground cumin

pinch of saffron

1 bay leaf

salt and pepper

chilli purée (paste) (optional)

fresh parsley, chopped

1 Cut off the squid tentacles and cut into bite-sized pieces. Slice the bodies into rings.

2 Place a large saucepan over a medium-low heat and add the chorizo. Cook for 5–10 minutes, stirring frequently, until it renders most of its fat. Remove with a slotted spoon and drain on paper towels.

3 Pour off all the fat from the pan and add the onion, celery, carrot and garlic. Cover and cook for 3–4 minutes until the onion is slightly softened.

4 Stir in the tomatoes, fish stock, cumin, saffron, bay leaf and chorizo.

5 Add the squid to the soup. Bring almost to the boil, reduce the heat, cover and cook gently for 40–45 minutes, or until the squid and carrot are tender, stirring occasionally.

6 Taste the soup and stir in a little chilli purée (paste) for a spicier flavour, if wished. Season with salt and pepper. Ladle into warm bowls, sprinkle with parsley and serve.

COOK'S TIP

Chorizo varies varies in the amount of fat and the degree of spiciness. A lean style is best for this soup.

Bean Soup

Pinto beans feature in Mexican cooking, and here they are used to give an exotic variation to European beans. They require soaking overnight.

NUTRITIONAL INFORMATION

Calories 188	Sugars 9g	
Protein 13g	Fat 1g	
Carbohydrate ...33g	Saturates 0.3g	

20 MINS   3 HOURS

SERVES 4

INGREDIENTS

175 g/6 oz pinto beans

1.25 litres/2¼ pints water

175–225 g/6–8 oz carrots, finely chopped

1 large onion, finely chopped

2–3 garlic cloves, crushed

½–1 chilli, seeded and finely chopped

1 litre /1¾ pints vegetable stock

2 tomatoes, peeled and finely chopped

2 celery sticks, very thinly sliced

salt and pepper

1 tbsp chopped coriander
   (cilantro) (optional)

CROUTONS

3 slices white bread, crusts removed

oil, for deep-frying

1–2 garlic cloves, crushed

VARIATION

Pinto beans are widely available, but if you cannot find them or you wish to vary the recipe, you can use cannellini beans or black-eyed beans (peas) as an alternative.

1 Soak the beans overnight in cold water; drain and place in a pan with the water. Bring to the boil and boil vigorously for 10 minutes. Lower the heat, cover and simmer for 2 hours, or until the beans are tender.

2 Add the carrots, onion, garlic, chilli and stock and bring back to the boil. Cover and simmer for a further 30 minutes, until very tender.

3 Remove half the beans and vegetables with the cooking juices and press through a strainer or process in a food processor or blender until smooth.

4 Return the bean purée to the saucepan and add the tomatoes and celery. Simmer for 10–15 minutes, or until the celery is just tender, adding a little more stock or water if necessary.

5 Meanwhile, make the croûtons. Dice the bread. Heat the oil with the garlic in a small frying pan (skillet) and fry the croûtons until golden brown. Drain on kitchen paper (paper towels).

6 Season the soup and stir in the chopped coriander (cilantro), if using. Transfer to a warm tureen and serve immediately with the croûtons.

White Bean Soup

In this elegant soup, the pungent green olive purée provides a pleasant counterpoint to the natural sweetness of the beans.

NUTRITIONAL INFORMATION

Calories 257	Sugars 5g
Protein 11g	Fat 13g
Carbohydrate ...27g	Saturates 2g

 20 MINS   2 HOURS

SERVES 8

INGREDIENTS

350 g/12 oz dried haricot (navy) beans

1 tbsp olive oil

1 large onion, finely chopped

1 large leek (white part only), thinly sliced

3 garlic cloves, finely chopped

2 stalk celery, finely chopped

2 small carrots, finely chopped

1 small fennel bulb, finely chopped

2 litres/3½ pints/8 cups water

¼ tsp dried thyme

¼ tsp dried marjoram

salt and pepper

TAPENADE:

1 garlic clove

1 small bunch fresh flat-leaf parsley, stems removed

240 g/8½ oz almond-stuffed green olives, drained

5 tbsp olive oil

2 Heat the oil in a large heavy-based saucepan over a medium heat. Add the onion and leek, cover and cook for 3–4 minutes, stirring occasionally, until just softened. Add the garlic, celery, carrots and fennel, and continue cooking for 2 minutes.

3 Add the water, drained beans and the herbs. When the mixture begins to bubble, reduce the heat to low. Cover and simmer gently, stirring occasionally, for about 1½ hours until the beans are very tender.

4 Meanwhile make the tapenade. Put the garlic, parsley and drained olives in a blender or food processor with the olive oil. Blend to a purée and scrape into a small serving bowl.

5 Allow the soup to cool slightly, then transfer to a blender or food processor and purée until smooth, working in batches if necessary. (If using a food processor, strain off the cooking liquid and reserve. Purée the soup solids with enough cooking liquid to moisten them, then combine with the remaining liquid.)

6 Return the puréed soup to the saucepan and thin with a little water, if necessary. Season with salt and pepper to taste, and simmer until heated through. Ladle into warm bowls and serve, stirring a generous teaspoon of the tapenade into each serving.

1 Pick over the beans, cover generously with cold water and leave to soak for 6 hours or overnight. Drain the beans, put in a saucepan and add cold water to cover by 5 cm/2 inches. Bring to the boil and boil for 10 minutes. Drain and rinse well.

Mixed Bean Soup

This is a really hearty soup, filled with colour, flavour and goodness, which may be adapted to any vegetables that you have at hand.

NUTRITIONAL INFORMATION

Calories	190	Sugars 9g
Protein	........10g	Fat 4g
Carbohydrate	...30g	Saturates 0.5g

 10 MINS   40 MINS

SERVES 4

INGREDIENTS

1 tbsp vegetable oil

1 red onion, halved and sliced

100 g/3½ oz/⅔ cup potato, diced

1 carrot, diced

1 leek, sliced

1 green chilli, sliced

3 garlic cloves, crushed

1 tsp ground coriander

1 tsp chilli powder

1 litre/1¾ pints/4 cups vegetable stock

450 g/1 lb mixed canned beans,
    such as red kidney, borlotti, black eye
    or flageolet, drained

salt and pepper

2 tbsp chopped coriander (cilantro),
    to garnish

1 Heat the vegetable oil in a large saucepan. Add the onion, potato, carrot and leek and sauté, stirring constantly, for about 2 minutes, until the vegetables are slightly softened.

2 Add the sliced chilli and crushed garlic and cook for a further 1 minute.

3 Stir in the ground coriander, chilli powder and the vegetable stock.

4 Bring the soup to the boil, reduce the heat and cook for 20 minutes, or until the vegetables are tender.

5 Stir in the beans, season well with salt and pepper and cook, stirring occasionally, for a further 10 minutes.

6 Transfer the soup to a warm tureen or individual bowls, garnish with chopped coriander (cilantro) and serve.

COOK'S TIP

Serve this soup with slices of warm corn bread or a cheese loaf.

Tuscan Bean Soup

A thick and creamy soup that is based on a traditional Tuscan recipe. If you use dried beans, the preparation and cooking times will be longer.

NUTRITIONAL INFORMATION

Calories 250	Sugars 4g
Protein 13g	Fat 10g
Carbohydrate ...29g	Saturates 2g

2 MINS   10 MINS

SERVES 4

INGREDIENTS

225 g/8 oz dried butter beans, soaked
  overnight, or 2 x 400 g/14 oz can butter
  beans

1 tbsp olive oil

2 garlic cloves, crushed

1 vegetable or chicken stock cube,
  crumbled

150 ml/¼ pint/⅔ cup milk

2 tbsp chopped fresh oregano

salt and pepper

1 If you are using dried beans that have been soaked overnight, drain them thoroughly. Bring a large pan of water to the boil, add the beans and boil for 10 minutes. Cover the pan and simmer for a further 30 minutes or until tender. Drain the beans, reserving the cooking liquid. If you are using canned beans, drain them thoroughly and reserve the liquid.

2 Heat the oil in a large frying pan (skillet) and fry the garlic for 2–3 minutes or until just beginning to brown.

3 Add the beans and 400 ml/14 fl oz/1⅔ cup of the reserved liquid to the pan (skillet), stirring. You may need to add a little water if there is insufficient liquid. Stir in the crumbled stock cube. Bring the

mixture to the boil and then remove the pan from the heat.

4 Place the bean mixture in a food processor and blend to form a smooth purée. Alternatively, mash the bean mixture to a smooth consistency. Season

to taste with salt and pepper and stir in the milk.

5 Pour the soup back into the pan and gently heat to just below boiling point. Stir in the chopped oregano just before serving.

Greek Bean Soup

This is based on a simple and variable bean soup typical in Greek home cooking.

NUTRITIONAL INFORMATION

Calories 186	Sugar 8g
Protein 10g	Fats 3g
Carbohydrates ...33g	Saturates 0g

 15 MINS   1 HOUR

SERVES 6

I N G R E D I E N T S

1 tbsp olive oil

1 large onion, finely chopped

1 large carrot, finely diced

2 stalks celery, finely chopped

4 tomatoes, skinned, deseeded and chopped, or 250 g/9 oz drained canned tomatoes

2 garlic cloves, finely chopped

2 x 400 g/14 oz cans cannellini or haricot beans, drained and rinsed well

1.2 litres/2 pints/5 cups water

1 courgette (zucchini), finely diced

grated rind of ½ lemon

1 tbsp chopped fresh mint, or ¼ tsp dried mint

1 tsp chopped fresh thyme, or ⅛ tsp dried thyme

1 bay leaf

400 g/14 oz can artichoke hearts

salt and pepper

1 Heat 1 teaspoon of the olive oil in a large saucepan over a medium heat. Add the onion and cook for 3–4 minutes, stirring occasionally, until the onion softens. Add the carrot, celery, tomatoes and garlic and continue cooking for a further 5 minutes, stirring frequently.

2 Add the beans and water. Bring to the boil, reduce the heat, cover and cook gently for about 10 minutes.

3 Add the courgette (zucchini), lemon rind, mint, thyme and bay leaf and season with salt and pepper. Cover and simmer about 40 minutes until all the vegetables are tender. Allow to cool slightly. Transfer 450 ml/16 fl oz/2 cups to a blender or food processor, purée until smooth and recombine.

4 Meanwhile, heat the remaining oil in a frying pan (skillet) over a medium heat, adding more if necessary to coat the bottom of the pan. Fry the artichokes, cut side down, until lightly browned. Turn over and fry long enough to heat through.

5 Ladle the soup into warm bowls and top each with an artichoke heart.

Vegetable & Bean Soup

This wonderful combination of cannellini beans, vegetables and vermicelli is made even richer by the addition of pesto and dried mushrooms.

NUTRITIONAL INFORMATION

Calories 294	Sugars 2g	
Protein 11g	Fat 16g	
Carbohydrate ...30g	Saturates 2g	

 30 MINS 🕐 30 MINS

SERVES 4

INGREDIENTS

1 small aubergine (eggplant)

2 large tomatoes

1 potato, peeled

1 carrot, peeled

1 leek

425 g/15 oz can cannellini beans

850 ml/1½ pints/3¾ cups hot vegetable or
    chicken stock

2 tsp dried basil

15 g/½ oz dried porcini mushrooms,
    soaked for 10 minutes in enough warm
    water to cover

50 g/1¾ oz/¼ cup vermicelli

3 tbsp pesto (use shop bought)

freshly grated Parmesan cheese, to serve
    (optional)

1 Slice the aubergine (eggplant) into rings about 1 cm/½ inch thick, then cut each ring into 4.

2 Cut the tomatoes and potato into small dice. Cut the carrot into sticks, about 2.5 cm/1 inch long and cut the leek into rings.

3 Place the cannellini beans and their liquid in a large saucepan. Add the aubergine (eggplant), tomatoes, potatoes, carrot and leek, stirring to mix.

4 Add the stock to the pan and bring to the boil. Reduce the heat and leave to simmer for 15 minutes.

5 Add the basil, dried mushrooms and their soaking liquid and the vermicelli and simmer for 5 minutes or until all of the vegetables are tender.

6 Remove the pan from the heat and stir in the pesto.

7 Serve with freshly grated Parmesan cheese, if using.

Bean & Pasta Soup

A dish with proud Mediterranean origins, this soup is a winter warmer.
Serve with warm, crusty bread and, if you like, a slice of cheese.

NUTRITIONAL INFORMATION

Calories 463	Sugars 5g	
Protein 13g	Fat 33g	
Carbohydrate . . .30g	Saturates 7g	

 5–10 MINS 1¼ HOURS

SERVES 4

INGREDIENTS

225 g/8 oz/generous 1 cup dried haricot
   (navy) beans, soaked, drained and rinsed

4 tbsp olive oil

2 large onions, sliced

3 garlic cloves, chopped

400 g/14 oz can chopped tomatoes

1 tsp dried oregano

1 tsp tomato purée (paste)

850 ml/1 ½ pints/3 ½ cups water

90 g/3 oz small pasta shapes, such as fusilli
   or conchigliette

125 g/4 ½ oz sun-dried tomatoes, drained
   and sliced thinly

1 tbsp chopped coriander (cilantro),
   or flat-leaf parsley

2 tbsp freshly grated Parmesan

salt and pepper

1 Put the soaked beans into a large pan,
cover with cold water and bring them
to the boil. Boil rapidly for 15 minutes to
remove any harmful toxins. Drain the
beans in a colander.

2 Heat the oil in a pan over a medium
heat and fry the onions until they are
just beginning to change colour. Stir in the
garlic and cook for 1 further minute. Stir

in the chopped tomatoes, oregano and the
tomato purée (paste) and pour on the
water. Add the beans, bring to the boil and
cover the pan. Simmer for 45 minutes or
until the beans are almost tender.

3 Add the pasta, season the soup with
salt and pepper to taste and stir in the
sun-dried tomatoes. Return the soup to

the boil, partly cover the pan and continue
cooking for 10 minutes, or until the pasta
is nearly tender.

4 Stir in the chopped coriander
(cilantro) or parsley. Taste the soup
and adjust the seasoning if necessary.
Transfer to a warmed soup tureen to serve.
Sprinkle with the cheese and serve hot.

Chickpea Soup

A thick vegetable soup which is a delicious meal in itself. Serve with Parmesan cheese and warm sun-dried tomato-flavoured ciabatta bread.

NUTRITIONAL INFORMATION

Calories	297	Sugars	.........0g
Protein	........11g	Fat	..........18g
Carbohydrate	...24g	Saturates	.......2g

5 MINS   15 MINS

SERVES 4

INGREDIENTS

2 tbsp olive oil

2 leeks, sliced

2 courgettes (zucchini), diced

2 garlic cloves, crushed

2 x 400 g/14 oz cans chopped tomatoes

1 tbsp tomato purée (paste)

1 fresh bay leaf

850 ml/1 ½ pints/3 ¾ cups chicken stock

400 g/14 oz can chick-peas (garbanzo beans), drained and rinsed

225 g/8 oz spinach

salt and pepper

TO SERVE

Parmesan cheese

sun-dried tomato bread

1 Heat the oil in a large saucepan, add the leeks and courgettes (zucchini) and cook briskly for 5 minutes, stirring constantly.

2 Add the garlic, tomatoes, tomato purée (paste), bay leaf, stock and chick-peas (garbanzo beans). Bring to the boil and simmer for 5 minutes.

3 Shred the spinach finely, add to the soup and cook for 2 minutes. Season.

4 Remove the bay leaf from the soup and discard.

5 Serve the soup with freshly grated Parmesan cheese and sun-dried tomato bread.

COOK'S TIP

Chick-peas (garbanzo beans) are used extensively in North African cuisine and are also found in Italian, Spanish, Middle Eastern and Indian cooking. They have a deliciously nutty flavour with a firm texture and are an excellent canned product.

Red Bean Soup

Beans feature widely in Italian soups, making them hearty and tasty.
The beans need to be soaked overnight, so prepare well in advance.

NUTRITIONAL INFORMATION

Calories	184	Sugars	.........5g
Protein	.........4g	Fat	...........11g
Carbohydrate	...19g	Saturates	.......2g

🍴 5–10 MINS 🕐 3¾ HOURS

SERVES 6

INGREDIENTS

175 g/6 oz/scant 1 cup dried red kidney
   beans, soaked overnight

1.7 litres/3 pints/7½ cups water

1 large ham bone or bacon knuckle

2 carrots, chopped

1 large onion, chopped

2 celery stalks, sliced thinly

1 leek, trimmed, washed and sliced

1–2 bay leaves

2 tbsp olive oil

2–3 tomatoes, peeled and chopped

1 garlic clove, crushed

1 tbsp tomato purée (paste)

60 g/2 oz/4½ tbsp arborio or Italian rice

125–175 g/4–6 oz green cabbage,
   shredded finely

salt and pepper

1 Drain the beans and place them in a
saucepan with enough water to cover.
Bring to the boil, then boil for 15 minutes
to remove any harmful toxins. Reduce the
heat and simmer for 45 minutes.

2 Drain the beans and put into a clean
saucepan with the water, ham bone or
knuckle, carrots, onion, celery, leek, bay
leaves and olive oil. Bring to the boil, then
cover and simmer for 1 hour or until the
beans are very tender.

3 Discard the bay leaves and bone,
reserving any ham pieces from the
bone. Remove a small cupful of the beans
and reserve. Purée or liquidize the soup in
a food processor or blender, or push
through a coarse sieve (strainer), and
return to a clean pan.

4 Add the tomatoes, garlic, tomato
purée (paste), rice and season. Bring
back to the boil and simmer for about
15 minutes or until the rice is tender.

5 Add the cabbage and reserved beans
and ham, and continue to simmer for
5 minutes. Adjust the seasoning and serve
very hot. If liked, a piece of toasted crusty
bread may be put in the base of each soup
bowl before ladling in the soup. If the
soup is too thick, add a little boiling water
or stock.

Brown Lentil & Pasta Soup

In Italy, this soup is called Minestrade Lentiche. A minestra is a soup cooked with pasta; here, farfalline, a small bow-shaped variety, is used.

NUTRITIONAL INFORMATION

Calories	225	Sugars	.........1g
Protein	........13g	Fat	...........8g
Carbohydrate	...27g	Saturates	.......3g

 5 MINS   25 MINS

SERVES 4

I N G R E D I E N T S

4 rashers streaky bacon, cut into small squares

1 onion, chopped

2 garlic cloves, crushed

2 sticks celery, chopped

50 g/1 ¾ oz/ ¼ cup farfalline or spaghetti, broken into small pieces

1 x 400 g/14 oz can brown lentils, drained

1.2 litres/2 pints/5 cups hot ham or vegetable stock

2 tbsp chopped, fresh mint

1 Place the bacon in a large frying pan (skillet) together with the onions, garlic and celery. Dry fry for 4–5 minutes, stirring, until the onion is tender and the bacon is just beginning to brown.

2 Add the pasta to the pan (skillet) and cook, stirring, for about 1 minute to coat the pasta in the oil.

3 Add the lentils and the stock and bring to the boil. Reduce the heat and leave to simmer for 12–15 minutes or until the pasta is tender.

4 Remove the pan (skillet) from the heat and stir in the chopped fresh mint.

5 Transfer the soup to warm soup bowls and serve immedately.

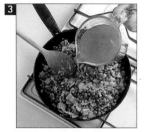

COOK'S TIP

If you prefer to use dried lentils, add the stock before the pasta and cook for 1–1¼ hours until the lentils are tender. Add the pasta and cook for a further 12–15 minutes.

Ravioli alla Parmigiana

This soup is traditionally served at Easter and Christmas in the province of Parma.

NUTRITIONAL INFORMATION

Calories 554	Sugars 3g	
Protein 26g	Fat 24g	
Carbohydrate . . .64g	Saturates 9g	

4½–5 HOURS   25 MINS

SERVES 4

INGREDIENTS

285 g/10 oz Basic Pasta Dough

1.2 litres/2 pints/5 cups veal stock

freshly grated Parmesan cheese, to serve

FILLING

125 ml/4 fl oz/ ½ cup Espagnole Sauce

100 g/3 ½ oz/1 cup freshly grated

Parmesan cheese

100 g/3 ½ oz/1 ⅔ cup fine white

  breadcrumbs

2 eggs

1 small onion, finely chopped

1 tsp freshly grated nutmeg

COOK'S TIP

It is advisable to prepare the Basic Pasta Dough and the Espagnole Sauce well in advance, or buy ready-made equivalents if you are short of time.

1 Make the Basic Pasta Dough and the Espagnole Sauce.

2 Carefully roll out 2 sheets of the pasta dough and cover with a damp tea towel (dish cloth) while you make the filling for the ravioli.

3 To make the filling, place the freshly grated Parmesan cheese, fine white breadcrumbs, eggs, Espagnole Sauce, finely chopped onion and the freshly grated nutmeg in a large mixing bowl, and mix together well.

4 Place spoonfuls of the filling at regular intervals on 1 sheet of pasta dough. Cover with the second sheet of pasta dough, then cut into squares and seal the edges.

5 Bring the veal stock to the boil in a large saucepan.

6 Add the ravioli to the pan and cook for about 15 minutes.

7 Transfer the soup and ravioli to warm serving bowls and serve, generously sprinkled with Parmesan cheese.

Minestrone

Minestrone translates as 'big soup' in Italian. It is made all over Italy, but this version comes from Livorno, a port on the western coast.

NUTRITIONAL INFORMATION

Calories	311	Sugars	........8g
Protein	........12g	Fat	..........19g
Carbohydrate	...26g	Saturates	.......5g

 10 MINS   30 MINS

SERVES 4

I N G R E D I E N T S

1 tbsp olive oil

100 g/3 ½ oz pancetta ham, diced

2 medium onions, chopped

2 cloves garlic, crushed

1 potato, peeled and cut into 1 cm/
⅓ inch cubes

1 carrot, peeled and cut into chunks

1 leek, sliced into rings

¼ green cabbage, shredded

1 stick celery, chopped

450 g/1 lb can chopped tomatoes

200 g/7 oz can flageolet (small navy)
beans, drained and rinsed

600 ml/1 pint/2 ½ cups hot ham or chicken
stock, diluted with 600 ml/1 pint/2 ½ cups
boiling water

bouquet garni (2 bay leaves, 2 sprigs
rosemary and 2 sprigs thyme, tied
together)

salt and pepper

freshly grated Parmesan cheese, to serve

1 Heat the olive oil in a large saucepan. Add the diced pancetta, chopped onions and garlic and fry for about 5 minutes, stirring, or until the onions are soft and golden.

2 Add the prepared potato, carrot, leek, cabbage and celery to the saucepan. Cook for a further 2 minutes, stirring frequently, to coat all of the vegetables in the oil.

3 Add the tomatoes, flageolet (small navy) beans, hot ham or chicken stock and bouquet garni to the pan, stirring to mix. Leave the soup to simmer, covered, for 15–20 minutes or until all of the vegetables are just tender.

4 Remove the bouquet garni, season with salt and pepper to taste and serve with plenty of freshly grated Parmesan cheese.

Minestrone with Pesto

This version of minestrone contains cannellini beans – these need to be soaked overnight, so prepare in advance.

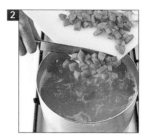

NUTRITIONAL INFORMATION

Calories	604	Sugars	.........3g
Protein	........26g	Fat	..........45g
Carbohydrate	...24g	Saturates	......11g

  10–15 MINS   1¾ HOURS

SERVES 6

INGREDIENTS

175 g/6 oz/scant 1 cup dried cannellini
   beans, soaked overnight

2.5 litres/4 ½ pints/10 cups water or stock

1 large onion, chopped

1 leek, trimmed and sliced thinly

2 celery stalks, sliced very thinly

2 carrots, chopped

3 tbsp olive oil

2 tomatoes, peeled and chopped roughly

1 courgette (zucchini), trimmed and
   sliced thinly

2 potatoes, diced

90 g/3 oz elbow macaroni (or other small
   macaroni)

salt and pepper

4–6 tbsp freshly grated Parmesan, to serve

PESTO

2 tbsp pine kernels (nuts)

5 tbsp olive oil

2 bunches basil, stems removed

4–6 garlic cloves, crushed

90 g /3 oz/ ½ cup Pecorino or Parmesan,
   grated

1 Drain the beans, rinse and put in a pan with the water or stock. Bring to the boil, cover and simmer for 1 hour.

2 Add the onion, leek, celery, carrots and oil. Cover and simmer for 4–5 minutes.

3 Add the tomatoes, courgette (zucchini), potatoes, macaroni and seasoning. Cover again and continue to simmer for about 30 minutes or until very tender.

4 Meanwhile, make the pesto. Fry the pine kernels (nuts) in 1 tablespoon of the oil until pale brown, then drain. Put the basil into a food processor or blender with the nuts and garlic. Process until well chopped. Alternatively, chop finely by hand and pound with a pestle and mortar. Gradually add the remaining oil until smooth. Turn into a bowl, add the cheese and seasoning, and mix thoroughly.

5 Stir 1½ tablespoons of the pesto into the soup until well blended. Simmer for a further 5 minutes and adjust the seasoning. Serve very hot, sprinkled with the cheese.

Red Pepper Soup

This soup has a real Mediterranean flavour, using sweet red peppers, tomato, chilli and basil. It is great served with a warm olive bread.

NUTRITIONAL INFORMATION

Calories 55	Sugar 10g	
Protein 2g	Fats 0.5g	
Carbohydrates ...11g	Saturates 0.1g	

 5 MINS   25 MINS

SERVES 4

INGREDIENTS

225 g/8 oz red (bell) peppers, seeded and sliced

1 onion, sliced

2 garlic cloves, crushed

1 green chilli, chopped

300 ml/½ pint/1½ cups passata (sieved tomatoes)

600 ml/1 pint/2½ cups vegetable stock

2 tbsp chopped basil

fresh basil sprigs, to garnish

1 Put the (bell) peppers in a large saucepan with the onion, garlic and chilli. Add the passata (sieved tomatoes) and vegetable stock and bring to the boil, stirring well.

2 Reduce the heat to a simmer and cook for 20 minutes or until the (bell) peppers have softened. Drain, reserving the liquid and vegetables separately.

3 Sieve the vegetables by pressing through a sieve (strainer) with the back of a spoon. Alternatively, blend in a food processor until smooth.

4 Return the vegetable purée to a clean saucepan with the reserved cooking liquid. Add the basil and heat through until hot. Garnish the soup with fresh basil sprigs and serve.

VARIATION

This soup is also delicious served cold with 150 ml/¼ pint/¼ cup of natural (unsweetened) yogurt swirled into it.

Tomato & Pepper Soup

Sweet red peppers and tangy tomatoes are blended together in a smooth vegetable soup that makes a perfect starter or light lunch.

NUTRITIONAL INFORMATION

Calories 52   Sugars 9g
Protein . . . . .3g   Fat 0.4g
Carbohydrate . . .10g   Saturates 0g

 1¼ HOURS   35 MINS

SERVES 4

INGREDIENTS

2 large red (bell) peppers

1 large onion, chopped

2 sticks celery, trimmed and chopped

1 garlic clove, crushed

600 ml/1 pint/2½ cups Fresh Vegetable Stock (see page 14)

2 bay leaves

2 x 400 g/14 oz cans plum tomatoes

salt and pepper

2 spring onions (scallions), finely shredded, to garnish

crusty bread, to serve

1 Preheat the grill (broiler) to hot. Halve and deseed the (bell) peppers, arrange them on the grill (broiler) rack and cook, turning occasionally, for 8–10 minutes until softened and charred.

2 Leave to cool slightly, then carefully peel off the charred skin. Reserving a small piece for garnish, chop the (bell) pepper flesh and place in a large saucepan.

3 Mix in the onion, celery and garlic. Add the stock and the bay leaves. Bring to the boil, cover and simmer for 15 minutes. Remove from the heat.

4 Stir in the tomatoes and transfer to a blender. Process for a few seconds until smooth. Return to the saucepan.

5 Season to taste and heat for 3–4 minutes until piping hot. Ladle into warm bowls and garnish with the reserved (bell) pepper cut into strips and the spring onion (scallion). Serve with crusty bread.

COOK'S TIP

If you prefer a coarser, more robust soup, lightly mash the tomatoes with a wooden spoon and omit the blending process in step 4.

Spiced Fruit Soup

This delicately flavoured apple and apricot soup is gently spiced with ginger and allspice, and finished with a swirl of soured cream.

NUTRITIONAL INFORMATION

Calories 147	Sugar 28g	
Protein 3g	Fats 0.4g	
Carbohydrates ...29g	Saturates 0g	

7³/₄ HOURS   25 MINS

SERVES 4–6

INGREDIENTS

125 g/4½oz/⅔ cup dried apricots, soaked overnight or no-need-to-soak dried apricots

500 g/1 lb 2 oz dessert apples, peeled, cored and chopped

1 small onion, chopped

1 tbsp lemon or lime juice

700 ml/1¼ pints/3 cups Fresh Chicken Stock (see page 14)

150 ml/¼ pint/⅔ cup dry white wine

¼ tsp ground ginger

good pinch of ground allspice

salt and pepper

TO GARNISH

4–6 tbsp soured cream or natural fromage frais

little ground ginger or ground allspice

1 Drain the apricot, if necessary and chop.

2 Put in a saucepan and add the apples, onion, lemon or lime juice and stock. Bring to the boil, cover and simmer gently for about 20 minutes.

3 Leave the soup to cool a little, then press through a sieve (strainer) or blend in a food processor or blender until smooth. Pour the fruit soup into a clean pan.

4 Add the wine and spices and season to taste. Bring back to the boil, then leave to cool. If too thick, add a little more stock or water and then chill thoroughly.

5 Put a spoonful of soured cream or fromage frais on top of each portion and lightly dust with ginger or allspice.

VARIATION

Other fruits can be combined with apples to make fruit soups — try raspberries, blackberries, blackcurrants or cherries. If the fruits have a lot of pips or stones (pits), the soup should be sieved (strained) after puréeing.

Spinach & Mascarpone

Spinach is the basis for this delicious soup, but use sorrel or watercress instead for a pleasant change.

NUTRITIONAL INFORMATION

Calories 537	Sugars 2g	
Protein 6g	Fat 53g	
Carbohydrate 9g	Saturates 29g	

5 MINS   35 MINS

SERVES 4

INGREDIENTS

60 g/2 oz/¼ cup butter

1 bunch spring onions (scallions), trimmed
and chopped

2 celery sticks, chopped

350 g/12 oz/3 cups spinach or sorrel, or
3 bunches watercress

850 ml /1 ½ pints/3 ½ cups vegetable stock

225 g/8 oz/1 cup Mascarpone cheese

1 tbsp olive oil

2 slices thick-cut bread, cut into cubes

½ tsp caraway seeds

salt and pepper

sesame bread sticks, to serve

1 Melt half the butter in a very large saucepan. Add the spring onions (scallions) and celery and cook gently for about 5 minutes, or until softened.

2 Pack the spinach, sorrel or watercress into the saucepan. Add the vegetable stock and bring to the boil; then reduce the heat and simmer, covered, for 15–20 minutes.

3 Transfer the soup to a blender or food processor and blend until smooth, or pass through a sieve. Return to the saucepan.

4 Add the Mascarpone cheese to the soup and heat gently, stirring, until smooth and blended. Taste and season with salt and pepper.

5 Heat the remaining butter with the oil in a frying pan (skillet). Add the bread cubes and fry in the hot oil until golden brown, adding the caraway seeds towards the end of cooking, so that they do not burn.

6 Ladle the soup into 4 warmed bowls. Sprinkle with the croûtons and serve at once, accompanied by the sesame bread sticks.

VARIATIONS

Any leafy vegetable can be used to make this soup to give variations to the flavour. For anyone who grows their own vegetables, it is the perfect recipe for experimenting with a glut of produce. Try young beetroot (beet) leaves or surplus lettuces for a change.

International Soups

Today people travel the world as a matter of course, and as we have access to more culinary influences our tastes have become more demanding. This chapter caters for that desire for

unusual recipes by featuring an international range of modern-day soups, incorporating unusual ingredients such as sweet potato and rocket combined with curry and chilli flavourings. Recipes have been drawn from Senegal, Eastern Europe, the Americas and the Caribbean; there is something for the most discerning of palates to enjoy.

Squash & Sweet Potato Soup

When there's a chill in the air, this vivid soup is just the thing to serve – it's very warm and comforting.

NUTRITIONAL INFORMATION

Calories ....128 Sugars 7g
Protein ....3g Fat 4g
Carbohydrate ...21g Saturates 2g

 15 MINS 1 HOUR 25 MINS

SERVES 6

INGREDIENTS

1 sweet potato, about 350 g/12 oz

1 acorn squash

4 shallots

olive oil

5–6 garlic cloves, unpeeled

850 ml/1½ pints/3¾ cups chicken stock

120 ml/4 fl oz/½ cup single (light) cream

salt and pepper

snipped chives, to garnish

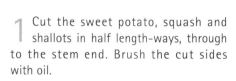

1 Cut the sweet potato, squash and shallots in half length-ways, through to the stem end. Brush the cut sides with oil.

2 Put the vegetables, cut sides down, in a shallow roasting tin (pan). Add the garlic cloves. Roast in a preheated oven at 190oC/375oF/Gas Mark 5 for about 40 minutes until tender and light brown.

3 When cool, scoop the flesh from the potato and squash halves and put in a saucepan with the shallots. Remove the garlic peel and add the soft insides to the other vegetables.

4 Add the stock and a pinch of salt. Bring just to the boil, reduce the heat and simmer, partially covered, for about 30 minutes, stirring occasionally, until the vegetables are very tender.

5 Allow the soup to cool slightly, then transfer to a blender or food processor and purée until smooth, working in batches, if necessary. (If using a food processor, strain off the cooking liquid and reserve. Purée the soup solids with enough cooking liquid to moisten them, then combine with the remaining liquid.)

6 Return the soup to the saucepan and stir in the cream. Season to taste, then simmer for 5–10 minutes until completely heated through. Ladle into warm bowls to serve.

Corn Soup with Chillies

This soup is rich and exotic but relatively simple to make. Ancho chillies have a distinct smoky flavour.

NUTRITIONAL INFORMATION

Calories 848	Sugars 14g	
Protein 10g	Fat 75g	
Carbohydrate ...37g	Saturates 46g	

25 MINS   35 MINS

SERVES 4

INGREDIENTS

1 dried ancho chilli

4 tbsp butter

500 g/1 lb 2 oz defrosted frozen sweetcorn kernels

1 large onion, finely chopped

1 large garlic clove, finely chopped

1 red (bell) pepper, cored, deseeded and finely chopped

300 ml/10 fl oz/1¼ cups chicken stock or water

600 ml/1 pint/2½ cups whipping cream

½ tsp ground cumin

salt

chopped fresh coriander (cilantro) or parsley, to garnish

1 Put the chilli in a bowl and cover with boiling water. Stand about 15 minutes to soften.

2 Melt the butter in a frying pan (skillet) over a medium-low heat. Add the sweetcorn and turn to coat. Cook for about 15 minutes, stirring frequently, until it starts to brown slightly. Add the onion, garlic and (bell) pepper and cook for about 7–10 minutes, stirring frequently, until the onion is softened and the mixture starts to stick.

3 Transfer the mixture to a blender or food processor, add the stock and purée until smooth.

4 Put the cream in a large saucepan, stir in the puréed vegetables and bring almost to the boil. Add the cumin. Season with a little salt. Adjust the heat so the soup bubbles very gently and cook until the mixture is reduced by about one-quarter.

5 Remove the ancho chilli from its liquid and discard the core and the seeds. (Wash hands well after touching chillies.) Put the chilli into a blender or food processor with 4–5 tablespoons of the soaking water and purée until smooth. Stir 2–4 tablespoons of the purée into the soup, according to taste, and continue cooking for a further 5 minutes.

6 Taste the soup and adjust the seasoning, if necessary. Ladle the soup into warm bowls, garnish with coriander (cilantro) or parsley and serve.

Melon Gazpacho

Glass bowls are pretty for serving this soup, which makes a very light starter for warm days.

NUTRITIONAL INFORMATION

Calories	86	Sugar	. . . . .17g
Protein	. . . . .2g	Fats	. . . . .1g
Carbohydrates	. . .18g	Saturates	. . . . . .0g

10 MINS   10 MINS

SERVES 4

I N G R E D I E N T S

1 tsp oil

1 onion, finely chopped

1 large garlic clove, finely chopped

1 tsp chopped fresh chilli

700 g/1 lb 9 oz seedless Cantaloupe melon flesh, cubed

½ tsp raspberry vinegar, or 1 tsp lemon juice

pinch of salt

½ ripe green melon, such as Galia (about 500 g/1 lb 2 oz)

snipped chives, to garnish

1 Heat the oil in a small pan over a low heat. Add the onion, garlic and chilli, cover and cook for 6–7 minutes, stirring occasionally, until the onion is soft but not browned.

2 Put the Cantaloupe melon flesh in a blender or food processor, add the onion, garlic and chilli and purée until smooth, stopping to scrape down the sides as needed. (You may need to work in batches.) Add the vinegar or lemon juice with the salt and process to combine.

3 Chill for about 30 minutes, or until the mixture is cold.

4 Remove the seeds from the green melon, then cut into balls with a melon baller. Or alternatively, cut into cubes with a sharp knife.

5 Divide the soup among 4 shallow bowls and top with the green melon balls. Sprinkle lightly with chives to garnish and serve.

COOK'S TIP

If you are wary of using fresh chilli, omit it and add a few drops of shop-bought hot pepper sauce to taste, at the end of Step 2, to liven up the soup.

Tomato & Orange Soup

This soup is made from raw vegetables and fruit, so it is full of goodness as well as good taste and is wonderfully refreshing on a warm day.

NUTRITIONAL INFORMATION

Calories 107   Sugar 23g
Protein . . . . .3g   Fats 1g
Carbohydrates . . .24g   Saturates 0g

20 MINS   0 MINS

SERVES 4

I N G R E D I E N T S

3 large seedless oranges

4 ripe tomatoes

2 stalks celery, strings removed, chopped

3 carrots, grated

350 ml/12 fl oz/1½ cups tomato juice

salt

Tabasco sauce (optional)

1 tbsp chopped fresh mint

fresh mint sprigs, to garnish

1 Working over a bowl to catch the juices, peel the oranges. Cut down between the membranes and drop the orange segments into the bowl.

2 Put the tomatoes in a small bowl and pour over boiling water to cover. Allow to stand for 10 seconds, then drain. Peel off the skin and cut the tomatoes in half crossways. Scoop out the seeds into a sieve set over a bowl; reserve the tomato juices.

3 Put the tomatoes, celery and carrots in a blender (or food processor). Add the orange segments and their juice and the juice saved from the tomatoes. Purée until smooth.

4 Scrape into a bowl and stir in the tomato juice. Cover and chill until cold.

5 Taste the soup and add salt, if needed, and a few drops of Tabasco sauce to heighten the flavour, if wished. Stir in the chopped mint, ladle into cold bowls and garnish with fresh mint sprigs.

COOK'S TIP

This soup really needs to be made in a blender for the best texture. A food processor can be used but the soup will not be completely smooth.

Avocado & Almond Soup

This rich-tasting cold soup has an inviting colour and would make an appetizing start to a dinner party.

NUTRITIONAL INFORMATION

Calories 368   Sugar 5g
Protein . . . . .8g   Fats 34g
Carbohydrates . . . .9g   Saturates 5g

20 MINS   35 MINS

SERVES 4

I N G R E D I E N T S

600 ml/1 pint/2½ cups water

1 onion, finely chopped

1 stalk celery, finely chopped

1 carrot, grated

4 garlic cloves, chopped or crushed

1 bay leaf

½ tsp salt

100 g/3½ oz/ ¾ cup ground almonds

2 ripe avocados (about 450 g/1 lb)

3–4 tbsp fresh lemon juice

salt

snipped chives, to garnish

1 Combine the water, onion, celery, carrot, garlic and bay leaf in a saucepan with the salt. Bring to the boil, reduce the heat, cover and simmer for about 30 minutes, or until the vegetables are very tender.

2 Strain the soup base, reserving the liquid and vegetables separately.

3 Put the vegetables into a blender or food processor. Add the almonds and a small amount of the liquid and purée until very smooth, scraping down the sides as necessary. Add as much of the remaining liquid as the capacity of the blender or processor permits and process to combine. Scrape into a bowl, stir in any remaining liquid and chill until cold.

4 Cut the avocados in half, discard the stones and scoop the flesh into the blender or food processor. Add the cold soup base and purée until smooth, scraping down the sides as necessary. For a thinner consistency, add a few spoonfuls of cold water.

5 Add the lemon juice and season with salt to taste. Ladle into chilled small bowls and sprinkle each serving lightly with chives.

Chilled Borscht

There are innumerable versions of this soup of Eastern European origin. This refreshing vegetarian version is light and flavourful.

NUTRITIONAL INFORMATION

Calories 91   Sugars 12g
Protein . . . . .4g   Fat 3g
Carbohydrate . . .15g   Saturates 0g

15 MINS   1½ HOURS

SERVES 4

INGREDIENTS

¼ medium cabbage, cored and coarsely chopped

1 tbsp vegetable oil

1 onion, finely chopped

1 leek, halved lengthways and sliced

400 g/14 oz can peeled tomatoes in juice

1.2 litres/2 pints/5 cups water, plus extra if needed

1 carrot, thinly sliced

1 small parsnip, finely chopped

3 beetroot (raw or cooked), peeled and cubed

1 bay leaf

350 ml/12 fl oz/1½ cups tomato juice

2–3 tbsp chopped fresh dill

fresh lemon juice (optional)

salt and pepper

soured cream or yogurt, to garnish

1 Cover the cabbage generously with cold water in a pan. Bring to the boil, boil for 3 minutes, then drain.

2 Heat the oil in a large saucepan over a medium-low heat. Add the onion and leek, cover and cook for about 5 minutes, stirring occasionally, until the vegetables begin to soften.

3 Add the tomatoes, water, carrot, parsnip, beetroot and bay leaf. Stir in the blanched cabbage and add a large pinch of salt. Bring to the boil, reduce the heat and simmer for about 1¼ hours until all the vegetables are tender. Remove the bay leaf, if possible.

4 Allow the soup to cool slightly, then transfer to a blender or food processor and purée until smooth, working in batches if necessary. (If using a food processor, strain off the cooking liquid and reserve. Purée the soup solids with enough cooking liquid to moisten them, then combine with the remaining liquid.)

5 Scrape the soup into a large container and stir in the tomato juice. Allow to cool and refrigerate until cold.

6 Add the dill and stir. Thin the soup with more tomato juice or water, if wished. Season to taste with salt and pepper and, if you prefer it less sweet, add a few drops of lemon juice. Ladle into chilled soup bowls, top each with a spiral of soured cream or a dollop of yogurt.

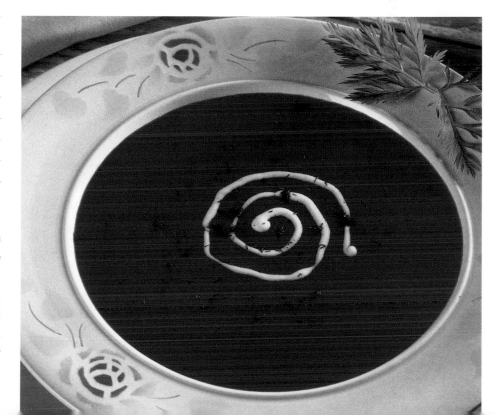

Iced Salsa Soup

A chunky mix of colourful vegetables, highlighted with Mexican flavours, this cold soup makes a lively starter to any meal.

NUTRITIONAL INFORMATION

Calories	136	Sugar	........12g
Protein	.........4g	Fats	...........4g
Carbohydrates	...21g	Saturates	......1g

15 MINS   20 MINS

SERVES 4

INGREDIENTS

2 large corn-on-the-cobs, or 225 g/ 8 oz frozen sweetcorn kernels

1 tbsp olive oil

1 orange or red (bell) pepper, cored, deseeded and finely chopped

1 green (bell) pepper, cored, deseeded and finely chopped

1 sweet onion, such as Vidalia, finely chopped

3 ripe tomatoes, skinned, deseeded and chopped

½ tsp chilli powder, or to taste

120 ml/4 fl oz/ ½ cup water

450 ml/16 fl oz/2 cups tomato juice

chilli purée (paste) (optional)

salt and pepper

TO GARNISH

3–4 spring onions (scallions), finely chopped

fresh coriander leaves (cilantro)

1 Cut the corn kernels from the cobs, or if using frozen sweetcorn, defrost and drain.

2 Heat the oil in a saucepan over a medium-high heat. Add the (bell) peppers and cook, stirring briskly, for 3 minutes. Add the onion and continue cooking for about 2 minutes, or until it starts to colour slightly.

3 Add the tomatoes, corn and chilli powder. Continue cooking, stirring frequently, for 1 minute. Pour in the water and when it bubbles, reduce the heat, cover and cook for a further 4–5 minutes, or until the (bell) peppers are just barely tender.

4 Transfer the mixture to a large container and stir in the tomato juice. Season with salt and pepper and add more chilli powder if wished. Cover and refrigerate until cold.

5 Taste and adjust the seasoning. For a more spicy soup, stir in a little chilli purée (paste) to taste. For a thinner soup, add a small amount of iced water. Ladle into chilled bowls and garnish with spring onion (scallion) and fresh coriander leaves (cilantro).

Sweet Potato & Apple Soup

This soup makes a marvellous late autumn or winter starter.
It has a delicious texture and cheerful golden colour.

NUTRITIONAL INFORMATION

Calories . . . . . . .235 Sugar 20g
Protein . . . . .3g Fats 10g
Carbohydrates . . .36g Saturates 6g

 15 MINS   50 MINS

SERVES 4

I N G R E D I E N T S

1 tbsp butter

3 leeks, thinly sliced

1 large carrot, thinly sliced

2 sweet potatoes, peeled and cubed

2 large tart eating apples, peeled and cubed

1.2 litres/2 pints/5 cups water

freshly grated nutmeg

225 ml/8 fl oz/1 cup apple juice

225 ml/8 fl oz/1 cup whipping or single
   (light) cream

salt and pepper

snipped fresh chives or fresh coriander
   leaves (cilantro), to garnish

1 Melt the butter in a large saucepan over a medium-low heat. Add the leeks, cover and cook for 6–8 minutes, or until softened, stirring frequently.

2 Add the carrot, sweet potatoes, apples and water. Season lightly with salt, pepper and nutmeg. Bring to the boil, reduce the heat and simmer, covered, for about 20 minutes, stirring occasionally, until the vegetables are very tender.

3 Allow the soup to cool slightly, then transfer to a blender or food processor and purée until smooth, working in batches if necessary. (If using a food processor, strain off the cooking liquid and reserve. Purée the soup solids with enough cooking liquid to moisten them, then combine with the remaining liquid.)

4 Return the puréed soup to the saucepan and stir in the apple juice. Place over a low heat and simmer for about 10 minutes until heated through.

5 Stir in the cream and continue simmering for about 5 minutes, stirring frequently, until heated through. Taste and adjust the seasoning, adding more salt, pepper and nutmeg, if necessary. Ladle the soup into warm bowls, garnish with chives or coriander (cilantro) and serve.

Sweet Potato & Onion Soup

This simple recipe uses the sweet potato with its distinctive flavour and colour, combined with a hint of orange and coriander.

NUTRITIONAL INFORMATION

Calories 320	Sugars 26g
Protein 7g	Fat 7g
Carbohydrate . . .62g	Saturates 1g

15 MINS   30 MINS

SERVES 4

I N G R E D I E N T S

2 tbsp vegetable oil

900 g/2 lb sweet potatoes, diced

1 carrot, diced

2 onions, sliced

2 garlic cloves, crushed

600 ml/1 pint/2½ cups vegetable stock

300 ml/½ pint/1¼ cups unsweetened
 orange juice

225 ml/8 fl oz/1 cup low-fat natural yogurt

2 tbsp chopped fresh coriander (cilantro)

salt and pepper

TO GARNISH

coriander (cilantro) sprigs

orange rind

1 Heat the vegetable oil in a large saucepan and add the diced sweet potatoes and carrot, sliced onions and garlic. Sauté the vegetables gently for 5 minutes, stirring constantly.

2 Pour in the vegetable stock and orange juice and bring them to the boil.

3 Reduce the heat to a simmer, cover the saucepan and cook the vegetables for 20 minutes or until the sweet potato and carrot cubes are tender.

4 Transfer the mixture to a food processor or blender in batches and process for 1 minute until puréed. Return the purée to the rinsed-out saucepan.

5 Stir in the natural yogurt and chopped coriander (cilantro) and season to taste.

6 Serve the soup in warm bowls and garnish with coriander (cilantro) sprigs and orange rind.

VARIATION

This soup can be chilled before serving, if preferred. If chilling it, stir the yogurt into the dish just before serving. Serve in chilled bowls.

Corn & Spinach Soup

Fresh sweetcorn retains a little crunch when cooked, adding a pleasing texture to this soup.

 15 MINS   40 MINS

SERVES 4

I N G R E D I E N T S

3 corn-on-the-cobs, cooked

1 tsp butter

1 tsp oil

1 large onion, finely chopped

1 leek, thinly sliced

1 carrot, finely chopped

1 large potato, diced

1.2 litres/2 pints/5 cups water

120 ml/4 fl oz/ ½ cup double (heavy) cream

120 ml/4 fl oz/ ½ cup milk

freshly grated nutmeg

175 g/6 oz spinach leaves, finely chopped

salt and pepper

1 Cut the kernels from the corn, without cutting all the way down to the cob. Using the back of a knife, scrape the cobs to extract the milky liquid; reserve.

2 Heat the butter and oil in a large saucepan over a medium heat and add the onion and leek. Cover and cook for 3–4 minutes, stirring frequently, until softened.

3 Add the carrot, potato and water with a large pinch of salt. Bring just to the boil and stir in the corn kernels and the liquid scraped from the cobs. Reduce the heat to low, cover and simmer for about 25 minutes, or until the carrot and potato are tender.

4 Allow the soup to cool slightly, then transfer about half of it to a blender or food processor and purée until smooth.

5 Return the puréed soup to the saucepan, add the cream and milk and stir to blend. Thin with a little more milk, if preferred. Season with salt, pepper and nutmeg. Simmer over a low heat until reheated.

6 Add the spinach and cook for 4–5 minutes, stirring frequently, just until the spinach is completely wilted. Taste and adjust the seasoning, if necessary, then ladle the soup into warm bowls. Serve at once.

COOK'S TIP

To cut corn kernels off the cob, lay on its side on a cutting board and slice lengthwise, rotating until all kernels are removed. Then stand on its stem and scrape down to extract the remaining pulp and juice.

Cheese & Vegetable Chowder

For this soup, the root vegetables should be cut into small dice so that they all cook in the same amount of time.

NUTRITIONAL INFORMATION

Calories 651	Sugar 9g
Protein 25g	Fats 48g
Carbohydrates . . .30g	Saturates 30g

 15 MINS   50 MINS

SERVES 4

I N G R E D I E N T S

25 g/1 oz/2 tbsp butter

1 large onion, finely chopped

1 large leek, split lengthways and thinly sliced

1–2 garlic cloves, crushed

50 g/2 oz/6 tbsp plain (all-purpose) flour

1.2 litres/2 pints/5 cups chicken or vegetable stock

3 carrots, finely diced

2 stalks celery, finely diced

1 turnip, finely diced

1 large potato, finely diced

3–4 sprigs fresh thyme, or ⅛ tsp dried thyme

1 bay leaf

350 ml/12 fl oz/1½ cups single (light) cream

300 g/10½ oz mature Cheddar cheese, grated

2 tbsp chopped mixed fresh parsley, tarragon and chives

fresh chopped parsley, to garnish

salt and pepper

1 Melt the butter in a large heavy-based saucepan over a medium-low heat. Add the onion, leek and garlic. Cover and cook for about 5 minutes, stirring frequently, until the vegetables start to soften.

2 Stir the flour into the veg-etables and continue cooking for 2 minutes. Add a little of the stock and stir well, scraping the bottom of the pan to mix in the flour. Bring to the boil, stirring frequently, and slowly stir in the rest of the stock.

3 Add the carrots, celery, turnip, potato, thyme and bay leaf. Reduce the heat, cover and cook gently for about 35 minutes, stirring occasionally, until the vegetables are tender. Remove the bay leaf and the thyme branches.

4 Stir in the cream and simmer over a very low heat for 5 minutes. Add the cheese a handful at a time, stirring constantly for 1 minute after each addition, to make sure it is completely melted. Taste the soup and adjust the seasoning, adding salt if needed, and pepper to taste. Ladle immediately into warm bowls, sprinkle with fresh chopped parsley and serve.

Vegetable & Corn Chowder

This is a really filling soup, which should be served before a light main course. It is easy to prepare and filled with flavour.

NUTRITIONAL INFORMATION

Calories 378	Sugars 20g
Protein 16g	Fat 13g
Carbohydrate ...52g	Saturates 6g

 15 MINS   30 MINS

SERVES 4

INGREDIENTS

1 tbsp vegetable oil

1 red onion, diced

1 red (bell) pepper, seeded and diced

3 garlic cloves, crushed

1 large potato, diced

2 tbsp plain (all-purpose) flour

600 ml/1 pint/2½ cups milk

300 ml/½ pint/1¼ cups vegetable stock

50 g/1¾ oz broccoli florets

300 g/10½ oz/3 cups canned
    sweetcorn (corn), drained

75 g/2¾ oz/¾ cup Cheddar cheese, grated

salt and pepper

1 tbsp chopped coriander (cilantro),
    to garnish

COOK'S TIP

Vegetarian cheeses are made with rennets of non-animal origin, using microbial or fungal enzymes.

1 Heat the oil in a large saucepan. Add the onion, (bell) pepper, garlic and potato and sauté over a low heat, stirring frequently, for 2–3 minutes.

2 Stir in the flour and cook, stirring for 30 seconds. Gradually stir in the milk and stock.

3 Add the broccoli and sweetcorn (corn). Bring the mixture to the boil, stirring constantly, then reduce the heat and simmer for about 20 minutes, or until all the vegetables are tender.

4 Stir in 50 g/1¾ oz/½ cup of the cheese until it melts.

5 Season and spoon the chowder into a warm soup tureen. Garnish with the remaining cheese and the coriander (cilantro) and serve.

Lettuce & Rocket Soup

Cooked lettuce tastes similar to sorrel, but lettuce is much easier to find and cheaper.

NUTRITIONAL INFORMATION

Calories 236	Sugars 7g	
Protein 3g	Fat 17g	
Carbohydrate ...19g	Saturates 10g	

15 MINS   55 MINS

SERVES 4

INGREDIENTS

1 tbsp butter

1 large sweet onion, halved and sliced

2 leeks, sliced

1.5 litres/2¾ pints/6¼ cups chicken stock

80 g/3 oz/6 tbsp white rice

2 carrots, thinly sliced

3 garlic cloves

1 bay leaf

2 heads soft round lettuce (about 500 g/1 lb 2 oz), cored and chopped

175 ml/6 fl oz/¾ cup double (heavy) cream

freshly grated nutmeg

80 g/3 oz rocket (arugula) leaves, finely chopped

salt and pepper

1 Heat the butter in a large saucepan over a medium heat and add the onion and leeks. Cover and cook for 3–4 minutes, stirring frequently, until the vegetables begin to soften.

2 Add the stock, rice, carrots, garlic and bay leaf with a large pinch of salt. Bring just to the boil. Reduce the heat, cover and simmer for 25–30 minutes, or until the rice and vegetables are tender. Remove the bay leaf.

3 Add the lettuce and cook for 10 minutes, until the leaves are soft, stirring occasionally.

4 Allow the soup to cool slightly, then transfer to a blender or food processor and purée until smooth, working in batches if necessary. (If using a food processor, strain off the cooking liquid and reserve. Purée the soup solids with enough cooking liquid to moisten them, then combine with the remaining liquid.)

5 Return the soup to the saucepan and place over a medium-low heat. Stir in the cream and a grating of nutmeg. Simmer for about 5 minutes, stirring occasionally, until the soup is reheated. Add more water or cream if you prefer a thinner soup.

6 Add the rocket (arugula) and simmer for 2–3 minutes, stirring occasionally, until it is wilted. Adjust the seasoning and ladle the soup into warm bowls.

Curried Tuna Chowder

This tasty soup uses canned tuna and tomatoes, two store-cupboard favourites that you are likely to have on hand.

NUTRITIONAL INFORMATION

Calories 265	Sugar 8g	
Protein 17g	Fats 11g	
Carbohydrates ...26g	Saturates 7g	

 10 MINS   35 MINS

SERVES 4

INGREDIENTS

200 g/7 oz can light meat tuna packed in water

1½ tbsp butter

1 onion, finely chopped

1 garlic clove, finely chopped

2 tbsp plain (all purpose) flour

2 tsp mild curry powder

400 g/14 oz can plum tomatoes in juice

3 tbsp white rice

1 courgette (zucchini), finely diced

120 ml/4 fl oz/ ½ cup light (single) cream

salt and pepper

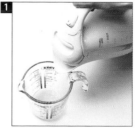  

1 Drain the tuna over a measuring jug (cup) and add boiling water to make up to 600 ml/1 pint/2 ½ cups.

2 Melt the butter in a large saucepan over a medium-low heat. Add the onion and garlic and cook for about 5 minutes until the onion is softened, stirring frequently.

3 Stir in the flour and curry powder. Continue cooking for 2 minutes.

4 Slowly add about half of the tuna juice and water mixture and stir well, scraping the bottom of the pan to mix in the flour. Pour in the remaining mixture and bring just to the boil, stirring frequently. Add the tomatoes and break up with a spoon. When the soup almost comes back to the boil, stir in the rice, reduce the heat, cover and simmer for 10 minutes.

5 Add the tuna and courgette (zucchini) and continue cooking for about 15 minutes, or until the vegetables and rice are tender.

6 Stir in the cream, season with salt and pepper to taste and continue simmering for 3–4 minutes until heated through. Ladle into warm bowls and serve.

Caribbean Seafood Soup

This soup It is traditionally made with the roots and leaves of local tuberous vegetables, but potato and spinach make a practical alternative.

NUTRITIONAL INFORMATION

Calories 134	Sugars 4g	
Protein 15g	Fat 4g	
Carbohydrate 11g	Saturates 2g	

15 MINS   50 MINS

SERVES 4

I N G R E D I E N T S

150 g/5½ oz peeled medium prawns (shrimp)

200 g/7 oz skinless firm white fish fillets, cubed

¾ tsp ground coriander

¼ tsp ground cumin

1 tsp chilli purée (paste), or to taste

3 tbsp fresh lemon juice, or to taste

1 tbsp butter

1 onion, halved and thinly sliced

2 large leeks, thinly sliced

3 garlic cloves, finely chopped

1 large potato, diced

1.2 litres/2 pints/5 cups chicken or vegetable stock

250 g/9 oz spinach leaves

120 ml/4 fl oz/ ½ cup coconut milk

salt and pepper

1 Put the prawns (shrimp) and fish in a bowl with the coriander, cumin, chilli purée (paste) and lemon juice and leave to marinate.

2 Melt the butter in a large saucepan over a medium heat. Add the onion and leeks, cover and cook for about 10 minutes, stirring occasionally, until they are soft. Add the garlic and cook for a further 3–4 minutes.

3 Add the potato and stock, together with a large pinch of salt, if using unsalted stock. Bring to the boil, reduce the heat, cover and cook gently for 15–20 minutes until the potato is tender. Stir in the spinach and continue cooking, uncovered, for about 3 minutes until it is just wilted.

4 Allow the soup to cool slightly, then transfer to a blender or food processor, working in batches if necessary. Purée the soup until smooth. (If using a food processor, strain off the cooking liquid and reserve. Purée the soup solids with enough cooking liquid to moisten them, then combine with the remaining liquid.)

5 Return the soup to the saucepan and stir in the coconut milk. Add the fish and prawns (shrimp) with their marinade. Simmer over a medium-low heat for about 8 minutes, stirring frequently, until the soup is heated through and the fish is cooked and flakes easily.

6 Taste and adjust the seasoning, adding more chilli purée (paste) and/or lemon juice if wished. Ladle into warm bowls and serve.

COOK'S TIP

Add a handful of fresh coriander leaves (cilantro) to the spinach.

Seafood Chowder

The proportions of fish and prawns are flexible – use more or less as you wish.

NUTRITIONAL INFORMATION

Calories	.310	Sugars	.5g
Protein	.29g	Fat	.14g
Carbohydrate	.17g	Saturates	.8g

 15 MINS   35 MINS

SERVES 4

INGREDIENTS

1 kg/2 lb 4 oz mussels

4 tbsp plain (all-purpose) flour

1.5 litres/2¾ pints/6¼ cups fish stock

1 tbsp butter

1 large onion, finely chopped

350 g/12 oz skinless white fish fillets, such as cod, sole or haddock

200 g/7 oz cooked or raw peeled prawns (shrimp)

300 ml/10 fl oz/1¼ cups whipping cream or double (heavy) cream

salt and pepper

snipped fresh dill, to garnish

1 Discard any broken mussels and those with open shells that do not close when tapped. Rinse, pull off any 'beards', and if there are barnacles, scrape them off with a knife under cold running water. Put the mussels in a large heavy-based saucepan. Cover tightly and cook over a high heat for about 4 minutes, or until the mussels open, shaking the pan occasionally. When they are cool enough to handle, remove the mussels from the shells, adding any additional juices to the cooking liquid. Strain the cooking liquid through a muslin-lined sieve and reserve.

2 Put the flour in a mixing bowl and very slowly whisk in enough of the stock to make a thick paste. Whisk in a little more stock to make a smooth liquid.

3 Melt the butter in heavy-based saucepan over a medium-low heat. Add the onion, cover and cook for about 5 minutes, stirring frequently, until it softens.

4 Add the remaining fish stock and bring to the boil. Slowly whisk in the flour mixture until well combined and bring back to the boil, whisking constantly. Add the mussel cooking liquid. Season with salt, if needed, and pepper. Reduce the heat and simmer, partially covered, for 15 minutes.

5 Add the fish and mussels and continue simmering, stirring occasionally, for about 5 minutes, or until the fish is cooked and begins to flake.

6 Stir in the prawns (shrimp) and cream. Taste and adjust the seasoning. Simmer for a few minutes longer to heat through. Ladle into warm bowls, sprinkle with dill and serve.

Shellfish & Tomato Soup

This soup is swimming with seafood. Depending on availability, you could substitute skinless, boneless white fish for the scallops or prawns

NUTRITIONAL INFORMATION

Calories 316   Sugars 3g
Protein ....26g   Fat 14g
Carbohydrate ...21g   Saturates 8g

15 MINS   35 MINS

SERVES 4

INGREDIENTS

1 kg/2 lb 4 oz mussels

2 tbsp butter

2 shallots, finely chopped

4 tbsp plain (all-purpose) flour

4 tbsp dry white wine

600 ml/1 pint/2½ cups fish stock

200 g/7 oz queen (bay) scallops

200 g/7 oz cooked peeled prawns (shrimp)

120 ml/4 fl oz/½ cup double (heavy) cream

4 tomatoes, skinned, deseeded and chopped

2 tbsp snipped fresh chives

2 tbsp chopped fresh parsley

salt and pepper

1 Discard any broken mussels and those with open shells that do not close when tapped. Rinse, pull off any 'beard', and if there are barnacles, scrape them off with a knife under cold running water. Put the mussels in a large heavy-based saucepan, cover tightly and cook for 4–5 minutes, or until the mussels open, shaking the pan occasionally.

2 When they are cool enough to handle, remove the mussels from the shells, adding additional juices to the cooking liquid. Strain the liquid through a muslin-lined sieve. Top it up with water to make 450 ml/16 fl oz/2 cups.

3 Melt the butter in a large saucepan over a medium-low heat. Add the shallots and cook for 3–4 minutes, stirring frequently, until soft. Stir in the flour and continue cooking for 2 minutes. Add the wine.

4 Slowly add the fish stock and stir well, scraping the bottom of the pan to mix in the flour. Pour in the remaining mussel cooking liquid and water and bring just to the boil, stirring frequently. Reduce the heat, cover and simmer for 10 minutes.

5 Add the scallops, prawns (shrimp) and mussels, and continue cooking for 1 minute.

6 Stir in the cream, tomatoes, chives, lemon juice and parsley. Season to taste with salt. Sprinkle with parsley and serve.

Fennel & Tomato Soup

This light and refreshing soup is also good served cold.

NUTRITIONAL INFORMATION

Calories 117	Sugars 9g	
Protein 10g	Fat 2g	
Carbohydrate ...15g	Saturates 0g	

 10 MINS 45 MINS

SERVES 4

I N G R E D I E N T S

2 tsp olive oil

1 large onion, halved and sliced

2 large fennel bulbs, halved and sliced

1 small potato, diced

850 ml/1½ pints/3¾ cups water

400 ml/14 fl oz/1⅔ cups tomato juice

1 bay leaf

125 g/4½ oz cooked peeled small prawns (shrimp)

2 tomatoes, skinned, deseeded and chopped

½ tsp snipped fresh dill

salt and pepper

dill sprigs or fennel fronds, to garnish

1 Heat the olive oil in a large saucepan over a medium heat. Add the onion and fennel and cook for 3–4 minutes, stirring occasionally, until the onion is just softened.

2 Add the potato, water, tomato juice and bay leaf with a large pinch of salt. Reduce the heat, cover and simmer for about 25 minutes, stirring once or twice, until the vegetables are soft.

3 Allow the soup to cool slightly, then transfer to a blender or food processor and purée until smooth, working in batches if necessary. (If using a food processor, strain off the cooking liquid and reserve. Purée the soup solids with enough cooking liquid to moisten them, then combine with the remaining liquid.)

4 Return the soup to the saucepan and add the prawns (shrimp). Simmer gently for about 10 minutes, to reheat the soup and allow it to absorb the prawn (shrimp) flavour.

5 Stir in the tomatoes and dill. Taste and adjust the seasoning, adding salt, if needed, and pepper. Thin the soup with a little more tomato juice, if wished. Ladle into warm bowls, garnish with dill or fennel fronds and serve.

Scallops in Garlic Broth

This soup is both simple and very elegant. Its lightness makes it particularly suitable as a starter.

NUTRITIONAL INFORMATION

Calories . . . . .112 Sugars 4g
Protein . . . . .16g Fat 1g
Carbohydrate . . . .11g Saturates 0g

 10 MINS   50 MINS

SERVES 4

INGREDIENTS

1.2 litres/2 pints/5 cups water

1 large garlic bulb (about 100 g/3½ oz),
    separated into unpeeled cloves

1 stalk celery, chopped

1 carrot, chopped

1 onion, chopped

10 peppercorns

5–6 parsley stems

1 tbsp oil

225 g/8 oz large sea scallops
    or queen scallops

salt and pepper

fresh coriander leaves (cilantro), to garnish

1 Combine the garlic cloves, celery, carrot, onion, peppercorns, parsley stems and water in a saucepan with a good pinch of salt. Bring to the boil, reduce the heat and simmer, partially covered, for 30–45 minutes.

VARIATION

Use fish stock instead of water to make the garlic stock if you want a more fishy flavour, or add Oriental fish sauce, such as nam pla, to taste.

2 Strain the stock into a clean saucepan. Taste and adjust the seasoning, and keep hot.

3 If using sea scallops, slice in half crossways to form 2 thinner rounds from each. (If the scallops are very large, slice them into 3 rounds.) Sprinkle with salt and pepper.

4 Heat the oil in a frying pan (skillet) over a medium-high heat and cook the scallops on one side for 1–2 minutes until lightly browned and the flesh becomes opaque.

5 Divide the scallops between 4 warm shallow bowls, arranging them browned-side up. Ladle the soup over the scallops, then float a few coriander leaves (cilantro) on top. Serve at once.

Clam & Corn Chowder

Fresh clams make this chowder that bit more special, but they can be expensive. Canned baby clams or razor shell clams can be used instead.

NUTRITIONAL INFORMATION

Calories 344   Sugar 11g
Protein . . . . .20g   Fats 10g
Carbohydrates . . .45g   Saturates 6g

15 MINS   40 MINS

SERVES 4

INGREDIENTS

750 g/1 lb 10 oz clams, or 280 g/
    10 oz can clams

2 tbsp dry white wine (if needed)

4 tsp butter

1 large onion, finely chopped

1 small carrot, finely diced

3 tbsp plain (all-purpose) flour

300 ml/10 fl oz/1¼ cups fish stock

200 ml/7 fl oz/¾ cup water (if needed)

450 g/1 lb potatoes, diced

125 g/4 oz/1 cup cooked or defrosted
    frozen sweetcorn

450 ml/16 fl oz/2 cups full-fat (whole) milk

salt and pepper

chopped fresh parsley, to garnish

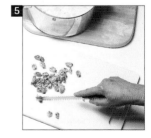

1 If using fresh clams, put them into a heavy-based saucepan with the wine. Cover tightly, set over a medium-high heat and cook for 2–4 minutes, or until they open, shaking the pan occasionally. Remove the clams from the shells and strain the cooking liquid through a very fine mesh sieve; reserve both. If using canned clams, drain and rinse well.

2 Melt the butter in a large saucepan over a medium-low heat. Add the onion and carrot and cook for 3–4 minutes, stirring frequently, until the onion is softened. Stir in the flour and continue cooking for 2 minutes.

3 Slowly add about half the stock and stir well, scraping the bottom of the pan to mix in the flour. Pour in the remaining stock and the reserved clam cooking liquid, or the water if using canned clams, and bring just to the boil, stirring.

4 Add the potatoes, sweetcorn and milk and stir to combine. Reduce the heat and simmer gently, partially covered, for about 20 minutes, stirring occasionally, until all the vegetables are tender.

5 Chop the clams, if large. Stir in the clams and continue cooking for about 5 minutes until heated through. Taste and adjust the seasoning, if needed.

6 Ladle the soup into bowls and sprinkle with parsley.

Mexican Beef & Rice Soup

For this tasty and unusual soup, boneless leg is a good cut of beef to use, as it is generally lean and any fat is easily trimmed off.

NUTRITIONAL INFORMATION

Calories	.501	Sugars	.14g
Protein	.45g	Fat	.18g
Carbohydrate	.36g	Saturates	.5g

 15 MINS   2 HOURS

SERVES 4

INGREDIENTS

3 tbsp olive oil

500 g/1 lb 2 oz boneless stewing beef, cut into 2.5 cm/1 inch pieces

150 ml/5 fl oz/²⁄₃ cup red wine

1 onion, finely chopped

1 green (bell) pepper, cored, deseeded and finely chopped

1 small fresh red chilli, deseeded and finely chopped

2 garlic cloves, finely chopped

1 carrot, finely chopped

¼ tsp ground coriander

¼ tsp ground cumin

⅛ tsp ground cinnamon

¼ tsp dried oregano

1 bay leaf

grated rind of ½ orange

400 g/14 oz can chopped tomatoes

1.2 litres/2 pints/5 cups beef stock

50 g/1¾ oz/¼ cup long-grain white rice

25 g/1 oz/3 tbsp raisins

15 g/½ oz plain semi-sweet chocolate, melted

chopped fresh coriander (cilantro), to garnish

1 Heat half the oil in a large frying pan (skillet) over a medium-high heat. Add the meat in one layer and cook until well browned, turning to colour all sides. Remove the pan from the heat and pour in the wine.

2 Heat the remaining oil in a large saucepan over a medium heat. Add the onion, cover and cook for about 3 minutes, stirring occasionally, until just softened. Add the green (bell) pepper, chilli, garlic and carrot, and continue cooking, covered, for 3 minutes.

3 Add the coriander, cumin, cinnamon, oregano, bay leaf and orange rind. Stir in the tomatoes and stock, along with the beef and wine. Bring almost to the boil and when the mixture begins to bubble, reduce the heat to low. Cover and simmer gently, stirring occasionally, for about 1 hour until the meat is tender.

4 Stir in the rice, raisins and chocolate, and continue cook-ing, stirring occasionally, for about 30 minutes until the rice is tender.

5 Ladle into warm bowls and garnish with coriander (cilantro).

Cabbage Soup with Sausage

Spicy or smoky sausages add substance to this soup, which makes a hearty and warming supper, served with crusty bread and green salad.

NUTRITIONAL INFORMATION

Calories 160   Sugar 7g
Protein ....10g   Fats 8g
Carbohydrates ...12g   Saturates 2g

 10 MINS   1¼ HOURS

SERVES 4

INGREDIENTS

350 g/12 oz lean sausages, preferably highly seasoned

2 tsp oil

1 onion, finely chopped

1 leek, halved lengthways and thinly sliced

2 carrots, halved and thinly sliced

400 g/14 oz can chopped tomatoes

350 g/12 oz young green cabbage, cored and coarsely shredded

1-2 garlic cloves, finely chopped

pinch dried thyme

1.5 litres/2¾ pints/6¼ cups chicken or meat stock

salt and pepper

freshly grated Parmesan cheese, to serve

1 Put the sausages in water to cover generously and bring to the boil. Reduce the heat and simmer until firm. Drain the sausages and, when cool enough to handle, remove the skin, if you wish, and slice thinly.

2 Heat the oil in a large saucepan over a medium heat, add the onion, leek and carrots and cook for 3–4 minutes, stirring frequently, until the onion starts to soften.

3 Add the tomatoes, cabbage, garlic, thyme, stock and sausages. Bring to the boil, reduce the heat to low and cook gently, partially covered, for about 40 minutes until the vegetables are tender.

4 Taste the soup and adjust the seasoning, if necessary. Ladle into warm bowls and serve with Parmesan cheese.

VARIATION

If you don't have fresh stock available, use water instead, with 1 stock cube only dissolved in it. Add a little more onion and garlic, plus a bouquet garni (remove it before serving).

Hunter's Soup

This soup is perfect for the sweet meat of rabbit, which is traditionally paired with tomatoes and mushrooms.

NUTRITIONAL INFORMATION

Calories	358	Sugar	.........10g
Protein	........35g	Fats	..........17g
Carbohydrates	...12g	Saturates	......6g

 25 MINS   1½ HOURS

SERVES 4

I N G R E D I E N T S

1-2 tbsp olive oil

900 g/2 lb rabbit, jointed

1 onion, finely chopped

2-3 garlic cloves, finely chopped or crushed

100 g/3½ oz lean smoked back bacon, finely chopped

120 ml/4 fl oz/ ½ cup white wine

1.2 litres/2 pints/5 cups chicken stock

450 ml/16 fl oz/2 cups tomato juice

2 tbsp tomato purée (paste)

2 carrots, halved lengthways and sliced

1 bay leaf

¼ tsp dried thyme

¼ tsp dried oregano

1 tbsp butter

300 g/10½ oz mushrooms, quartered if small or sliced

chopped fresh parsley, to garnish

1 Heat the oil in a large saucepan or flameproof casserole over a medium-high heat. Add the rabbit, in batches if necessary to avoid crowding, and cook until lightly browned on all sides, adding a little more oil if needed. Remove the pieces when browned.

2 Reduce the heat a little and add the onion, garlic and bacon to the pan. Cook, stirring frequently, for a further 2 minutes.

3 Add the wine and bubble for 1 minute. Add the stock and return the rabbit to the pan with any juices. Bring to the boil and skim off any foam that rises to the surface. Reduce the heat and stir in the tomato juice, tomato purée (paste), carrots, bay leaf, thyme and oregano. Season with salt and pepper. Cover and simmer gently for 1 hour, or until very tender.

4 Remove the rabbit pieces with a slotted spoon and, when cool enough to handle, remove the meat from the bones. Discard any fat or gristle, along with the bones. Cut the meat into bite-sized pieces and return to the soup.

5 Melt the butter in a frying pan (skillet) over a medium-high heat. Add the mushrooms and season with salt and pepper. Fry gently until lightly golden, then add to the soup. Simmer for 10-15 minutes to blend. Season to taste and serve sprinkled with parsley.

Chicken, Corn & Bean Soup

This soup is especially tasty using fresh sweetcorn kernels cut from 3 or 4 corn-on-the-cobs.

NUTRITIONAL INFORMATION

Calories 256	Sugars 6g	
Protein 19g	Fat 7g	
Carbohydrate ...32g	Saturates 3g	

 10 MINS   45 MINS

SERVES 4

I N G R E D I E N T S

1 ½ tbsp butter

1 large onion, finely chopped

1 garlic clove, finely chopped

3 tbsp plain (all-purpose) flour

600 ml/1 pint/2½ cups water

1 litre/1¾ pints/4 cups chicken stock

1 carrot, quartered and thinly sliced

175 g/6 oz green beans, trimmed
   and cut into short pieces

400 g/14 oz can butter beans, drained and
   rinsed

350 g/12 oz cooked sweetcorn or frozen
   sweetcorn kernels

225 g/8 oz cooked chicken meat

salt and pepper

1 Melt the butter in a large saucepan over a medium-low heat. Add the onion and garlic and cook, stirring frequently, for 3–4 minutes until just softened.

2 Stir in the flour and continue cooking for 2 minutes, stirring occasionally.

3 Gradually pour in the water, stirring constantly and scraping the bottom of the pan to mix in the flour. Bring to the boil, stirring frequently, and cook for 2 minutes. Add the stock and stir until smooth.

4 Add the carrot, green beans, butter beans, sweetcorn and chicken meat. Season with salt and pepper. Bring back to the boil, reduce the heat to medium-low, cover and simmer for about 35 minutes until the vegetables are tender.

5 Taste the soup and adjust the seasoning, adding salt, if needed, and plenty of pepper.

6 Ladle the soup into warm, deep bowls and serve.

VARIATION

Replace the butter beans with 300 g/10½ oz cooked fresh broad beans, peeled if wished, or lima beans. You could also substitute sliced runner beans for the green beans.

Senegalese Soup

This delicately curried chicken soup requires a flavourful stock. Its velvety texture makes it an elegant starter.

NUTRITIONAL INFORMATION

Calories 428	Sugars 6g	
Protein 16g	Fat 26g	
Carbohydrate ...34g	Saturates 15g	

15 MINS   40 MINS

SERVES 4

INGREDIENTS

1.2 litres/2 pints/5 cups chicken stock

1 small onion, thinly sliced

1 small carrot, finely chopped

1 stalk celery, finely chopped

½ small eating apple, peeled, cored and chopped

1–2 garlic cloves, halved

1 tsp mild curry powder

200 g/7 oz skinless, boneless chicken breast

2 egg yolks

4 tbsp cornflour (cornstarch)

225 ml/8 fl oz/1 cup whipping cream

freshly grated nutmeg

salt and white pepper

toasted coconut strips or pecans, to garnish

1 Heat the stock in a large saucepan. Add the onion, carrot, celery, apple, garlic and curry powder with a large pinch of salt, if the stock is unsalted. Bring to the boil, reduce the heat and simmer, covered, for 20 minutes.

2 Trim any fat from the chicken. Add the chicken to the stock and continue

simmering for 10 minutes, or until the chicken is tender. Remove the chicken with a slotted spoon.

3 Strain the stock and discard the stock vegetables. Spoon off any fat. When cool enough to handle, cut the chicken into thin slivers.

4 Put the strained stock in a large heavy-based saucepan and put over a medium heat. When starting to bubble around the edge, adjust the heat so it continues to bubble gently at the edge but remains still in the centre.

5 Put the egg yolks in a bowl. Add the cornflour (cornstarch) and cream and whisk until smooth. Whisk one-quarter of the hot stock into the cream mixture, then pour it all back into the saucepan, whisking constantly. With a wooden spoon, stir constantly for 10 minutes until the soup thickens slightly. Do not allow it to boil or the soup may curdle. If you see the soup beginning to boil, take the pan off the heat and stir more quickly until it cools down.

6 Stir in the chicken and reduce the heat to low. Season the soup with salt, pepper and nutmeg. Ladle into warm soup bowls, garnish with toasted coconut strips or pecans and serve.

Chicken Gumbo

This soup contains okra, an essential ingredient in a gumbo. It helps thicken the soup

NUTRITIONAL INFORMATION

Calories 242   Sugars 5g
Protein ....17g   Fat 10g
Carbohydrate ...23g   Saturates 2g

15 MINS   60 MINS

SERVES 4

INGREDIENTS

2 tbsp olive oil

4 tbsp plain (all-purpose) flour

1 onion, finely chopped

1 small green (bell) pepper, cored, deseeded and finely chopped

1 stalk celery, finely chopped

1.2 litres/2 pints/5 cups chicken stock

400 g/14 oz can chopped tomatoes in juice

3 garlic cloves, finely chopped or crushed

125 g/4½ oz okra, stems removed, cut into 5 mm/¼ inch thick slices

50 g/1¾ oz/4 tbsp white rice

200 g/7 oz cooked chicken, cubed

115 g/4 oz cooked garlic sausage, sliced or cubed

1 Heat the oil in a large heavy-based saucepan over a medium-low heat and stir in the flour. Cook for about 15 minutes, stirring occasionally, until the mixture is a rich golden brown (see Cook's Tip).

2 Add the onion, green (bell) pepper and celery and continue cooking for about 10 minutes until the onion softens.

3 Slowly pour in the stock and bring to the boil, stirring well and scraping the bottom of the pan to mix in the flour. Remove the pan from the heat.

4 Add the tomatoes and garlic. Stir in the okra and rice and season. Reduce the heat, cover and simmer for 20 minutes, or until the okra is tender.

5 Add the chicken and sausage and continue simmering for about 10 minutes. Taste and adjust the seasoning, if necessary, and ladle into warm bowls to serve.

COOK'S TIP

Keep a watchful eye on the roux (flour and oil) as it begins to darken. The soup gains a lot of flavour from this traditional Cajun base, but if it burns the soup will be bitter. If you prefer, omit it and start by cooking the onion, green (bell) pepper and celery in the oil, adding the flour when they are softened.

Turkey & Mushrooms Soup

This is a warming wintery soup, substantial enough to serve as a main course, with lots of crusty bread.

NUTRITIONAL INFORMATION

Calories 465	Sugar 3g	
Protein 18g	Fats 30g	
Carbohydrates ...33g	Saturates 18g	

15 MINS   60 MINS

SERVES 4

INGREDIENTS

3 tbsp butter

1 onion, finely chopped

1 stalk celery, finely chopped

25 large fresh sage leaves, finely chopped

4 tbsp plain (all-purpose) flour

1.2 litres/2 pints/5 cups turkey or chicken stock

100 g/3½ oz/⅔ cup brown rice

250 g/9 oz mushrooms, sliced

200 g/7 oz cooked turkey

200 ml/7 fl oz/ ¾ cup double (heavy) cream

freshly grated Parmesan cheese, to serve

1 Melt half the butter in a large saucepan over a medium-low heat. Add the onion, celery and sage and cook for 3-4 minutes until the onion is softened, stirring frequently. Stir in the flour and continue cooking for 2 minutes.

2 Slowly add about one quarter of the stock and stir well, scraping the bottom of the pan to mix in the flour. Pour in the remaining stock, stirring to combine completely, and bring just to the boil.

3 Stir in the rice and season with salt and pepper. Reduce the heat and simmer gently, partially covered, for about 30 minutes until the rice is just tender, stirring occasionally.

4 Meanwhile, melt the remaining butter in a large frying pan (skillet) over a medium heat. Add the mushrooms and season with salt and pepper. Cook for about 8 minutes until they are golden brown, stirring occasionally at first, then more often after they start to colour. Add the mushrooms to the soup.

5 Add the turkey to the soup and stir in the cream. Continue simmering for about 10 minutes until heated through. Taste and adjust the seasoning, if necessary. Ladle into warm bowls and serve with Parmesan cheese.

Confetti Bean Soup

This soup uses the colourful dried bean mixes available that include a variety of different beans.

NUTRITIONAL INFORMATION

Calories 241   Sugar 6g
Protein . . . . .16g   Fats 2g
Carbohydrates . . .41g   Saturates 0g

15 MINS   1¾ HOURS

SERVES 4

I N G R E D I E N T S

500 g/1 lb 2 oz mixed dried beans

1 tbsp olive oil

2 onions, finely chopped

1 yellow or orange (bell) pepper, cored, deseeded and finely chopped

3 garlic cloves, finely chopped or crushed

2 carrots, cubed

1 parsnip, cubed

2 stalks celery, halved lengthways and cut into 5 mm/¼ inch pieces

100 g/3½ oz lean smoked gammon or ham, cubed

2 litres/3½ pints/8 cups water

2 tbsp tomato purée (paste)

⅛ tsp dried thyme

1 bay leaf

1 potato, finely diced

1 tbsp chopped fresh marjoram

2 tbsp chopped fresh parsley

salt and pepper

1 Pick over the beans, cover generously with cold water and leave to soak for 6 hours or overnight. Drain the beans, put in a saucepan and add enough cold water to cover by 5 cm/2 inches. Bring to the boil and boil for 10 minutes, skimming off the foam as it accumulates. Drain and rinse well.

2 Heat the oil in a large saucepan over a medium heat. Add the onions and (bell) pepper, cover and cook for 3–4 minutes, stirring occasionally, until the onion is just softened. Add the garlic, carrots, parsnip, celery and gammon or ham and continue cooking for 2–3 minutes, or until the onion begins to colour.

3 Add the water, drained beans, tomato purée (paste), thyme and bay leaf. Bring just to the boil, cover and simmer, occasionally stirring, for 1¼ hours, or until the beans and vegetables are tender.

4 Put the potato in a small saucepan and ladle over just enough of the bean cooking liquid to cover the potatoes. Bring to the boil, cover the pan, reduce the heat and boil gently for about 12 minutes or until the potato is very tender.

5 Put the potato and its cooking liquid into a blender or food processor, then add 3 ladlefuls of the beans with a small amount of their liquid and purée until completely smooth.

6 Scrape the purée into the saucepan, add the marjoram and parsley and stir to blend. Season the soup to taste, adding salt and pepper generously. Reheat gently over a medium-low heat until hot and ladle the soup into warm bowls.

Black Bean & Pumpkin Soup

Pumpkin, a greatly underrated vegetable, balances the spicy heat in this soup and gives it a splash of colour, too.

NUTRITIONAL INFORMATION

Calories	174	Sugar	.........7g
Protein	........10g	Fats	...........2g
Carbohydrates	...30g	Saturates	......0g

10 MINS   2¹/₂ HOURS

SERVES 4

INGREDIENTS

250 g/9 oz dried kidney beans

1 tbsp olive oil

2 onions, finely chopped

4 garlic cloves, finely chopped

1 stalk celery, thinly sliced

1 carrot, halved and thinly sliced

2 tsp tomato purée (paste)

¹/₈ tsp dried thyme

¹/₈ tsp dried oregano

¹/₈ tsp ground cumin

1.2 litres/2 pints/5 cups water

1 bay leaf

400 g/14 oz can chopped tomatoes
in juice

250 g/9 oz peeled pumpkin flesh, diced

¹/₄ tsp chilli purée (paste), or to taste

salt and pepper

fresh coriander leaves (cilantro), to garnish

2 Heat the oil in a large sauce-pan over a medium heat. Add the onions and cook, covered, for 3–4 minutes until they are just softened, stirring occasionally. Add the garlic, celery and carrot, and continue cooking for 2 minutes.

3 Add the water, drained beans, tomato purée (paste), thyme, oregano, cumin, water and bay leaf. When the mixture begins to bubble, reduce the heat to low. Cover and simmer gently for 1 hour, stirring occasionally.

4 Stir in the tomatoes, pumpkin and chilli purée (paste) and continue simmering for about 1 hour more, or until the beans and pumpkin are tender, stirring from time to time.

5 Taste and season the soup, stir in a little more chilli purée (paste) if liked. Ladle the soup into bowls, garnish with coriander (cilantro) and serve.

1 Pick over the beans, cover generously with cold water and leave to soak for 6 hours or overnight. Drain the beans, put in a saucepan and add enough cold water to cover by 5 cm/2 inches. Bring to the boil and boil for 10 minutes. Drain and rinse well.

Rice & Black-Eye Bean Soup

This soup is satisfying and very healthy. Brown rice gives a pleasing chewy texture, but white rice could be used instead.

NUTRITIONAL INFORMATION

Calories 260   Sugar 8g
Protein . . . . .15g   Fats 4g
Carbohydrates . . .44g   Saturates 1g

15 MINS   1³/₄ HOURS

SERVES 4

INGREDIENTS

250 g/9 oz dried black-eye beans (peas)

1 tbsp olive oil

1 large onion, finely chopped

2 garlic cloves, finely chopped or crushed

2 carrots, finely chopped

2 stalks celery, finely chopped

1 small red (bell) pepper, deseeded and finely chopped

80 g/3 oz lean smoked ham, finely diced

½ tsp fresh thyme leaves, or ⅛ tsp dried thyme

1 bay leaf

1.2 litres/2 pints/5 cups chicken or vegetable stock

600 ml/1 pint/2½ cups water

100 g/3½ oz/ ½ cup brown rice

chopped fresh parsley or chives, to garnish

1 Pick over the beans, cover generously with cold water and leave to soak for at least 6 hours or overnight. Drain the beans, put in a saucepan and add enough cold water to cover by 5 cm/2 inches. Bring to the boil and boil for 10 minutes. Drain and rinse well.

2 Heat the oil in a large heavy-based saucepan over a medium heat. Add the onion, cover and cook for 3–4 minutes, stirring frequently, until just softened. Add the garlic, carrots, celery and (bell) pepper, stir well and cook for a further 2 minutes.

3 Add the drained beans, ham, thyme, bay leaf, stock and water. Bring to the boil, reduce the heat, cover and simmer gently, stirring occasionally, for 1 hour, or until the beans are just tender.

4 Stir in the rice and season the soup with salt, if needed, and pepper. Continue cooking for 30 minutes, or until the rice and beans are tender.

5 Taste the soup and adjust the seasoning, if necessary. Ladle into warm bowls and serve garnished with parsley or chives.

Traditional Soups

The range of soups found in this chapter is guaranteed to provide good old-fashioned nourishment and are perfect served as a main course accompanied by a hearty chunk of

fresh bread or perhaps a salad or a hunk of strong-tasting cheese. Wholesome treats include the traditional Scots recipe for Partan Bree, lentil and ham soup and delicious fresh mushroom soup. To make the most of these soups, remember that they are only as good as their ingredients, so be sure to pick good quality produce.

Celeriac, Leek & Potato Soup

It is hard to imagine that celeriac, a coarse, knobbly vegetable, can taste so sweet. It makes a wonderfully flavourful soup.

NUTRITIONAL INFORMATION

Calories	123	Sugars	.........8g
Protein	.........4g	Fat	...........4g
Carbohydrate	...17g	Saturates	......2g

 15 MINS 35 MINS

SERVES 4

INGREDIENTS

1 tbsp butter

1 onion, chopped

2 large leeks, halved lengthways and sliced

1 large celeriac (about 750 g/
    1 lb 10 oz), peeled and cubed

1 potato, cubed

1 carrot, quartered and thinly sliced

1.2 litres/2 pints/5 cups water ⅛ tsp dried
    marjoram

1 bay leaf

freshly grated nutmeg

salt and pepper

celery leaves, to garnish

1 Melt the butter in a large saucepan over a medium-low heat. Add the onion and leeks and cook for about 4 minutes, stirring frequently, until just softened; do not allow to colour.

2 Add the celeriac, potato, carrot, water, marjoram and bay leaf, with a large pinch of salt. Bring to the boil, reduce the heat, cover and simmer for about 25 minutes until the vegetables are tender. Remove the bay leaf.

3 Allow the soup to cool slightly. Transfer to a blender or food processor and purée until smooth. (If using food processor, strain off cooking liquid and reserve. Purée the soup solids with enough cooking liquid to moisten them, then combine with remaining liquid.)

4 Return the puréed soup to the saucepan and stir to blend. Season with salt, pepper and nutmeg. Simmer over a medium-low heat until reheated.

5 Ladle the soup into warm bowls, garnish with celery leaves and serve.

Baked Leek & Cabbage Soup

A flavourful stock is important for this delicious and filling soup, which is a typical peasant-style bread soup, perfect for supper.

NUTRITIONAL INFORMATION

Calories 448	Sugar 7g
Protein 23g	Fats 29g
Carbohydrates . . .26g	Saturates 17g

 15 MINS   1 HOUR 25 MINS

SERVES 4

INGREDIENTS

2 tbsp butter

2 large leeks, halved lengthways and thinly sliced

1 large onion, halved and thinly sliced

3 garlic cloves, finely chopped

250 g/9 oz finely shredded green cabbage

1 litre/1¾ pints/4 cups chicken or meat stock

4 slices firm bread, cut in half, or 8 slices baguette

250 g/9 oz grated Gruyère cheese

1 Melt the butter in a large saucepan over a medium heat. Add the leeks and onion and cook for 4–5 minutes, stirring frequently, until just softened.

COOK'S TIP

A large soufflé dish or earthenware casserole at least 10 cm/4 inches deep, or an enamelled cast-iron casserole, is good for baking the soup. If the soup fills the dish to the top, put a baking tray with a rim underneath to catch any overflow.

2 Add the garlic and cabbage, stir to combine and continue cooking for about 5 minutes until the cabbage is wilted.

3 Stir in the stock and simmer for 10 minutes. Taste and season with salt and pepper.

4 Arrange the bread in the base of a large deep 3 litre/5 pint/12 cups ovenproof dish. Sprinkle about half the cheese over the bread.

5 Ladle over the soup and top with the remaining cheese. Bake in a preheated oven at 180oC/350oC/Gas Mark 4 for 1 hour. Serve at once.

Leek, Potato & Carrot Soup

A quick chunky soup, ideal for a snack or a quick lunch. The leftovers can be puréed to make one portion of creamed soup for the next day.

NUTRITIONAL INFORMATION

Calories 156   Sugars 7g
Protein . . . . .4g   Fat 6g
Carbohydrate . . .22g   Saturates 0.7g

  10 MINS   🕐 25 MINS

SERVES 2

INGREDIENTS

1 leek, about 175 g/6 oz

1 tbsp sunflower oil

1 garlic clove, crushed

700 ml/1¼ pints/3 cups vegetable stock

1 bay leaf

¼ tsp ground cumin

175 g/6 oz/1 cup potatoes, diced

125 g/4½ oz/1 cup coarsely grated carrot

salt and pepper

chopped parsley, to garnish

PUREED SOUP

5–6 tbsp milk

1–2 tbsp double (heavy) cream, crème
    fraîche or soured cream

1 Trim off and discard some of the coarse green part of the leek, then slice thinly and rinse thoroughly in cold water. Drain well.

2 Heat the sunflower oil in a heavy-based saucepan. Add the leek and garlic, and fry over a low heat for about 2–3 minutes, until soft, but barely coloured. Add the vegetable stock, bay leaf and cumin and season to taste with salt and pepper. Bring the mixture to the boil, stirring constantly.

3 Add the diced potato to the saucepan, cover and simmer over a low heat for 10–15 minutes until the potato is just tender, but not broken up.

4 Add the grated carrot and simmer for a further 2–3 minutes. Adjust the seasoning, discard the bay leaf and serve sprinkled liberally with chopped parsley.

5 To make a puréed soup, first process the leftovers (about half the original soup) in a blender or food processor or press through a strainer until smooth and then return to a clean saucepan with the milk. Bring to the boil and simmer for 2–3 minutes. Adjust the seasoning and stir in the cream or crème fraîche before serving sprinkled with chopped parsley.

Cauliflower & Cider Soup

This soup was inspired by a visit to Normandy where cider and cream are plentiful, and are combined in many local specialities.

  15 MINS   60 MINS

SERVES 4

I N G R E D I E N T S

25 g/1 oz/2 tbsp butter

1 onion, finely chopped

1 garlic clove, crushed

1 carrot, thinly sliced

500 g/1 lb 2 oz cauliflower florets (from 1 medium head)

600 ml/1 pint/2½ cups dry (hard) cider

freshly grated nutmeg

120 ml/4 fl oz/ ½ cup milk

120 ml/4 fl oz/ ½ cup double (heavy) cream

salt and pepper

snipped chives, to garnish

1 Melt the butter in a saucepan over a medium heat. Add the onion and garlic and cook for about 5 minutes, stirring occasionally, until just softened.

2 Add the carrot and cauliflower to the pan and pour over the cider. Season with salt, pepper and a generous grating of nutmeg. Bring to the boil, then reduce the heat to low. Cover and cook gently for about 50 minutes until the vegetables are very soft.

3 Allow the soup to cool slightly, then transfer to a blender or food processor and purée until smooth, working in batches if necessary. (If using a food processor, strain off the cooking liquid and reserve. Purée the soup solids with enough cooking liquid to moisten them, then combine with the remaining liquid.)

4 Return the soup to the saucepan and stir in the milk and cream. Taste and adjust the seasoning, if necessary. Simmer the soup over a low heat, stirring occasionally, until heated through.

5 Ladle the soup into warm bowls, garnish with chives and serve.

COOK'S TIP

If you don't have dry cider, substitute 120 ml/4 fl oz/¹/₂ cup each white wine, apple juice and water.

Cauliflower & Broccoli Soup

Full of flavour, this creamy cauliflower and broccoli soup is simple to make and absolutely delicious to eat.

NUTRITIONAL INFORMATION

Calories 378   Sugars 14g
Protein . . . . .18g   Fat 26g
Carbohydrate . . .20g   Saturates 7g

 10 MINS   35 MINS

SERVES 4

INGREDIENTS

3 tbsp vegetable oil

1 red onion, chopped

2 garlic cloves, crushed

300 g/10½ oz cauliflower florets

300 g/10½ oz broccoli florets

1 tbsp plain (all-purpose) flour

600 ml/1 pint/2½ cups milk

300 ml/½ pint/1¼ cups vegetable stock

75 g/2¾ oz/¾ cup Gruyère cheese, grated

pinch of paprika

150 ml/¼ pint/⅔ cup single (light) cream

paprika and Gruyère cheese shavings,
   to garnish

1 Heat the oil in a large, heavy-based saucepan. Add the onion, garlic, cauliflower florets and broccoli florets and sauté over a low heat, stirring constantly, for 3–4 minutes. Add the flour and cook, stirring constantly for a further 1 minute.

2 Gradually stir in the milk and stock and bring to the boil, stirring constantly. Reduce the heat and simmer for 20 minutes.

3 Remove about a quarter of the vegetables with a slotted spoon and set aside. Put the remaining soup in a food processor or blender and process for about 30 seconds, until smooth. Alternatively, press the vegetables through a strainer with the back of a wooden spoon. Transfer the soup to a clean saucepan.

4 Return the reserved vegetable pieces to the soup. Stir in the grated cheese, paprika and single (light) cream and heat through over a low heat, without boiling, for 2–3 minutes, or until the cheese starts to melt.

5 Transfer to warmed individual serving bowls, garnish with shavings of Gruyère and dust with paprika and serve immediately.

COOK'S TIP

The soup must not start to boil after the cream has been added, otherwise it will curdle. Use natural (unsweetened) yogurt instead of the cream if preferred, but again do not allow it to boil.

Asparagus Soup

Fresh asparagus is now available for most of the year, so this soup can be made at any time. It can also be made using canned asparagus.

NUTRITIONAL INFORMATION

Calories ....196 Sugars 7g
Protein ....7g Fat 12g
Carbohydrate ...15g Saturates 4g

 5–10 MINS   55 MINS

SERVES 6

I N G R E D I E N T S

1 bunch asparagus, about 350 g/12 oz,
   or 2 packs mini asparagus,
   about 150 g/5½ oz each

700 ml/1¼ pints/3 cups vegetable stock

60 g/2 oz/¼ cup butter or margarine

1 onion, chopped

3 tbsp plain (all-purpose) flour

¼ tsp ground coriander

1 tbsp lemon juice

450 ml/16 fl oz/2 cups milk

4–6 tbsp double (heavy) or single
   (light) cream

salt and pepper

COOK'S TIP

If using canned asparagus, drain off the liquid and use as part of the measured stock. Remove a few small asparagus tips for garnish and chop the remainder. Continue as above.

1 Wash and trim the asparagus, discarding the woody part of the stem. Cut the remainder into short lengths, keeping a few tips for garnish. Mini asparagus does not need to be trimmed.

2 Cook the tips in the minimum of boiling salted water for 5–10 minutes. Drain and set aside.

3 Put the asparagus in a saucepan with the stock, bring to the boil, cover and simmer for about 20 minutes, until soft. Drain and reserve the stock.

4 Melt the butter or margarine in a saucepan. Add the onion and fry over a low heat until soft, but only barely coloured. Stir in the flour and cook for 1 minute, then gradually whisk in the reserved stock and bring to the boil.

5 Simmer for 2–3 minutes, until thickened, then stir in the cooked asparagus, seasoning, coriander and lemon juice. Simmer for 10 minutes, then cool a little and either press through a strainer or process in a blender or food processor until smooth.

6 Pour into a clean pan, add the milk and reserved asparagus tips and bring to the boil. Simmer for 2 minutes. Stir in the cream, reheat gently and serve.

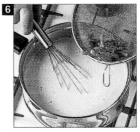

Mushroom & Barley Soup

This old-fashioned soup is nourishing and warming, with distinctive flavours and a nice chewy texture.

NUTRITIONAL INFORMATION

Calories	128	Sugar	.........5g
Protein	.........4g	Fats	...........4g
Carbohydrates	...19g	Saturates	......2g

15 MINS   1¼ HOURS

SERVES 4

I N G R E D I E N T S

60 g/2 oz/⅓ cup pearl barley

1.5 litres/2¾ pints/6¼ cups chicken or vegetable stock

1 bay leaf

1 tbsp butter

350 g/12 oz mushrooms, thinly sliced

1 tsp olive oil

1 onion, finely chopped

2 carrots, thinly sliced

1 tbsp chopped fresh tarragon

1 tbsp chopped fresh parsley or tarragon, to garnish

1 Rinse the barley and drain. Bring 450 ml/16 fl oz/2 cups of the stock to the boil in a small saucepan. Add the bay leaf and, if the stock is unsalted, add a large pinch of salt. Stir in the barley, reduce the heat, cover and simmer for 40 minutes.

2 Melt the butter in a large frying pan (skillet) over a medium heat. Add the mushrooms and season with salt and pepper. Cook for about 8 minutes until they are golden brown, stirring occasionally at first, then more often after they start to colour. Remove the mushrooms from the heat.

3 Heat the oil in a large sauce-pan over a medium heat and add the onion and carrots. Cover and cook for about 3 minutes, stirring frequently, until the onion is softened.

4 Add the remaining stock and bring to the boil. Stir in the barley with its cooking liquid and add the mushrooms. Reduce the heat, cover and simmer gently for about 20 minutes, or until the carrots are tender, stirring occasionally.

5 Stir in the tarragon and parsley. Taste and adjust the seasoning, if necessary. Ladle into warm bowls, garnish with fresh parsley or tarragon and serve.

COOK'S TIP

The barley will continue to absorb liquid if the soup is stored, so if making ahead, you may need to add a little more stock or water when reheating.

Fresh Mushroom Soup

When you see mushrooms at a special price in your local supermarket,

NUTRITIONAL INFORMATION

Calories	225	Sugars	.........5g
Protein	.........6g	Fat	..........17g
Carbohydrate	...12g	Saturates	.....10g

10 MINS   40 MINS

SERVES 4

INGREDIENTS

40 g/1½ oz/3 tbsp butter

700 g/1 lb 9 oz mushrooms, sliced

1 onion, finely chopped

1 shallot, finely chopped

25 g/1 oz/3 tbsp plain (all-purpose) flour

2–3 tbsp dry white wine or sherry

1.4 litres/2½ pints/6 cups chicken
   or vegetable stock

150 ml/5 fl oz/ ⅔ cup single (light) cream

2 tbsp chopped fresh parsley

fresh lemon juice (optional)

salt and pepper

4 tbsp soured cream or crème fraîche,
   to garnish

2 Melt the remaining butter in a saucepan over a medium heat, add the onion and shallot and cook for 2–3 minutes until just softened. Stir the flour into the pan and continue cooking for 2 minutes. Add the wine and stock and stir well.

3 Set aside about one-quarter of the mushrooms. Add the remainder to the pan. Reduce the heat, cover and cook gently for 20 minutes, stirring occasionally.

4 Allow the soup to cool slightly, then transfer to a blender or food processor and purée until smooth, working in batches, if necessary. (If using a food processor, strain off the cooking liquid and reserve. Purée the soup solids with enough cooking liquid to moisten them, then combine with the remaining liquid.)

5 Return the soup to the saucepan and stir in the reserved mushrooms, the cream and parsley. Cook for about 5 minutes to heat through. Taste and adjust the seasoning, adding a few drops of lemon juice if wished. Ladle into warm bowls and decorate with soured cream.

1 Melt half the butter in a large frying pan (skillet) over a medium heat. Add the mushrooms and season with salt and pepper. Cook for about 8 minutes until they are golden brown, stirring occasionally at first, then more often after they start to colour. Remove the mushrooms from the heat.

Celery & Stilton Soup

This soup combines two ingredients that have been paired since Victorian times.

NUTRITIONAL INFORMATION

Calories 380	Sugar 6g	
Protein 10g	Fats 35g	
Carbohydrates 7g	Saturates 21g	

 15 MINS   40 MINS

SERVES 4

INGREDIENTS

2 tbsp butter

1 onion, finely chopped

4 large stalks celery, peeled and finely chopped

1 large carrot, finely chopped

1 litre/1¾ pints/4 cups chicken or vegetable stock

3–4 thyme sprigs

1 bay leaf

120 ml/4 fl oz/ ½ cup double (heavy) cream

150 g/5½ oz Stilton cheese, crumbled

freshly grated nutmeg

salt and pepper

celery and carrot and continue cooking for 3 minutes. Season lightly with salt and pepper.

2 Add the stock, thyme and bay leaf and bring to the boil. Reduce the heat, cover and simmer gently for about 25 minutes, stirring occasionally, until the vegetables are very tender.

3 Allow the soup to cool slightly and remove the bouquet garni. Transfer the soup to a blender or food processor and purée until smooth, working in batches, if necessary. (If using a food processor, strain off the cooking liquid and reserve. Purée the soup solids with enough cooking liquid to moisten them, then combine with the remaining liquid.)

4 Return the puréed soup to the saucepan and stir in the cream. Simmer over a low heat for 5 minutes.

5 Add the Stilton slowly, stirring constantly, until smooth. (Do not allow the soup to boil.) Taste and adjust the seasoning, adding salt, if needed, plenty of pepper and nutmeg to taste.

6 Ladle into warm bowls, garnish with celery leaves and serve.

1 Melt the butter in a large saucepan over a medium-low heat. Add the onion and cook for 3-4 minutes, stirring frequently, until just softened. Add the

VARIATION

Substitute matured Cheddar or Gruyére for the Stilton.

Trout & Celeriac Soup

The cooking liquid in which the fish is poached becomes a delicious fish stock. If you just want stock, poach fish heads and trimmings.

NUTRITIONAL INFORMATION

Calories	369	Sugars	.........4g
Protein	........24g	Fat	..........21g
Carbohydrate	...17g	Saturates	.....10g

 25 MINS 1¼ HOURS

SERVES 4

INGREDIENTS

700 g/1 lb 9 oz whole trout

200 g/7 oz celeriac, peeled and diced

150 ml/2 fl oz/ ¼ cup double (heavy) cream

3 tbsp cornflour (cornstarch), dissolved in 3 tbsp water

chopped fresh chervil or parsley, to garnish

FISH STOCK BASE

1 tbsp butter

I onion, thinly sliced

I carrot, thinly sliced

I leek, thinly sliced

225 ml/8 fl oz/l cup dry white wine

1.2 litres/2 pints/5 cups water

1 bay leaf

3 Put the fish into the liquid (if necessary, cut the fish in pieces to fit in). Bring back to the boil and skim off any foam that rises to the top. Reduce the heat to low and simmer gently for 20 minutes.

4 Remove the fish and set aside. Strain the stock through a muslin-lined sieve into a clean saucepan. Remove any fat from the stock. (There should be about 1.5 litres/2¾pints/6 cups stock.)

5 Bring the stock to the boil. Add the celeriac and boil gently, uncovered, for 15–20 minutes until it is tender and the liquid has reduced by about one-third.

6 When the fish is cool enough to handle, peel off the skin and remove the flesh from the bones. Discard the skin, bones, head and tail.

7 Add the cream to the soup and when it comes back to the boil, stir in the dissolved cornflour (cornstarch). Boil gently for 2–3 minutes until slightly thickened, stirring frequently. Return the fish to the soup. Cook for 3–4 minutes to reheat. Taste and adjust the seasoning, if necessary. Ladle into warm bowls and garnish with chervil or parsley.

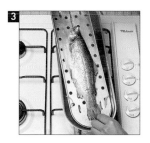

1 To make the fish stock base, melt the butter in a fish kettle, a large saucepan or cast-iron casserole over a medium-high heat. Add the onion, carrot and leek and cook for about 3 minutes, or until the onion starts to soften.

2 Add the wine, water and bay leaf. Bring to the boil, reduce the heat a little, cover and boil gently for 15 minutes.

Haddock & Potato Soup

This chunky aromatic soup is perfect for a cold weather lunch or supper served with crusty bread and a salad.

NUTRITIONAL INFORMATION

Calories	404	Sugar	........17g
Protein	........24g	Fats	..........11g
Carbohydrates	...55g	Saturates	......4g

15 MINS   40 MINS

SERVES 4

I N G R E D I E N T S

1 tbsp oil

60 g/2 oz smoked streaky bacon, cut into thin matchsticks

1 large onion, finely chopped

2 tbsp plain (all-purpose) flour

1 litre/1¾ pints/4 cups milk

700 g/1 lb 9 oz potatoes, cut into 1 cm/½ inch cubes

175 g/6 oz skinless smoked haddock

salt and pepper

finely chopped fresh parsley, to garnish

1 Heat the oil in a large saucepan over a medium heat. Add the bacon and cook for 2 minutes. Stir in the onion and continue cooking for 5–7 minutes, stirring frequently, until the onion is soft and the bacon golden. Tip the pan and spoon off as much fat as possible.

2 Stir in the flour and continue cooking for 2 minutes. Add half of the milk and stir well, scraping the bottom of the pan to mix in the flour.

3 Add the potatoes and remaining milk and season with pepper. Bring just to the boil, stirring frequently, then reduce the heat and simmer, partially covered, for 10 minutes.

4 Add the fish and continue cooking, stirring occasionally, for about 15 minutes, or until the potatoes are tender and the fish breaks up easily.

5 Taste the soup and adjust the seasoning (salt may not be needed). Ladle into a warm tureen or bowls and sprinkle generously with chopped parsley.

COOK'S TIP

Cutting the potatoes into small cubes not only looks attractive, but it allows them to cook more quickly and evenly.

Salmon & Leek Soup

Salmon is a favourite with almost everyone. This delicately flavoured and pretty soup is perfect for entertaining.

NUTRITIONAL INFORMATION

Calories 322	Sugar 6g
Protein 18g	Fats 21g
Carbohydrates ...15g	Saturates 8g

 15 MINS   40 MINS

SERVES 4

I N G R E D I E N T S

1 tbsp olive oil

1 large onion, finely chopped

3 large leeks, including green parts, thinly sliced

1 potato, finely diced

450 ml/16 fl oz/2 cups fish stock

700 ml/1¼ pints/3 cups water

1 bay leaf

300 g/10½ oz skinless salmon fillet, cut into 1 cm/½ inch cubes

80 ml/3 fl oz/ ⅓ cup double (heavy) cream

salt and pepper

fresh lemon juice (optional)

snipped fresh chervil or parsley, to garnish

1 Heat the oil in a heavy-based saucepan over a medium heat. Add the onion and leeks and cook for about 3 minutes until they begin to soften.

2 Add the potato, stock, water and bay leaf with a large pinch of salt. Bring to the boil, reduce the heat, cover and cook gently for about 25 minutes until the vegetables are tender. Remove the bay leaf.

3 Allow the soup to cool slightly, then transfer about half of it to a blender or food processor and purée until smooth. (If using a food processor, strain off the cooking liquid and reserve. Purée half the soup solids with enough cooking liquid to moisten them, then combine with the remaining liquid.)

4 Return the puréed soup to the saucepan and stir to blend. Reheat gently over a medium-low heat.

5 Season the salmon with salt and pepper and add to the soup. Continue cooking for about 5 minutes, stirring occasionally, until the fish is tender and starts to break up. Stir in the cream, taste and adjust the seasoning, adding a little lemon juice if wished. Ladle into warm bowls, sprinkle with chervil or parsley and serve.

Prawn Bisque

This soup utilises every part of the prawns. You could leave the prawn flesh out of the soup as most of the flavour comes from the shells.

NUTRITIONAL INFORMATION

Calories ....227 Sugars 7g
Protein ....25g Fat 4g
Carbohydrate ...22g Saturates 1g

 15 MINS   1 HOUR 20 MINS

SERVES 4

INGREDIENTS

500 g/1 lb 2 oz cooked prawns (shrimp) in the shell

2 tsp oil

2 large onions, halved and sliced

1 carrot, grated

1 stalk celery, sliced

1–2 garlic cloves, finely chopped or crushed

1.5 litres/2¾ pints/6¼ cups water

1 bay leaf

2 tsp butter

80 g/3 oz/6 tbsp white rice

1 tbsp tomato purée (paste)

fresh lemon juice

salt and pepper

snipped fresh dill or chopped parsley, to garnish

1 Peel the prawns (shrimp) and keep the shells for the soup. Reserve the prawn (shrimp) flesh, covered, in the refrigerator.

2 Heat the oil in a large saucepan. Add the prawn (shrimp) shells and cook over a high heat, stirring frequently, until they start to brown. Reduce the heat and add one-quarter of the onions, the carrot, celery and garlic. Cover and cook for 4–5 minutes, stirring frequently, until the

onions soften. Add the water and bay leaf with a small pinch of salt. Bring to the boil, reduce the heat, cover and simmer gently for 25 minutes. Strain the prawn (shrimp) stock

3 Heat the butter in a large saucepan over a medium heat and add the remaining onions. Cover and cook for 5–6 minutes, stirring frequently, until they soften and just begin to colour. Add the prawn (shrimp) stock, rice and tomato purée (paste). Bring to the boil. Reduce the heat, cover and simmer for 30 minutes, or until rice is very soft.

4 Allow the soup to cool slightly, then transfer to a blender or food processor and purée until smooth, working in batches if necessary. (If using a food processor, strain off the cooking liquid and reserve. Purée the soup solids with enough cooking liquid to moisten them, then combine with the remaining liquid.)

5 Return the soup to the saucepan and place over a medium-low heat. Add the reserved prawns (shrimp) and a few drops of lemon juice, or to taste. Simmer for about 8 minutes, stirring occasionally, until the soup is reheated. Taste and adjust the seasoning if necessary. Ladle into warm bowls, sprinkle with dill or parsley and serve.

Vegetable Beef Soup

A wonderful way to use fresh garden produce, but frozen vegetables are equally colourful and nutritious. No need to defrost them first.

NUTRITIONAL INFORMATION

Calories	186	Sugar	.........9g
Protein	........22g	Fats	...........5g
Carbohydrates	...15g	Saturates	......1g

 10 MINS   2 HOURS

SERVES 6

INGREDIENTS

450 g/1 lb stewing steak

2 x 400 g/14 oz cans chopped tomatoes in juice

2 onions, finely chopped

2-3 garlic cloves, finely chopped

3 carrots, diced

2 stalks celery, sliced

150 g/5½ oz green cabbage, thinly sliced

1 bay leaf

5-6 allspice berries

¼ tsp dried thyme

¼ tsp dried marjoram

1 litre/1¾ pints/4 cups water

1 litre/1¾ pints/4 cups beef stock

200 g/7 oz green beans, cut into short pieces

150 g/5½ oz peas

150 g/5½ oz sweetcorn

salt and pepper

1 Trim all visible fat from the steak and cut into 1 cm/½ inch cubes. Put in a large saucepan with the tomatoes, onions, garlic, carrots, celery, cabbage, bay leaf, allspice, thyme, marjoram and water.

2 Bring to the boil over a medium-high heat, skimming off any foam that rises to the surface. Stir in the stock, reduce the heat and regulate it so that the soup boils very gently. Season with salt and pepper. Cook, partially covered, for 1 hour, stirring occasionally.

3 Add the green beans, peas and sweetcorn. Continue cooking for 1 hour longer, or until the meat and vegetables are very tender.

4 Taste and adjust the seasoning, adding salt and pepper as necessary. Ladle into warm bowls and serve.

COOK'S TIP

For quick beef stock, dilute 1 stock cube in 1 litre/1¾pints/4 cups water, or use a can of beef consommé made up to that quantity with water. Alternatively, you can use all water and add 1 tsp salt.

Beef, Herb & Vegetable Broth

This light, lean soup is studded with small diced vegetables and fragrant herbs. The stock may be used as a basis for other soups.

NUTRITIONAL INFORMATION

Calories	25	Sugars	........4g
Protein	.........1g	Fat	..........0g
Carbohydrate	....5g	Saturates	......0g

15 MINS   5 HOURS

SERVES 4

INGREDIENTS

200 g/7 oz celeriac, peeled and finely diced

2 large carrots, finely diced

2 tsp chopped fresh marjoram leaves

2 tsp chopped fresh parsley

2 plum tomatoes, skinned, deseeded and diced

salt and pepper

BEEF STOCK

550 g/1 lb 4 oz boneless beef shin or stewing steak, cut into large cubes

750 g/1 lb 10 oz veal, beef or pork bones

2 onions, quartered

2.5 litres/4⅓ pints/10 cups water

4 garlic cloves, sliced

2 carrots, sliced

1 large leek, sliced

1 stalk celery, cut into 5 cm/2 inch pieces

1 bay leaf

4–5 sprigs fresh thyme, or ¼ tsp dried thyme

salt

1 To make the stock, trim as much fat as possible from the beef and put in a large roasting tin (pan) with the bones and onions. Roast in a preheated oven at 190°C/375°F/Gas Mark 5 for 30–40 minutes until browned, turning once or twice. Transfer the ingredients to a large soup kettle or flameproof casserole and discard the fat.

2 Add the water (it should cover by at least 5 cm/2 inches) and bring to the boil. Skim off any foam that rises to the surface. Reduce the heat and add the sliced garlic, carrots, leek, celery, bay leaf, thyme and a pinch of salt. Simmer very gently, uncovered, for 4 hours, skimming occasionally. Do not stir. If the ingredients emerge from the liquid, top up with water.

3 Gently ladle the stock through a muslin-lined sieve into a large container and remove as much fat as possible. Save the meat for another purpose, if wished, and discard the bones and vegetables. (There should be about 2 litres/3½ pints/8 cups of stock.)

4 Boil the stock very gently until it is reduced to 1.5 litres/2¾ pints/6¼ cups, or if the stock already has concentrated flavour, measure out that amount and save the rest for another purpose. Taste the stock and adjust the seasoning if necessary.

5 Bring a saucepan of salted water to the boil and drop in the celeriac and carrots. Reduce the heat, cover and boil gently for about 15 minutes until tender. Drain.

6 Add the herbs to the boiling beef stock. Divide the cooked vegetables and tomatoes among warm bowls, ladle over the boiling stock and serve.

Scotch Broth

This traditional winter soup is full of goodness, with lots of tasty golden vegetables along with tender barley and lamb.

NUTRITIONAL INFORMATION

Calories ....166 Sugar 7g
Protein ....13g Fats 5g
Carbohydrates ...18g Saturates 2g

  15 MINS 🕐 1½ MINS

SERVES 4

I N G R E D I E N T S

60 g/2 oz/⅓ cup pearl barley

300 g/10½ oz lean boneless lamb, such as shoulder or neck fillet, trimmed of fat and cut into 1 cm/
½ inch cubes

700 ml/1¼ pints/3 cups water

1 onion, finely chopped

2 garlic cloves, finely chopped or crushed

1 litre/1¾ pints/4 cups chicken or meat stock1 bay leaf

1 large leek, quartered lengthways and sliced

2 large carrots, finely diced

1 parsnip, finely diced

125 g/4½ oz peeled swede (rutabaga), diced

2 tbsp chopped fresh parsley

salt and pepper

COOK'S TIP

This soup is lean when the lamb is trimmed. By making it beforehand, you can remove any hardened fat before reheating.

1 Rinse the barley under cold running water. Put in a saucepan and cover generously with water. Bring to the boil and boil for 3 minutes, skimming off the foam from the surface. Set aside, covered, in the saucepan.

2 Put the lamb in a large saucepan with the water and bring to the boil. Skim off the foam that rises to the surface.

3 Stir in the garlic, stock, onion and bay leaf. Reduce the heat and boil very gently, partially covered, for 15 minutes.

4 Drain the barley and add to the soup. Add the leek, carrots, parsnip and swede (rutabaga). Continue simmering for about 1 hour, or until the lamb and vegetables are tender, stirring occasionally.

5 Taste and adjust the seasoning. Stir in the parsley and ladle into warm bowls to serve.

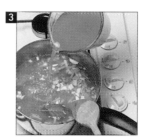

Chicken & Noodle Broth

A flavourful stock is essential, but meat stock would be equally good.

NUTRITIONAL INFORMATION

Calories	87	Sugar	.........0g
Protein	.........5g	Fats	...........4g
Carbohydrates	....8g	Saturates	......2g

20 MINS   15 MINS

SERVES 4

INGREDIENTS

1 egg yolk

25 g/1 oz/⅓ cup freshly grated Parmesan
 cheese

2 tbsp plain (all-purpose) flour

freshly grated nutmeg

1 tsp water, or as needed

1.2 litres/2 pints/5 cups chicken stock

1 tbsp shredded basil leaves or chopped
 tarragon leaves

2 tsp finely chopped fresh parsley

salt and pepper

freshly grated Parmesan cheese,
 to serve

1 Combine the egg yolk, Parmesan cheese and flour in a mixing bowl. Add a good grating of nutmeg, a pinch of salt and plenty of freshly ground pepper.

2 Add the water and stir with a fork until the dough comes together and pulls away from the sides of the bowl. (It should be very stiff.) If the dough is too crumbly, add more water by half teaspoons. If the dough is too sticky, add more flour by teaspoons until it holds together and does not stick to your hands.

3 Cut the dough in quarters. Working with one quarter at a time, roll the

dough into a sausage shape until it exceeds the width of your two hands. Break in half and roll into thin strings, 3 mm/⅛ inch in diameter or less (as thin as possible); break into shorter lengths as needed. Lay the strings on a cutting board, well spaced. Repeat with the remaining dough. Leave to dry for 15–45 minutes and cut into 2.5 cm/1 inch lengths.

4 Put the stock in a large saucepan and bring to the boil. Reduce the heat and regulate it so the liquid bubbles gently. Taste and season with salt and pepper. Drop in the noodles and cook for 5–6 minutes until they are tender. Stir in the shredded basil and chopped parsley. Ladle into warm bowls and serve with freshly grated Parmesan cheese.

Pumpkin Soup

This is an American classic that has now become popular worldwide.
When pumpkin is out of season use butternut squash in its place.

NUTRITIONAL INFORMATION

Calories	112	Sugars	7g
Protein	4g	Fat	7g
Carbohydrate	8g	Saturates	2g

 10 MINS   30 MINS

SERVES 6

INGREDIENTS

about 1 kg/2 lb 4 oz pumpkin

40 g/1½ oz/3 tbsp butter or margarine

1 onion, sliced thinly

1 garlic clove, crushed

900 ml/1½ pints/3½ cups vegetable stock

½ tsp ground ginger

1 tbsp lemon juice

3–4 thinly pared strips of orange
   rind (optional)

1–2 bay leaves or 1 bouquet garni

300 ml/½ pint/1¼ cups milk

salt and pepper

TO GARNISH

4–6 tablespoons single (light) or double
   (heavy) cream, natural yogurt
   or fromage frais

snipped chives

1 Peel the pumpkin, remove the seeds and then cut the flesh into 2.5 cm/ 1 inch cubes.

2 Melt the butter or margarine in a large, heavy-based saucepan. Add the onion and garlic and fry over a low heat until soft but not coloured.

3 Add the pumpkin and toss with the onion for 2–3 minutes.

4 Add the stock and bring to the boil over a medium heat. Season to taste with salt and pepper and add the ginger, lemon juice, strips of orange rind, if using, and bay leaves or bouquet garni. Cover and simmer over a low heat for about 20 minutes, until the pumpkin is tender.

5 Discard the orange rind, if using, and the bay leaves or bouquet garni. Cool the soup slightly, then press through a strainer or process in a food processor until smooth. Pour into a clean saucepan.

6 Add the milk and reheat gently. Adjust the seasoning. Garnish with a swirl of cream, natural yogurt or fromage frais and snipped chives, and serve.

Chicken & Asparagus Soup

This delectable soup is best made with fairly large asparagus with long stems.

NUTRITIONAL INFORMATION

Calories	308	Sugar	.........5g
Protein	........17g	Fats	..........24g
Carbohydrates	....7g	Saturates	.....14g

20 MINS   45 MINS

SERVES 4

I N G R E D I E N T S

350 g/12 oz asparagus

2 tsp butter

1 onion, halved and sliced

1 leek, sliced

60 g/2 oz/4 tbsp white rice

1 litre/1 ¾ pints/4 cups chicken stock

1 bay leaf

150 ml/5 fl oz/ ⅔ cup double (heavy) cream

175 g/6 oz cooked chicken, cut into thin slices

salt and pepper

1 Remove and discard woody bases of the asparagus. Using a vegetable peeler, peel the asparagus stems. Cut off the tips and set aside. Chop the stems into small pieces.

2 Bring a small saucepan of salted water to the boil and drop in the asparagus tips. Cook for 1–2 minutes until

bright green and barely tender. If they are large, slice in half lengthways. Reserve the asparagus tips.

3 Heat the butter in a large saucepan over a medium heat and add the onion and leek. Cover and cook for 3–4 minutes, stirring frequently, until the onion is soft.

4 Add the asparagus stems, rice, stock and bay leaf with a pinch of salt. Bring just to the boil, reduce the heat, cover and simmer for 30–35 minutes or until the rice and vegetables are very soft. Remove the bay leaf.

5 Allow the soup to cool slightly, then transfer to a blender or food processor and purée until smooth, working in batches if necessary. (If using a food processor, strain off the cooking liquid and reserve. Purée the soup solids with enough cooking liquid to moisten them, then combine with the remaining liquid.)

6 Return the soup to the saucepan and place over a medium-low heat. Stir in the chicken and reserved asparagus tips, then the cream. Taste and adjust the seasoning, adding salt, if needed, and pepper. Simmer for 5–10 minutes until heated through, stirring occasionally. Ladle the soup into warm bowls and serve.

Chicken, Leek & Celery Soup

This gently flavoured pale green soup is well balanced and very satisfying. It is suitable either for a starter or light lunch.

NUTRITIONAL INFORMATION

Calories	258	Sugars	.........3g
Protein	........19g	Fat	..........12g
Carbohydrate	...20g	Saturates	......6g

15 MINS   1¼ HOURS

SERVES 4

INGREDIENTS

1 litre/1¾ pints/4 cups chicken stock

1 bay leaf

200 g/7 oz skinless boned chicken breast

4 tbsp plain (all-purpose) flour

2 tsp butter

1 small onion, finely chopped

3 large leeks, including green parts, thinly sliced

2 stalks celery, peeled and thinly sliced

2 tbsp double (heavy) cream

freshly grated nutmeg

salt and pepper

fresh coriander leaves (cilantro) or parsley, to garnish

3 Heat the butter in a heavy-based saucepan over a medium-low heat. Add the onion, leeks and half of the celery. Cook for about 5 minutes, stirring frequently, until the leeks begin to soften.

4 Slowly pour in the flour and stock mixture and bring to the boil, stirring constantly. Stir in the remaining stock, with a large pinch of salt if it is unsalted. Reduce the heat, cover and cook gently for about 25 minutes until the vegetables are tender.

5 Allow the soup to cool slightly, then transfer to a blender or food processor and purée until smooth, working in batches, if necessary. (If using a food processor, strain off the cooking liquid and reserve for later. Purée the soup solids with enough cooking liquid to moisten them, then combine with the remaining liquid.)

6 Return the soup to the saucepan and stir in the cream and nutmeg. Season with salt, if needed, and pepper. Place over a medium-low heat. Add the chicken breast and remaining celery to the soup. Simmer for about 15 minutes, until the celery is just tender, stirring occasionally. Taste and adjust the seasoning, ladle into warm bowls and sprinkle with coriander (cilantro) or parsley.

1 Heat the stock in a small saucepan with the bay leaf until it is steaming. Add the chicken breast and simmer gently for 20 minutes, or until firm to the touch. Discard the bay leaf. Remove the chicken and, when cool enough to handle, cut into small cubes.

2 Put the flour in a bowl. Very slowly whisk in enough of the stock to make a smooth liquid, adding about half the chicken stock.

Lentil & Parsnip Pottage

Smooth and delicious, this soup has the most glorious golden colour and a fabulous flavour.

NUTRITIONAL INFORMATION

Calories	82	Sugars	........4g
Protein	.........6g	Fat	...........1g
Carbohydrate	...13g	Saturates	.....0.3g

5 MINS

55 MINS

SERVES 4

INGREDIENTS

3 slices lean streaky bacon, chopped

1 onion, chopped

2 carrots, chopped

2 parsnips, chopped

60 g/2 oz/⅓ cup red lentils

1 litre/1¾ pints/4 cups vegetable stock or water

salt and pepper

chopped fresh chives to garnish

1 Heat a large saucepan, add the bacon and dry-fry for 5 minutes until crisp and golden.

2 Add the onion, carrots and parsnips and cook for about 5 minutes without browning.

3 Add the lentils to the saucepan and stir to mix with the vegetables.

4 Add the stock or water to the pan and bring to the boil. Cover and simmer for 30–40 minutes until tender.

5 Transfer the soup to a blender or food processor and blend for about 15 seconds until smooth. Alternatively, press the soup through a sieve (strainer).

6 Return to the saucepan and reheat gently until almost boiling.

7 Season the soup with salt and pepper to taste.

8 Garnish the lentil and parsnip pottage with chopped fresh chives and serve at once.

COOK'S TIP

For a meatier soup, use a knuckle of ham in place of the streaky bacon. Cook it for 1½–2 hours before adding the vegetables and lentils and use the ham's cooking liquid as the stock.

Beef & Vegetable Soup

This comforting broth is perfect for a cold day and is just as delicious made with lean lamb or pork fillet.

NUTRITIONAL INFORMATION

Calories	138	Sugars	.........2g
Protein	........13g	Fat	..........3g
Carbohydrate	...15g	Saturates	......1g

12 HOURS   1 ¼ HOURS

SERVES 4

I N G R E D I E N T S

60 g/2 oz/⅓ cup pearl barley, soaked overnight

1.2 litres/2 pints/5 cups beef stock

1 tsp dried mixed herbs

225 g/8 oz lean rump or sirloin beef

1 large carrot, diced

1 leek, shredded

1 medium onion, chopped

2 sticks celery, sliced

salt and pepper

2 tbsp fresh parsley, chopped, to garnish

crusty bread, to serve

1 Place the pearl barley in a large saucepan. Pour over the stock and add the mixed herbs. Bring to the boil, cover and simmer gently over a low heat for 10 minutes.

  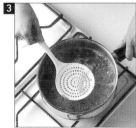

VARIATION

A vegetarian version can be made by omitting the beef and beef stock and using vegetable stock instead. Just before serving, stir in 175 g/6 oz fresh bean curd (tofu), drained and diced.

2 Meanwhile, trim any fat from the beef and cut the meat into thin strips.

3 Skim away any scum that has risen to the top of the stock with a flat ladle.

4 Add the beef, carrot, leek, onion and celery to the pan. Bring back to the boil, cover and simmer for about 1 hour or until the barley, meat and vegetables are just tender.

5 Skim away any remaining scum that has risen to the top of the soup with a flat ladle. Blot the surface with absorbent kitchen paper to remove any fat. Adjust the seasoning according to taste.

6 Ladle the soup into warm bowls and sprinkle with freshly chopped parsley. Serve piping hot, accompanied with crusty bread.

Chunky Potato & Beef Soup

This is a real winter warmer – pieces of tender beef and chunky mixed vegetables are cooked in a liquor flavoured with sherry.

NUTRITIONAL INFORMATION

Calories 187   Sugars 3g
Protein . . . . .14g   Fat 9g
Carbohydrate . . .12g   Saturates 2g

5 MINS   35 MINS

SERVES 4

I N G R E D I E N T S

2 tbsp vegetable oil

225 g/8 oz lean braising or frying steak, cut into strips

225 g/8 oz new potatoes, halved

1 carrot, diced

2 celery sticks, sliced

2 leeks, sliced

850 ml/1½ pints/3¾ cups beef stock

8 baby sweetcorn cobs, sliced

1 bouquet garni

2 tbsp dry sherry

salt and pepper

chopped fresh parsley, to garnish

1 Heat the vegetable oil in a large saucepan.

2 Add the strips of meat to the saucepan and cook for 3 minutes, turning constantly.

3 Add the halved potatoes, diced carrot and sliced celery and leeks. Cook for a further 5 minutes, stirring.

4 Pour the beef stock into the saucepan and bring to the boil. Reduce the heat until the liquid is simmering, then add the sliced baby sweetcorn cobs and the bouquet garni.

5 Cook the soup for a further 20 minutes or until cooked through.

6 Remove the bouquet garni from the saucepan and discard. Stir the dry sherry into the soup and then season to taste with salt and pepper.

7 Pour the soup into warmed bowls and garnish with the chopped fresh parsley. Serve at once with crusty bread.

COOK'S TIP

Make double the quantity of soup and freeze the remainder in a rigid container for later use. When ready to use, leave in the refrigerator to defrost thoroughly, then heat until piping hot.

Lentil & Ham Soup

This is a good hearty soup, based on a stock made from a ham knuckle, with plenty of vegetables and red lentils to thicken it and add flavour.

NUTRITIONAL INFORMATION

Calories	.219	Sugars	.4g
Protein	.17g	Fat	.3g
Carbohydrate	.33g	Saturates	.1g

2¼ HOURS   1¾ HOURS

SERVES 4–6

INGREDIENTS

225 g/8 oz/1 cup red lentils

1.5 litres/2¾ pints/6¼ cups stock or water

2 onions, chopped

1 garlic clove, crushed

2 large carrots, chopped

1 lean ham knuckle or 175 g/6 oz lean bacon, chopped

4 large tomatoes, skinned and chopped

2 fresh or dried bay leaves

250 g/9 oz potatoes, chopped

1 tbsp white wine vinegar

¼ tsp ground allspice

salt and pepper

chopped spring onions (scallions) or chopped fresh parsley, to garnish

1 Put the lentils and stock or water in a saucepan and leave to soak for 1–2 hours.

2 Add the onions, garlic, carrots, ham knuckle or bacon, tomatoes, bay leaves and seasoning.

3 Bring the mixture in the saucepan to the boil, cover and simmer for about 1 hour until the lentils are tender, stirring occasionally to prevent the lentils from sticking to the bottom of the pan.

4 Add the potatoes and continue to simmer for about 20 minutes until the potatoes and ham knuckle are tender.

5 Discard the bay leaves. Remove the knuckle and chop 125 g/4½ oz/¾ cup of the meat and reserve. If liked, press half the soup through a sieve (strainer) or blend in a food processor or blender until smooth. Return to the pan with the rest of the soup.

6 Adjust the seasoning, add the vinegar and allspice and the reserved chopped ham. Simmer gently for a further 5–10 minutes. Serve sprinkled liberally with spring onions (scallions) or chopped parsley.

Lamb & Barley Broth

Warming and nutritious, this broth is perfect for a cold winter's day. The slow cooking allows you to use one of the cheaper cuts of meat.

NUTRITIONAL INFORMATION

Calories 304	Sugars 4g
Protein 29g	Fat 14g
Carbohydrate . . .16g	Saturates 6g

15 MINS   2¼ HOURS

SERVES 4

I N G R E D I E N T S

1 tbsp vegetable oil

500 g/1 lb 2 oz lean neck of lamb

1 large onion, sliced

2 carrots, sliced

2 leeks, sliced

1 litre/1¾ pints/4 cups vegetable stock

1 bay leaf

few sprigs of fresh parsley

60 g/2 oz/⅓ cup pearl barley

1 Heat the vegetable oil in a large, heavy-based saucepan and add the pieces of lamb, turning them to seal and brown on both sides.

2 Lift the lamb out of the pan and set aside until required.

3 Add the onion, carrots and leeks to the saucepan and cook gently for about 3 minutes.

4 Return the lamb to the saucepan and add the vegetable stock, bay leaf, parsley and pearl barley to the saucepan.

5 Bring the mixture in the pan to the boil, then reduce the heat. Cover and simmer for 1½–2 hours.

6 Discard the parsley sprigs. Lift the pieces of lamb from the broth and allow them to cool slightly.

7 Remove the bones and any fat and chop the meat. Return the lamb to the broth and reheat gently.

8 Ladle the lamb and parsley broth into warmed bowls and serve immediately.

COOK'S TIP

This broth will taste even better if made the day before, as this allows the flavours to fully develop. It also means that any fat will solidify on the surface so you can then lift it off. Keep the broth in the refrigerator until required.

Chicken & Leek Soup

This satisfying soup can be served as a main course. You can add rice and peppers to make it even more hearty, as well as colourful.

NUTRITIONAL INFORMATION

Calories	183	Sugar	.........4g
Protein	........21g	Fats	..........9g
Carbohydrates	....4g	Saturates	......5g

5 MINS   1¼ HOURS

SERVES 4–6

I N G R E D I E N T S

25 g/1 oz/2 tbsp butter

350 g/12 oz boneless chicken

350 g/12 oz leeks, cut into 2.5-cm/
  1-inch pieces

1.2 litres/2 pints/5 cups Fresh Chicken
  Stock (see page 14)

1 bouquet garni sachet

8 pitted prunes, halved

salt and white pepper

cooked rice and diced (bell) peppers
  (optional)

1 Melt the butter in a large saucepan.

2 Add the chicken and leeks to the saucepan and fry for 8 minutes.

3 Add the chicken stock and bouquet garni sachet and stir well.

4 Season well with salt and pepper to taste.

5 Bring the soup to the boil and simmer for 45 minutes.

6 Add the prunes to the saucepan with some cooked rice and diced (bell) peppers (if using) and simmer for about 20 minutes.

7 Remove the bouquet garni sachet from the soup and discard. Serve the chicken and leek soup immediately.

VARIATION

Instead of the bouquet garni sachet, you can use a bunch of fresh mixed herbs, tied together with string. Choose herbs such as parsley, thyme and rosemary.

Partan Bree

This traditional Scottish soup is thickened with a purée of rice and crab meat cooked in milk. Add soured cream, if liked, at the end of cooking.

NUTRITIONAL INFORMATION

Calories 112   Sugars 5g
Protein . . . . .7g   Fat 2g
Carbohydrate . . .18g   Saturates 0.3g

 1 HOUR   🕐 35 MINS

SERVES 6

I N G R E D I E N T S

1 medium-sized boiled crab

90 g/3 oz/scant ½ cup long-grain rice

600 ml/1 pint/2½ cups skimmed milk

600 ml/1 pint/2½ cups Fish Stock
  (see page 15)

1 tbsp anchovy essence (paste)

2 tsp lime or lemon juice

1 tbsp chopped fresh parsley or I tsp
  chopped fresh thyme

3–4 tbsp soured cream (optional)

salt and pepper

snipped chives, to garnish

1 Remove and reserve all the brown and white meat from the crab, then crack the claws and remove and chop that meat; reserve the claw meat.

COOK'S TIP

If you are unable to buy a whole crab, use about 175 g/6 oz frozen crab meat and thaw thoroughly before use; or a 175 g/6 oz can of crab meat which just needs thorough draining.

2 Put the rice and milk into a saucepan and bring slowly to the boil. Cover and simmer gently for about 20 minutes.

3 Add the reserved white and brown crab meat and seasoning and simmer for a further 5 minutes.

4 Cool a little, then press through a sieve (strainer), or blend in a food processor or blender until smooth.

5 Pour the soup into a clean saucepan and add the fish stock and the reserved claw meat. Bring slowly to the boil, then add the anchovy essence (paste) and lime or lemon juice and adjust the seasoning.

6 Simmer for a further 2–3 minutes. Stir in the parsley or thyme and then swirl soured cream (if using) through each serving. Garnish with snipped chives.

Smoked Haddock Soup

Smoked haddock gives this soup a wonderfully rich flavour, while the mashed potatoes and cream thicken and enrich the stock.

NUTRITIONAL INFORMATION

Calories 169   Sugars 8g
Protein ....16g   Fat 5g
Carbohydrate ...16g   Saturates 3g

25 MINS   40 MINS

SERVES 4–6

INGREDIENTS

225 g/8 oz smoked haddock fillet

1 onion, chopped finely

1 garlic clove, crushed

600 ml/1 pint/2½ cups water

600 ml/1 pint/2½ cups skimmed milk

225–350 g/8–12 oz/1–1½ cups hot mashed potatoes

30 g/1 oz/2 tbsp butter

about 1 tbsp lemon juice

6 tbsp low-fat natural fromage frais

4 tbsp fresh parsley, chopped

salt and pepper

1 Put the fish, onion, garlic and water into a saucepan. Bring to the boil, cover and simmer for 15–20 minutes.

2 Remove the fish from the pan, strip off the skin and remove all the bones. Flake the flesh finely.

3 Return the skin and bones to the cooking liquor and simmer for 10 minutes. Strain, discarding the skin and bone. Pour the liquor into a clean pan.

4 Add the milk, flaked fish and seasoning to the pan, bring to the boil and simmer for about 3 minutes.

5 Gradually whisk in sufficient mashed potato to give a fairly thick soup, then stir in the butter and sharpen to taste with lemon juice.

6 Add the fromage frais and 3 tablespoons of the chopped parsley. Reheat gently and adjust the seasoning. Sprinkle with the remaining parsley and serve immediately.

COOK'S TIP

Undyed smoked haddock may be used in place of the bright yellow fish; it will give a paler colour but just as much flavour. Alternatively, use smoked cod or smoked whiting.

LOW-FAT SOUPS

Soups are a traditional first course, but served with fresh crusty
bread they can also be a satisfying meal in their own right –

and, depending on the choice of ingredients
– one that is low in calories. For the best
results, use homemade stock from the liquid
left over from cooking vegetables and the
juices from casseroles. Potatoes can also be

added to the soup to thicken it as opposed to the traditional
thickeners of flour or fat and water.

Cucumber & Tomato Soup

Although this chilled soup is not an authentic Indian dish, it is wonderful served as a 'cooler' between hot, spicy courses.

NUTRITIONAL INFORMATION

Calories	73	Sugar	16g
Protein	2g	Fats	1g
Carbohydrates	16g	Saturates	0.2g

12 HOURS   0 MINS

SERVES 6

INGREDIENTS

4 tomatoes, peeled and deseeded

1.5 kg/3 lb 5 oz watermelon, seedless if available

10 cm/4 inch piece cucumber, peeled and deseeded

2 spring onions (scallions), green part only, chopped

1 tbsp chopped fresh mint

salt and pepper

fresh mint sprigs, to garnish

1 Using a sharp knife, cut 1 tomato into 1 cm/½ inch dice.

2 Remove the rind from the melon, and remove the seeds if it is not seedless.

3 Put the 3 remaining tomatoes into a blender or food processor and, with the motor running, add the deseeded cucumber, chopped spring onions (scallions) and watermelon. Blend until smooth.

4 If not using a food processor, push the deseeded watermelon through a sieve (strainer). Stir the diced tomatoes and mint into the melon mixture. Adjust the seasoning to taste. Chop the cucumber, spring onions (scallions) and the 3 remaining tomatoes finely and add to the melon.

5 Chill the cucumber and tomato soup overnight in the refrigerator. Check the seasoning and transfer to a serving dish. Garnish with mint sprigs.

COOK'S TIP

Although this soup does improve if chilled overnight, it is also delicious as a quick appetizer if whipped up just before a meal, and served immediately.

Chilled Cucumber Soup

Serve this soup over ice on a warm summer day as a refreshing starter. It has the fresh tang of yogurt and a dash of spice from the Tabasco sauce.

NUTRITIONAL INFORMATION

Calories 83	Sugars 7g
Protein 12g	Fat 1g
Carbohydrate 7g	Saturates 0.3g

1¼ HOURS   0 MINS

SERVES 4

I N G R E D I E N T S

1 cucumber, peeled and diced

400 ml/14 fl oz/1⅔ cups Fresh Fish Stock, chilled (see page 15)

150 ml/5 fl oz/⅔ cup tomato juice

150 ml/5 fl oz/⅔ cup low-fat natural (unsweetened) yogurt

150 ml/5 fl oz/⅔ cup low-fat fromage frais (or double the quantity of yogurt)

125 g/4½ oz peeled prawns (shrimp), thawed if frozen, roughly chopped

few drops Tabasco sauce

1 tbsp fresh mint, chopped

salt and white pepper

ice cubes, to serve

T O   G A R N I S H

sprigs of mint

cucumber slices

whole peeled prawns (shrimp)

VARIATION

Instead of prawns (shrimp), add white crab meat or minced chicken. For a vegetarian version of this soup, omit the prawns (shrimp) and add an extra 125 g/4½ oz finely diced cucumber. Use fresh vegetable stock instead of fish stock.

1 Place the diced cucumber in a blender or food processor and work for a few seconds until smooth. Alternatively, chop the cucumber finely and push through a sieve.

2 Transfer the cucumber to a bowl. Stir in the stock, tomato juice, yogurt, fromage frais (if using) and prawns (shrimp), and mix well.

3 Add the Tabasco sauce and season to taste.

4 Stir in the chopped mint, cover and chill for at least 2 hours.

5 Ladle the soup into glass bowls and add a few ice cubes. Serve garnished with mint, cucumber slices and whole prawns (shrimp).

Beetroot & Potato Soup

A deep red soup makes a stunning first course. Adding a swirl of soured cream and a few sprigs of dill gives a very pretty effect.

NUTRITIONAL INFORMATION

Calories	120	Sugars	........11g
Protein	.........4g	Fat	...........2g
Carbohydrate	...22g	Saturates	......1g

20 MINS   30 MINS

SERVES 6

INGREDIENTS

1 onion, chopped

350 g/12 oz potatoes, diced

1 small cooking apple, peeled, cored and grated

3 tbsp water

1 tsp cumin seeds

500 g/1 lb 2 oz cooked beetroot, peeled and diced

1 dried bay leaf

pinch of dried thyme

1 tsp lemon juice

600 ml/1 pint/2½ cups hot vegetable stock

4 tbsp soured cream

salt and pepper

few sprigs of fresh dill, to garnish

1 Place the onion, potatoes, apple and water in a large bowl. Cover and cook on HIGH power for 10 minutes.

2 Stir in the cumin seeds and cook on HIGH power for 1 minute.

3 Stir in the beetroot, bay leaf, thyme, lemon juice and stock. Cover and cook on HIGH power for 12 minutes, stirring halfway through. Leave to stand, uncovered, for 5 minutes.

4 Remove and discard the bay leaf. Strain the vegetables and reserve the liquid in a jug.

5 Purée the vegetables with a little of the reserved liquid in a food processor or blender, until they are smooth and creamy. Alternatively, either mash the soup or press it through a sieve (strainer).

6 Pour the vegetable purée into a clean bowl with the reserved liquid and mix well. Season with salt and pepper to taste. Cover and cook on HIGH power for 4–5 minutes until piping hot.

7 Serve the soup in warmed bowls. Swirl 1 tablespoon of soured cream into each serving and garnish with a few sprigs of fresh dill.

Yogurt & Spinach Soup

Whole young spinach leaves add vibrant colour to this unusual soup.
Serve with hot, crusty bread for a nutritious light meal.

NUTRITIONAL INFORMATION

Calories 227	Sugars 13g
Protein 14g	Fat 7g
Carbohydrate ...29g	Saturates 2g

15 MINS   30 MINS

SERVES 4

INGREDIENTS

600 ml/1 pint/2½ cups chicken stock

60 g/2 oz/4 tbsp long-grain rice, rinsed and drained

4 tbsp water

1 tbsp cornflour (cornstarch)

600 ml/1 pint/2½ cups low-fat natural yogurt

juice of 1 lemon

3 egg yolks, lightly beaten

350 g/12 oz young spinach leaves, washed and drained

salt and pepper

1 Pour the stock into a large pan, season and bring to the boil. Add the rice and simmer for 10 minutes, until barely cooked. Remove from the heat.

2 Combine the water and cornflour (cornstarch) to make a smooth paste.

3 Pour the yogurt into a second pan and stir in the cornflour (cornstarch) mixture. Set the pan over a low heat and bring the yogurt slowly to the boil, stirring with a wooden spoon in one direction only. This will stabilize the yogurt and prevent it from separating or curdling on contact with the hot stock. When the yogurt has reached boiling point, stand the pan on a heat diffuser and leave to simmer slowly for 10 minutes. Remove the pan from the heat and allow the mixture to cool slightly before stirring in the beaten egg yolks.

4 Pour the yogurt mixture into the stock, stir in the lemon juice and stir to blend thoroughly. Keep the soup warm, but do not allow it to boil.

5 Blanch the washed and drained spinach leaves in a large pan of boiling, salted water for 2-3 minutes until they begin to soften but have not wilted. Tip the spinach into a colander, drain well and stir it into the soup. Let the spinach warm through. Taste the soup and adjust the seasoning if necessary. Serve in wide shallow soup plates, with hot, fresh crusty bread.

Red Lentil Soup with Yogurt

Tasty red lentil soup flavoured with chopped coriander. The yogurt adds a light piquancy to the soup .

NUTRITIONAL INFORMATION

Calories 280	Sugars 6g
Protein 17g	Fat 7g
Carbohydrate . . .40g	Saturates 4g

5 MINS   30 MINS

SERVES 4

I N G R E D I E N T S

25 g/1 oz/2 tbsp butter

1 onion, chopped finely

1 celery stick, chopped finely

1 large carrot, grated

1 dried bay leaf

225 g/8 oz/1 cup red lentils

1.2 litres/2 pints/5 cups hot vegetable or chicken stock

2 tbsp chopped fresh coriander (cilantro)

4 tbsp low-fat natural (unsweetened) yogurt

salt and pepper

fresh coriander (cilantro) sprigs, to garnish

1 Place the butter, onion and celery in a large bowl. Cover and cook on HIGH power for 3 minutes.

2 Add the carrot, bay leaf and lentils. Pour over the stock. Cover and cook on HIGH power for 15 minutes, stirring halfway through.

3 Remove from the microwave oven and stand, covered, for 5 minutes.

4 Remove the bay leaf, then blend in batches in a food processor, until smooth. Alternatively, press the soup through a sieve (strainer).

5 Pour into a clean bowl. Season with salt and pepper to taste and stir in the coriander (cilantro). Cover and cook on HIGH power for 4–5 minutes until piping hot.

6 Serve in warmed bowls. Stir 1 tablespoon of yogurt into each serving and garnish with sprigs of fresh coriander (cilantro).

COOK'S TIP

For an extra creamy soup try adding low-fat crème fraîche or soured cream instead of yogurt.

Spicy Lentil Soup

For a warming, satisfying meal on a cold day, this lentil dish is packed full of taste and goodness.

NUTRITIONAL INFORMATION

Calories ....155 Sugars 4g
Protein ....11g Fat 3g
Carbohydrate ...22g Saturates 0.4g

1 HOUR   1¼ HOURS

SERVES 4

INGREDIENTS

125 g/4½ oz/½ cup red lentils

2 tsp vegetable oil

1 large onion, chopped finely

2 garlic cloves, crushed

1 tsp ground cumin

1 tsp ground coriander

1 tsp garam masala

2 tbsp tomato purée (paste)

1 litre/1¾ pints/4½ cups Fresh Vegetable
   Stock (see page 14)

about 350 g/12 oz can sweetcorn, drained

salt and pepper

TO SERVE

low-fat natural (unsweetened) yogurt

chopped fresh parsley

warmed pitta (pocket) bread

1 Rinse the red lentils in cold water. Drain the lentils well and put to one side.

2 Heat the oil in a large non-stick saucepan and fry the onion and garlic gently until softened but not browned.

3 Stir in the cumin, coriander, garam masala, tomato purée (paste) and 4 tablespoons of the stock. Mix well and simmer gently for 2 minutes.

4 Add the lentils and pour in the remaining stock. Bring to the boil, reduce the heat and simmer, covered, for 1 hour until the lentils are tender and the soup thickened. Stir in the sweetcorn and heat through for 5 minutes. Season well.

5 Ladle into warmed soup bowls and top each with a spoonful of yogurt and a sprinkling of parsley. Serve with warmed pitta (pocket) bread.

COOK'S TIP

Many of the ready-prepared ethnic breads available today either contain fat or are brushed with oil before baking. Always check the ingredients list for fat content.

Mushroom & Ginger Soup

Thai soups are very quickly and easily put together, and are cooked so that each ingredient can still be tasted in the finished dish.

NUTRITIONAL INFORMATION

Calories 74   Sugars 1g
Protein . . . . .3g   Fat 3g
Carbohydrate . . . .9g   Saturates 0.4g

     1½ HOURS   15 MINS

SERVES 4

I N G R E D I E N T S

15 g/½ oz/¼ cup dried Chinese
   mushrooms or 125 g/4½ oz/1⅓ cups field
   or chestnut (crimini) mushrooms

1 litre/1¾ pints/4 cups hot Fresh
   Vegetable Stock (see page 14)

125 g/4½ oz thread egg noodles

2 tsp sunflower oil

3 garlic cloves, crushed

2.5 cm/1 inch piece ginger,
   shredded finely

½ tsp mushroom ketchup

1 tsp light soy sauce

125 g/4½ oz/2 cups bean sprouts

coriander (cilantro) leaves, to garnish

1 Soak the dried Chinese mushrooms (if using) for at least 30 minutes in 300 ml/½ pint/1¼ cups of the hot vegetable stock. Remove the stalks and discard, then slice the mushrooms. Reserve the stock.

2 Cook the noodles for 2–3 minutes in boiling water. Drain and rinse. Set them aside.

3 Heat the oil over a high heat in a wok or large, heavy frying pan (skillet). Add the garlic and ginger, stir and add the mushrooms. Stir over a high heat for 2 minutes.

4 Add the remaining vegetable stock with the reserved stock and bring to the boil. Add the mushroom ketchup and soy sauce.

5 Stir in the bean sprouts and cook until tender. Put some noodles in each bowl and ladle the soup on top. Garnish with coriander (cilantro) leaves and serve immediately.

COOK'S TIP

Rice noodles contain no fat and are ideal for for anyone on a low–fat diet.

Carrot & Cumin Soup

Carrot soups are very popular and and here cumin, tomato, potato and celery give the soup both richness and depth.

NUTRITIONAL INFORMATION

Calories 114	Sugars 8g	
Protein 3g	Fat 6g	
Carbohydrate . . .12g	Saturates 4g	

2¼ HOURS   45 MINS

SERVES 4–6

INGREDIENTS

45 g/1½ oz/3 tbsp butter or margarine

1 large onion, chopped

1–2 garlic cloves, crushed

350 g/12 oz carrots, sliced

900 ml/1½ pints/3½ cups Chicken or Vegetable Stock (see page 15)

¾ tsp ground cumin

2 celery sticks, sliced thinly

125 g/4 oz potato, diced

2 tsp tomato purée (paste)

2 tsp lemon juice

2 fresh or dried bay leaves

about 300 ml/½ pint/1¼ cups skimmed milk

salt and pepper

celery leaves to garnish

1 Melt the butter or margarine in a large saucepan. Add the onion and garlic and fry very gently until the onion begins to soften.

2 Add the carrots and continue to fry gently for a further 5 minutes, stirring frequently and taking care they do not brown.

3 Add the stock, cumin, seasoning, celery, potato, tomato purée (paste), lemon juice and bay leaves and bring to the boil. Cover and simmer gently for about 30 minutes until all the vegetables are very tender.

4 Discard the bay leaves, cool the soup a little and then press it through a sieve (strainer) or blend in a food processor or blender until smooth.

5 Pour the soup into a clean pan, add the milk and bring slowly to the boil. Taste and adjust the seasoning.

6 Garnish each serving with a small celery leaf and serve.

COOK'S TIP

This soup can be frozen for up to 3 months. Add the milk when reheating.

Consommé

A traditional clear soup made from beef bones and lean minced beef. Thin strips of vegetables provide a colourful garnish.

NUTRITIONAL INFORMATION

Calories 109   Sugars 6g
Protein . . . . .13g   Fat 3g
Carbohydrate . . . .7g   Saturates 1g

    6¼ HOURS   1¼ HOURS

SERVES 4–6

I N G R E D I E N T S

1.25 litres/2¼ pints/5 cups strong beef stock

225 g/8 oz/1 cup extra lean minced (ground) beef

2 tomatoes, skinned, seeded and chopped

2 large carrots, chopped

1 large onion, chopped

2 celery sticks, chopped

1 turnip, chopped (optional)

1 Bouquet Garni

2–3 egg whites

shells of 2–4 eggs, crushed

1–2 tbsp sherry (optional)

salt and pepper

Melba Toast, to serve

TO GARNISH

julienne strips of raw carrot, turnip, celery or celeriac (celery root) or a one-egg omelette, cut into julienne strips

1 Put the stock and minced (ground) beef in a saucepan. Leave for 1 hour. Add the tomatoes, carrots, onion, celery, turnip (if using), bouquet garni, 2 of the egg whites, the crushed shells of 2 of the eggs and plenty of seasoning. Bring to almost boiling point, whisking hard all the time with a flat whisk.

2 Cover and simmer for 1 hour, taking care not to allow the layer of froth on top of the soup to break.

3 Pour the soup through a jelly bag or scalded fine cloth, keeping the froth back until the last, then pour the ingredients through the cloth again into a clean pan. The resulting liquid should be clear.

4 If the soup is not quite clear, return it to the pan with another egg white and the crushed shells of 2 more eggs. Repeat the whisking process as before and then boil for 10 minutes; strain again.

5 Add the sherry (if using) to the soup and reheat gently. Place the garnish in the warmed soup bowls and carefully pour in the soup. Serve with melba toast.

Bacon, Bean & Garlic Soup

A mouth-wateringly healthy vegetable, bean and bacon soup with a garlic flavour. Serve with granary or wholemeal bread.

🍲 5 MINS   🕐 20 MINS

SERVES 4

I N G R E D I E N T S

225 g/8 oz lean smoked back bacon slices

1 carrot, sliced thinly

1 celery stick, sliced thinly

1 onion, chopped

1 tbsp oil

3 garlic cloves, sliced

700 ml/1¼ pints/3 cups hot vegetable stock

200 g/7 oz can chopped tomatoes

1 tbsp chopped fresh thyme

about 400 g/14 oz can cannellini beans, drained

1 tbsp tomato purée (paste)

salt and pepper

grated Cheddar cheese, to garnish

  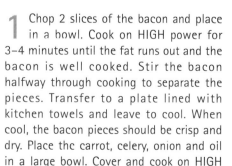

COOK'S TIP

For a more substantial soup add 60 g/2 oz cup small pasta shapes or short lengths of spaghetti when you add the stock and tomatoes. You will also need to add an extra 150 ml/ ¼ pint/²/₃ cup vegetable stock.

1 Chop 2 slices of the bacon and place in a bowl. Cook on HIGH power for 3–4 minutes until the fat runs out and the bacon is well cooked. Stir the bacon halfway through cooking to separate the pieces. Transfer to a plate lined with kitchen towels and leave to cool. When cool, the bacon pieces should be crisp and dry. Place the carrot, celery, onion and oil in a large bowl. Cover and cook on HIGH power for 4 minutes.

2 Chop the remaining bacon and add to the bowl with the garlic. Cover and cook on HIGH power for 2 minutes.

3 Add the stock, the contents of the can of tomatoes, the thyme, beans and tomato purée (paste). Cover and cook on HIGH power for 8 minutes, stirring halfway through. Season to taste. Ladle the soup into warmed bowls and sprinkle with the crisp bacon and grated cheese.

Special Occasion Soups

The selection of soups in this chapter offers something a little different. Special occasion soups are appropriate for entertaining, either because of their festive ingredients or their suitability for an informal gathering, or perhaps because they requires a little more preparation time than a family supper normally demands. The cold soups included in the chapter are also great for special occasions and home entertaining, and are equally welcome on a hot summer's day as a refreshing treat.

Minted Pea & Yogurt Soup

A deliciously refreshing, summery soup that is full of goodness. It is also extremely tasty served chilled.

NUTRITIONAL INFORMATION

Calories 208	Sugars 9g	
Protein 10g	Fat 7g	
Carbohydrate ...26g	Saturates 2g	

 15 MINS   25 MINS

SERVES 6

INGREDIENTS

2 tbsp vegetable ghee or sunflower oil

2 onions, coarsely chopped

225 g/8 oz potato, coarsely chopped

2 garlic cloves, crushed

2.5 cm/1 inch root ginger, chopped

1 tsp ground coriander

1 tsp ground cumin

1 tbsp plain (all-purpose) flour

850 ml/1½ pints/3½ cups vegetable stock

500 g/1 lb 2 oz frozen peas

2-3 tbsp chopped mint

salt and pepper

150 ml/¼ pint/⅔ cup strained
    Greek yogurt, plus extra to serve

½ tsp cornflour (cornstarch)

300 ml/½ pint/1¼ cups milk

mint sprigs, to garnish

1 Heat the vegetable ghee or sunflower oil in a saucepan, add the onions and potato and cook over a low heat, stirring occasionally, for about 3 minutes, until the onion is soft and translucent.

2 Stir in the garlic, ginger, coriander, cumin and flour and cook, stirring constantly, for 1 minute.

3 Add the vegetable stock, peas and the chopped mint and bring to the boil, stirring. Reduce the heat, cover and simmer gently for 15 minutes, or until the vegetables are tender.

4 Process the soup, in batches, in a blender or food processor. Return the mixture to the pan and season with salt

and pepper to taste. Blend the yogurt with the cornflour (cornstarch) to a smooth paste and stir into the soup.

5 Add the milk and bring almost to the boil, stirring constantly. Cook very gently for 2 minutes. Serve the soup hot, garnished with the mint sprigs and a swirl of extra yogurt.

Stilton & Walnut Soup

Full of flavour, this rich and creamy soup is very simple to make and utterly delicious to eat.

NUTRITIONAL INFORMATION

Calories	392	Sugars	.........8g
Protein	........15g	Fat	..........30g
Carbohydrate	...15g	Saturates	......16g

 10 MINS 30 MINS

SERVES 4

INGREDIENTS

60 g/2 oz/4 tbsp butter

2 shallots, chopped

3 celery sticks, chopped

1 garlic clove, crushed

2 tbsp plain (all-purpose) flour

600 ml/1 pint/2½ cups vegetable stock

300 ml/½ pint/1¼ cups milk

150 g/5½ oz/1½ cups blue Stilton cheese, crumbled, plus extra to garnish

2 tbsp walnut halves, roughly chopped

150 ml/¼ pint/⅔ cup natural (unsweetened) yogurt

salt and pepper

chopped celery leaves, to garnish

1 Melt the butter in a large, heavy-based saucepan and sauté the shallots, celery and garlic, stirring occasionally, for 2–3 minutes, until softened.

2 Lower the heat, add the flour and cook, stirring constantly, for 30 seconds.

3 Gradually stir in the vegetable stock and milk and bring to the boil.

4 Reduce the heat to a gentle simmer and add the crumbled blue Stilton cheese and walnut halves. Cover and simmer for 20 minutes.

5 Stir in the yogurt and heat through for a further 2 minutes without boiling.

6 Season the soup to taste with salt and pepper, then transfer to a warm soup tureen or individual serving bowls, garnish with chopped celery leaves and extra crumbled blue Stilton cheese and serve at once.

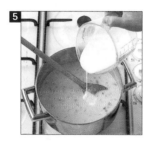

COOK'S TIP

As well as adding protein, vitamins and useful fats to the diet, nuts add important flavour and texture to vegetarian meals.

Carrot & Almond Soup

Carrots and almonds have a natural affinity that is obvious in this soup.

NUTRITIONAL INFORMATION

Calories	313	Sugars	........11g
Protein	........10g	Fat	..........23g
Carbohydrate	...17g	Saturates	......2g

15 MINS   55 MINS

SERVES 4

INGREDIENTS

2 tsp olive oil

1 onion, finely chopped

1 leek, thinly sliced

500 g/1 lb 2 oz carrots, thinly sliced

1.5 litres/2¾ pints/6¼ cups water

50 g/1¾ oz soft white breadcrumbs

200 g/7 oz/1½ cups ground almonds

1 tbsp fresh lemon juice, or to taste

salt and pepper

snipped fresh chives, to garnish

3 Soak the breadcrumbs in cold water to cover for 2–3 minutes, then strain them and press out the remaining water.

4 Put the almonds and breadcrumbs in a blender or food processor with a ladleful of the carrot cooking water and purée until smooth and paste-like.

5 Transfer the soup vegetables and remaining cooking liquid to the blender or food processor and purée until smooth, working in batches if necessary. (If using a food processor, strain off the cooking liquid and reserve. Purée the soup solids with enough cooking liquid to moisten them, then combine with the remaining liquid.)

6 Return the soup to the saucepan and simmer over a low heat, stirring occasionally, until heated through. Add lemon juice, salt and pepper to taste. Ladle the soup into warm bowls, garnish with chives and serve.

1 Heat the oil in a large saucepan over a medium heat and add the onion and leek. Cover and cook for about 3 minutes, stirring occasionally, until just softened; do not allow them to brown.

2 Add the carrots and water and season with a little salt and pepper. Bring to the boil, reduce the heat and simmer gently, partially covered, for about 45 minutes until the vegetables are tender.

Avocado & Mint Soup

A rich and creamy pale green soup made with avocados and enhanced by a touch of chopped mint. Serve chilled in summer or hot in winter.

NUTRITIONAL INFORMATION

Calories 199   Sugars 3g
Protein ....3g   Fat 18g
Carbohydrate ....7g   Saturates 6g

 15 MINS   35 MINS

SERVES 6

INGREDIENTS

40 g/1½ oz/3 tbsp butter or margarine

6 spring onions (scallions), sliced

1 garlic clove, crushed

25 g/1 oz/¼ cup plain (all-purpose) flour

600 ml/1 pint/2½ cups vegetable stock

2 ripe avocados

2–3 tsp lemon juice

pinch of grated lemon rind

150 ml/¼ pint/⅔ cup milk

150 ml/¼ pint/⅔ cup single (light) cream

1–1½ tbsp chopped mint

salt and pepper

mint sprigs, to garnish

MINTED GARLIC BREAD

125 g/4½ oz/½ cup butter

1–2 tbsp chopped mint

1–2 garlic cloves, crushed

1 wholemeal (whole wheat) or
white French bread stick

1 Melt the butter or margarine in a large, heavy-based saucepan. Add the spring onions (scallions) and garlic clove and fry over a low heat, stirring occasionally, for about 3 minutes, until soft and translucent.

2 Stir in the flour and cook, stirring, for 1–2 minutes. Gradually stir in the stock, then bring to the boil. Simmer gently while preparing the avocados.

3 Peel the avocados, discard the stones (pits) and chop coarsely. Add to the soup with the lemon juice and rind and seasoning. Cover and simmer for about 10 minutes, until tender.

4 Cool the soup slightly, then press through a strainer with the back of a spoon or process in a food processor or blender until a smooth purée forms. Pour into a bowl.

5 Stir in the milk and cream, adjust the seasoning, then stir in the mint. Cover and chill thoroughly.

6 To make the minted garlic bread, soften the butter and beat in the mint and garlic. Cut the loaf into slanting slices but leave a hinge on the bottom crust. Spread each slice with the butter and reassemble the loaf. Wrap in foil and place in a preheated oven, 180°C/350°F/Gas Mark 4, for about 15 minutes.

7 Serve the soup garnished with a sprig of mint and accompanied by the minted garlic bread.

Lobster Bisque

This rich and elegant starter soup is perfect for a special dinner. The lobster shell, made into a stock, contributes greatly to the flavour.

NUTRITIONAL INFORMATION

Calories 398	Sugars 6g
Protein 14g	Fat 22g
Carbohydrate ...30g	Saturates 14g

20 MINS   50 MINS

SERVES 4

I N G R E D I E N T S

450 g/1 lb cooked lobster

45 g/1½ oz/3 tbsp butter

1 small carrot, grated

1 stalk celery, finely chopped

1 leek, finely chopped

1 small onion, finely chopped

2 shallots, finely chopped

3 tbsp brandy or Cognac

50 ml/2 fl oz/ ¼ cup dry white wine

1.2 litres/2 pints/5 cups water

1 tbsp tomato purée (paste)

120 ml/4 fl oz/ ½ cup whipping cream, or to taste

6 tbsp plain (all-purpose) flour

salt and pepper

snipped fresh chives, to garnish

1 Pull off the lobster tail. With the legs up, cut the body in half lengthways. Scoop out the tomalley (the soft pale greenish-grey part) and, if it is a female, the roe (the solid red-orange part). Reserve these together, covered and refrigerated. Remove the meat and cut into bite-sized pieces; cover and refrigerate. Chop the shell into large pieces.

2 Melt half the butter in a large saucepan over a medium heat and add the lobster shell pieces. Fry until brown bits begin to stick on the bottom of the pan. Add the carrot, celery, leek, onion and shallots. Cook, stirring, for 1½–2 minutes (do not let it burn). Add the alcohol and bubble for 1 minute. Pour over the water, add the tomato purée (paste), a large pinch of salt and bring to the boil. Reduce the heat, simmer for 30 minutes and strain the stock, discarding the solids.

3 Melt the remaining butter in a small saucepan and add the tomalley and roe, if any. Add the cream, whisk to mix well, remove from the heat and set aside.

4 Put the flour in a small mixing bowl and very slowly whisk in 2–3 tablespoons of cold water. Stir in a little of the hot stock mixture to make a smooth liquid.

5 Bring the remaining lobster stock to the boil and whisk in the flour mixture. Boil gently for 4–5 minutes until the soup thickens, stirring frequently. Press the tomalley, roe and cream mixture through a sieve into the soup. Reduce the heat and add the reserved lobster meat. Simmer gently until heated through.

6 Taste the soup and adjust the seasoning, adding more cream if wished. Ladle into warm bowls, sprinkle with chives and serve.

Creamy Oyster Soup

This soup makes a rich and elegant starter. Serve it in shallow bowls so the oysters are visible, warm the bowls to keep the soup hot.

NUTRITIONAL INFORMATION

Calories ....299 Sugars 3g
Protein ....3g Fat 24g
Carbohydrate ...16g Saturates 15g

 20 MINS   30 MINS

SERVES 4

I N G R E D I E N T S

12 oysters

2 tbsp butter

2 shallots, finely chopped

5 tbsp white wine

300 ml/10 fl oz/1¼ cups fish stock

175 ml/6 fl oz/ ¾ cup whipping or double (heavy) cream

2 tbsp cornflour (cornstarch), dissolved in 2 tbsp cold water

salt and pepper

caviar or lumpfish roe, to garnish (optional)

2 Melt half the butter in a saucepan over a low heat. Add the shallots and cook gently for about 5 minutes until just softened, stirring frequently; do not allow them to brown.

3 Add the wine, bring to the boil and boil for 1 minute. Stir in the fish stock, bring back to the boil and boil for 3–4 minutes. Reduce the heat to a gentle simmer.

4 Add the oysters and their liquid and poach for about 1 minute until they become more firm but are still tender. Remove the oysters with a slotted spoon and reserve, covered. Strain the stock.

5 Bring the strained stock to the boil in a clean saucepan. Add the cream and bring back to the boil.

6 Stir the dissolved cornflour (cornstarch) into the soup and boil gently for 2–3 minutes, stirring frequently, until slightly thickened. Add the oysters and cook for 1–2 minutes to reheat them. Taste and adjust the seasoning, if necessary, and ladle the soup into warm bowls. Top each serving with a teaspoon of caviar or roe, if using.

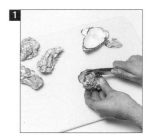

1 To open the oysters, hold flat-side up, over a sieve set over a bowl to catch the juices, and push an oyster knife into the hinge. Work it around until you can pry off the top shell. When all the oysters have been opened, strain the liquid through a sieve lined with damp muslin. Remove any bits of shell stuck to the oysters and reserve them in their liquid.

Bouillabaisse

This soup makes a festive seafood extravaganza worthy of a special celebration.

NUTRITIONAL INFORMATION

Calories . . . . . . .432 Sugar 9g
Protein . . . . .43g Fats 20g
Carbohydrates . . .21g Saturates 3g

20 MINS   1 HOUR

SERVES 4

I N G R E D I E N T S

450 g/1 lb king prawns (large shrimp)

750 g/1 lb 10 oz lb firm white fish fillets, such as sea bass, snapper and monkfish

4 tbsp olive oil

grated rind of 1 orange

1 large garlic clove, finely chopped

½ tsp chilli purée (paste) or harissa

1 large leek, sliced

1 onion, halved and sliced

1 red (bell) pepper, cored, deseeded and sliced

3–4 tomatoes, cored and cut into eighths

4 garlic cloves, sliced

1 bay leaf

pinch of saffron threads

½ tsp fennel seeds

600 ml/1 pint/2½ cups water

1.2 litres/2 pints/5 cups fish stock

1 fennel bulb, finely chopped

1 large onion, finely chopped

225 g/8 oz potatoes, peeled, halved and thinly sliced

250 g/9 oz scallops

salt and pepper

toasted French bread slices, to serve

ready-prepared aioli (garlic mayonnaise), to serve

1 Peel the prawns (shrimp) and reserve the shells. Cut the fish fillets into serving pieces about 5 cm/2 inches square. Trim off any ragged edges and reserve. Put the fish in a bowl with 2 tablespoons of the olive oil, the orange rind, crushed garlic and chilli purée (paste) or harissa. Turn to coat well, cover and chill the prawns (shrimp) and fish separately.

2 Heat 1 tablespoon of the olive oil in a large saucepan over a medium heat. Add the leek, sliced onion and red (bell) pepper. Cover and cook for about 5 minutes, stirring frequently, until the onion softens. Stir in the tomatoes, sliced garlic, bay leaf, saffron, fennel seeds, prawn (shrimp) shells, water and fish stock. Bring to the boil, reduce the heat and simmer, covered, for 30 minutes. Strain the stock, pressing with the back of a spoon to extract all the liquid.

3 To finish the soup, heat the remaining olive oil in a large saucepan. Add the fennel and finely chopped onion and cook for 4–5 minutes until the onion softens, stirring frequently. Add the stock and potatoes and bring to the boil. Reduce the heat slightly, cover and cook for 12–15 minutes, or until the potatoes are just tender.

4 Adjust the heat so the soup simmers gently and add the fish, starting with any thicker pieces and putting in the thinner ones after 2 or 3 minutes. Add the prawns (shrimp) and scallops and continue simmering gently until all the seafood is cooked and opaque throughout.

5 Taste the soup and adjust the seasoning. Ladle into warm bowls. Spread the garlic sauce on the toasted bread slices and arrange on top of the soup.

Cioppino

This tomato-based Californian soup is brimming with seafood, which can be varied according to availability. Serve it with olive bread or ciabatta.

NUTRITIONAL INFORMATION

Calories . . . . . . .211 Sugar 7g
Protein . . . . .26g Fats 4g
Carbohydrates . . .10g Saturates 1g

20 MINS   1¼ HOURS

SERVES 4

INGREDIENTS

500 g/1 lb 2 oz mussels

500 g/1 lb 2 oz clams, rinsed

300 ml/10 fl oz/1¼ cups dry
white wine

1 tbsp olive oil

1 large onion, finely chopped

1 stalk celery, finely chopped

1 yellow or green (bell) pepper, cored,
deseeded and fincly chopped

400 g/14 oz can chopped tomatoes
in juice

3 garlic cloves, very finely chopped

1 tbsp tomato purée (paste)

1 bay leaf

350 ml/12 fl oz/1½ cups fish
stock or water

175 g/6 oz small squid, cleaned and cut
into small pieces

225 g/8 oz skinless white fish fillets, such
as cod, sole or haddock

150 g/5½ oz small scallops, or cooked
shelled prawns (shrimp)

chopped fresh parsley, to garnish

1 Discard any broken mussels and those
with open shells that do not close
when tapped. Rinse, pull off any 'beards',
and if there are barnacles, scrape them
with a knife under cold running water. Put

the mussels in a large heavy-based saucepan. Cover tightly and cook over a high heat for about 4 minutes, or until the mussels open, shaking the pan occasionally.

2 When cool enough to handle, remove the mussels from the shells, adding any additional juices to the cooking liquid. Strain the cooking liquid through a muslin-lined sieve and reserve.

3 Put the clams into a heavy saucepan with 50 ml/2 fl oz/¼ cup of the wine. Cover tightly, place over a medium-high heat and cook for 2–4 minutes, or until they open. Remove the clams from the shells and strain the cooking liquid through a muslin-lined sieve and reserve.

4 Heat the olive oil in a large saucepan over a medium-low heat. Add the

onion, celery and (bell) pepper and cook for 3–4 minutes, until the onion softens, stirring occasionally. Add the remaining wine, tomatoes, garlic, tomato purée (paste) and bay leaf. Continue cooking for 10 minutes.

5 Stir in the fish stock or water, squid and reserved mussel and clam cooking liquids. Bring to the boil, reduce the heat and simmer for 35–40 minutes until the vegetables and squid are tender.

6 Add the fish, mussels and clams and simmer, stirring occasionally, for about 4 minutes until the fish becomes opaque. Stir in the scallops or prawns (shrimp) and continue simmering for 3–4 minutes until heated through. Remove the bay leaf, ladle into warm bowls and sprinkle with chopped parsley.

Bean & Sausage Tureen

The Mexican-style garnishes make this a festive dish for informal entertaining. Include some smoky or spicy sausages for added flavour.

20 MINS   2 HOURS

SERVES 4

INGREDIENTS

750 g/1 lb 10 oz/3⅔ cups dried black beans

1 tbsp olive oil

2 onions, finely chopped

4 garlic cloves, finely chopped

2 litres/3½ pints/8 cups water

2 x 400 g/14 oz cans plum tomatoes in juice

1 tbsp tomato purée (paste)

1 bay leaf

½ tsp ground cumin

¼ tsp dried oregano

½ tsp chilli purée (paste)

700 g/1 lb 9 oz lean sausages

salt and pepper

TO GARNISH

2–3 ripe avocados

3–4 tbsp lime juice

3 tomatoes, skinned, deseeded and chopped

about 300 ml/10 fl oz/1¼ cups soured cream

1 bunch spring onions (scallions), finely chopped

1 large bunch fresh coriander leaves (cilantro), chopped

1 Pick over the beans, cover generously with cold water and leave to soak for 6 hours or overnight. Drain the beans, put in a saucepan and add enough cold water to cover by 5 cm/2 inches. Bring to the boil and boil for 10 minutes. Drain and rinse well.

2 Heat the oil in a very large pot or flameproof casserole over a medium heat. Add the onions and cook for about 5 minutes, stirring frequently, until they start to colour. Add the garlic and continue cooking for 1 minute.

3 Add the water, tomatoes, tomato purée (paste) and drained beans. When the mixture begins to bubble, reduce the heat to low. Add the bay leaf, cumin, oregano and chilli purée (paste) and stir to mix well. Cover

and simmer gently for 1½–2 hours, stirring occasionally, until the beans are very tender. Season with salt and, if needed, pepper.

4 Meanwhile, bake the sausages in a preheated oven at 180oC/ 350oF/Gas Mark 4 for 40–45 minutes, turning 2 or 3 times for even browning. Drain, slice and add to the beans after they have been cooking for about 1 hour.

5 Peel and dice the avocado. Mix with the lime juice in a bowl and turn to coat. Put all the other garnishes in separate bowls.

6 When the beans are tender, taste the soup and adjust the seasoning. Ladle the soup into warm bowls. Serve with garnishes.

Poached Beef Soup

This lean, pretty soup makes an elegant light main course for 4, or it will serve 6 as a starter. A bit of last minute assembly is needed.

NUTRITIONAL INFORMATION

Calories 178   Sugars 6g
Protein ....16g   Fat 4g
Carbohydrate ...19g   Saturates 2g

 15 MINS   40 MINS

SERVES 4

INGREDIENTS

12 small new potatoes, quartered

4 slim carrots, quartered lengthways and cut into 4 cm/1½ inch lengths

150 g/5½ oz tiny French (green) beans, cut into 4 cm/1½ inch lengths

1.5 litres/2¾ pints/6 cups rich beef or meat stock

2 tbsp soy sauce

3 tbsp dry sherry

350 g/12 oz beef fillet (tenderloin), about 5 cm/2 inches thick

150 g/5½ oz shiitake mushrooms, sliced

1 tbsp chopped fresh parsley

1 tbsp chopped fresh chives

salt and pepper

  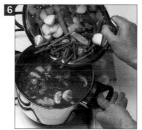

1 Bring a saucepan of salted water to the boil and drop in the potatoes and carrots. Reduce the heat, cover and boil gently for about 15 minutes until tender. Bring another saucepan of salted water to the boil, drop in the beans and boil for about 5 minutes until just tender. Drain the vegetables and reserve.

2 Bring the stock to the boil in a saucepan and add the soy sauce and sherry. Season with salt and pepper to taste. Reduce the heat and adjust so that the stock bubbles very gently around the edges. Add the beef and simmer for 10 minutes. (The beef should be very rare, as it will continue cooking in the bowls.)

3 Add the mushrooms and continue simmering for 3 minutes. Warm the bowls in a low oven.

4 Remove the meat from the stock and leave to rest on a carving board. Taste the stock and adjust the seasoning, if necessary. Bring the stock back to the boil.

5 Cut the meat in half lengthways and slice each half into pieces about 3 mm/⅛ inch thick. Season the meat lightly with salt and pepper and divide among the warm bowls.

6 Drop the reserved vegetables into the stock and heat through for about 1 minute. Ladle the stock over the meat, dividing the vegetables as evenly as possible. Sprinkle over the herbs and serve.

Chicken Soup with Pastry

This soup needs a rich, flavourful stock, and mushrooms that contribute plenty of flavour. The pastry top is baked separately to simplify serving.

NUTRITIONAL INFORMATION

Calories 560	Sugars 2g	
Protein 28g	Fat 33g	
Carbohydrate ...40g	Saturates 10g	

 15 MINS 1 HOUR

SERVES 4

I N G R E D I E N T S

1.5 litres/2¾ pints stock

4 skinless boned chicken breasts

2 garlic cloves, crushed

small bunch of fresh tarragon or
¼ tsp dried tarragon

1 tbsp butter

400 g/14 oz chestnut or horse mushrooms,
sliced

3 tbsp dry white wine

6 tbsp plain (all-purpose) flour

175 ml/6 fl oz/¾ cup whipping or double
(heavy) cream

375 g/13½ oz puff pastry

2 tbsp finely chopped fresh parsley

salt and pepper

1 Put the stock in a saucepan and bring just to the boil. Add the chicken, garlic and tarragon, reduce the heat, cover and simmer for 20 minutes, or until the chicken is cooked through. Remove the chicken and strain the stock. When the chicken is cool, cut into bite-sized pieces.

2 Melt the butter in a large frying pan (skillet) over a medium heat. Add the mushrooms and season with salt and pepper. Cook for 5–8 minutes until they are golden brown, stirring occasionally at first, then stirring more often after

they start to colour. Add the wine and bubble briefly. Remove the mushrooms from the heat.

3 Put the flour in a small mixing bowl and very slowly whisk in the cream to make a thick paste. Stir in a little of the stock to make a smooth liquid.

4 Bring the stock to the boil in a large saucepan. Whisk in the flour mixture and bring back to the boil. Boil gently for 3–4 minutes until the soup thickens, stirring frequently. Add the mushrooms and liquid, if any. Reduce the heat to low and simmer very gently, just to keep warm.

5 Cut out 6 rounds of pastry smaller in diameter than the soup bowls, using a plate as a guide. Put on a baking (cookie) sheet, prick with a fork and bake in a preheated oven at 200oC/400°F/Gas Mark 6 for about 15 minutes, or until deep golden.

6 Meanwhile, add the chicken meat to the soup. Taste and adjust the seasoning. Simmer for about 10 minutes until the soup is heated through. Stir in the parsley. Ladle the soup into warm bowls and place the pastry rounds on top. Serve immediately.

Chickpea & Fruit Soup

This main-course soup is Mexican in origin. Its appeal comes from an unusual combination of fruits and vegetables.

NUTRITIONAL INFORMATION

Calories	323	Sugars	........18g
Protein	........22g	Fat	..........10g
Carbohydrate	...38g	Saturates	......2g

25 MINS   1¹/₂ HOURS

SERVES 4

INGREDIENTS

800 g/1 lb 12 oz chicken legs or thighs, skinned

1 stalk celery, sliced

1 large carrot, halved and sliced

1 large onion, finely chopped

2 garlic cloves, finely chopped

2.5 litres/4⅓ pints/10 cups chicken stock

4–5 parsley stems

1 bay leaf

125 g/4½ oz lean smoked ham, diced

400 g/14 oz can chick-peas (garbanzo beans), drained and rinsed

1 large turnip, diced

2 courgettes (zucchini), halved and sliced

1 large potato, diced

1 sweet potato, diced

175 g/6 oz sweetcorn kernels

3 large pears, peeled, cored and cut into bite-sized pieces

3 tbsp fresh lime juice, or to taste

2 tbsp olive oil

2 very green, unripe bananas, cut into 5 mm/¼ inch slices

salt and pepper

chopped fresh parsley, to garnish

1 Put the chicken into a large 4 litre/7 pint/16 cup pot with the celery, carrot, onion, garlic, stock, parsley stems and bay leaf. Bring just to the boil over a medium-high heat and skim off any foam that rises to the surface. Reduce the heat and simmer, partially covered, for about 45 minutes, or until the chicken is tender.

2 Remove the chicken from the stock. When it is cool, remove the meat from the bones, cut into bite-sized pieces and reserve. Skim the fat as from the stock. Discard the parsley stems and bay leaf.

3 Bring the stock just to the boil. Add the ham, chick-peas (garbanzo beans), turnip, courgettes (zucchini), potato, sweet potato and sweetcorn. Return the meat to the stock. Adjust the heat so the soup simmers gently and cook, partially covered, for about 30 minutes, or until all the vegetables are tender.

4 Add the pears and lime juice to the soup and continue cooking for about 5 minutes, just until they are barely poached. Season to taste, add more lime juice if wished.

5 Heat the oil in a frying pan (skillet) over a medium-high heat. Fry the bananas until golden. Drain on paper towels and keep warm. Ladle the soup into bowls and top with fried banana slices.

Pheasant & Cider Soup

This an excellent soup to serve during the autumn, when pheasant are widely available.

NUTRITIONAL INFORMATION

Calories 471   Sugar 8g
Protein . . . . .12g   Fats 32g
Carbohydrates . . .32g   Saturates 19g

    30 MINS   1³/₄ HOURS

SERVES 4

INGREDIENTS

2 tbsp butter

3 shallots, finely chopped

2 garlic cloves, thinly sliced

300 ml/10 fl oz/1¼ cups dry (hard) cider

1.2 litres/2 pints /5 cups pheasant or chicken stock

1 carrot, finely chopped

1 stalk celery, finely chopped

1 bay leaf

1 pheasant

300 g/10½ oz potatoes, diced

250 g/9 oz small button mushrooms, halved or quartered

1 large eating apple, peeled and diced

300 ml/10 fl oz/1¼ cups double (heavy) cream

4 tbsp cornflour (cornstarch), diluted with 3 tbsp cold water

salt and pepper

TO GARNISH

2 tbsp olive oil, or as needed

30 sage leaves

1 Melt half of the butter in a large saucepan over a medium heat. Add the shallots and garlic and cook for 3–4 minutes, stirring frequently, until softened. Pour over the cider and bring to the boil.

Add the stock, carrot, celery, bay leaf and pheasant, which should be submerged. Bring back to the boil, reduce the heat, cover and simmer for about 1 hour, or until the pheasant is very tender. (Older pheasant may take longer.)

2 When the pheasant is cool enough to handle, remove the meat from the bones and cut into bite-sized pieces, discarding any fat. Strain the stock, pressing with the back of a spoon to extract all the liquid. Discard the vegetables and bay leaf. Remove as much fat as possible from the stock.

3 Put the pheasant stock in a large saucepan and bring to the boil. Adjust the heat so the liquid boils very gently. Add the potatoes and cook for about 15 minutes until they are just barely tender.

4 Meanwhile, melt the remaining butter in a large frying pan (skillet) over a medium heat. Add the mushrooms and season with salt and pepper. Cook for 5–8 minutes until they are golden brown, stirring on occasion, then more often once they start to change colour.

5 Add the mushrooms to the soup, together with the apple and cream, and cook for about 10 minutes until the apple and potatoes are tender. Whisk the diluted cornflour (cornstarch) into the soup. Boil gently for 2–3 minutes, whisking, until slightly thickened. Then, add the pheasant meat and simmer gently until the soup is hot.

6 Heat the oil in a small frying pan (skillet) until it starts to smoke. Add the sage leaves and fry for about 20 seconds until crispy. Drain on paper towels. Ladle the soup into warm bowls and garnish with crumbled fried sage.

Duck, Cabbage & Bean Soup

If you can't find the preserved duck or goose that is traditionally used for this dish, you could braise duck legs in stock.

NUTRITIONAL INFORMATION

Calories	479	Sugars	........8g
Protein	........29g	Fat	..........16g
Carbohydrate	...57g	Saturates	......7g

20 MINS   1¼ HOURS

SERVES 4

INGREDIENTS

2 preserved duck legs

1 tbsp duck fat or olive oil

1 onion, finely chopped

4 garlic cloves, finely chopped

2 carrots, sliced

1 large leek, halved lengthways and sliced

2 turnips, diced

200 g/7 oz dark leafy cabbage, such as cavolo nero or Savoy

1.2 litres/2 pints/5 cups chicken or duck stock

2 potatoes, diced

225 g/8 oz dried white beans, soaked and cooked, or 2 x 400 g/14 oz cans white beans

1 bay leaf

2 tbsp roughly chopped fresh parsley

12 slices baguette

150 g/5½ oz grated Gruyére cheese

salt and pepper

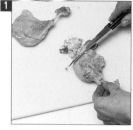  

1 Scrape as much fat as possible from the preserved duck. Remove the duck meat from the bones, keeping it in large pieces; discard the skin and bones.

2 Heat the duck fat or oil in a large soup kettle or flameproof casserole over a medium heat. Add the onion and three-quarters of the garlic. Cover and cook for 3–4 minutes until just softened. Add the carrots, leek and turnips, cover and continue cooking for 20 minutes, stirring occasionally. If the vegetables start to brown, add a tablespoon of water.

3 Meanwhile, bring a large saucepan of salted water to the boil. Drop in the cabbage and boil gently for 5 minutes. Drain well.

4 Add the stock to the stewed vegetables. Stir in the potatoes, beans, parboiled cabbage and bay leaf, adjust seasoning. Bring to the boil, reduce the heat and simmer for 15 minutes.

5 Chop together the parsley and remaining garlic. Stir into the soup with the preserved duck, cover again and simmer for about 20 minutes, stirring occasionally. Season to taste.

6 Toast the bread under a preheated hot grill (broiler) on one side. Turn and top with the cheese. Grill (broil) until the cheese melts. Ladle the soup into warm bowls and top with the cheese toasts.

Parmesan Pancakes in Broth

This delicious soup has a rich homemade Italian-style meat stock as a base. A perfect dinner party starter, it is very light.

NUTRITIONAL INFORMATION

Calories 37   Sugars 0g
Protein . . . . .3g   Fat 2g
Carbohydrate . . . .3g   Saturates 1g

25 MINS   2¹/₂ HOURS

SERVES 4

INGREDIENTS

1 tbsp plain (all-purpose) flour

2 tbsp milk

2 eggs

2 tbsp chopped fresh basil

3 tbsp freshly grated Parmesan cheese, plus extra to serve

MEAT STOCK

450 g/1 lb chicken wings and/or legs

250 g/9 oz lean boneless stewing beef, such as shin

1.4 litres/2½ pints/6 cups water

1 celery stalk, thinly sliced

1 carrot, thinly sliced

1 onion, halved and sliced

2 garlic cloves, crushed

3–4 parsley stems

1 bay leaf

½ tsp salt

pepper

1 To make the stock, put the chicken and beef in a large pot with the water, celery, carrot, onion, garlic, parsley stems, bay leaf and salt. Bring just to the boil and skim off the foam that rises to the surface. Reduce the heat and simmer very gently, uncovered, for 2 hours.

2 Strain the stock and remove as much fat as possible. Discard the vegetables and herbs. (Save the meat for another purpose.)

3 Bring the stock to the boil in a clean saucepan. If necessary, boil to reduce the stock to 1 litre/1 ¾ pints/4 cups. Taste and adjust the seasoning (be restrained with salt). Reduce the heat and simmer gently while making the pancakes.

4 To make the pancakes, put the flour in a bowl and add half the milk. Whisk until smooth, add the remaining milk and whisk again. Break in the eggs and whisk to combine well. Season with salt and pepper and stir in the basil and Parmesan.

5 Film the bottom of a small non-stick 15–18 cm/6–7 inch frying pan (skillet) with oil and heat until it begins to smoke. Pour in one-third of the batter (about 4 tablespoons) and tilt the pan so the batter covers the bottom. Cook for about 1 minute until mostly set around the edges. Turn the pancake and cook the other side for about 15 seconds. Turn out on to a plate. Continue making the remaining pancakes, adding more oil to the pan if needed.

6 Roll the pancakes up while warm, then cut into 3 mm/⅛ inch slices across the roll to make spirals. Divide the pancake spirals among bowls. Ladle over the hot broth and serve with Parmesan.

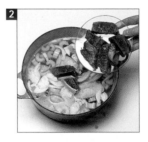

French Onion Soup

A rich, flavourful homemade stock is the key to this satisfying soup. While beef stock is traditional, chicken stock would be delicious as well.

NUTRITIONAL INFORMATION

Calories 417	Sugar 10g
Protein 16g	Fats 19g
Carbohydrates . . .41g	Saturates 9g

 15 MINS   1½ HOURS

SERVES 4

INGREDIENTS

1 tbsp butter

2 tbsp olive oil

1 kg/2 lb 4 oz large yellow onions, halved and sliced into half-circles

3 large garlic cloves, finely chopped

2 tbsp plain (all-purpose) flour

200 ml/7 fl oz/¾ cup dry white wine

2 litres/3½ pints/8 cups beef stock

3 tbsp Cognac or brandy

6 slices French bread

200 g/7 oz Gruyére cheese, grated

salt and pepper

1 Melt the butter with the oil in a large heavy-based saucepan over a medium heat. Add the onions and cook, covered, for 10–12 minutes until they soften, stirring occasionally. Add the garlic and sprinkle with salt and pepper.

COOK'S TIP

Don't try to hurry this soup. The rich flavour comes from cooking the onions slowly so their natural sugar caramelizes, then brewing them with the stock.

2 Reduce the heat a little and continue cooking, uncovered, for 30–35 minutes, or until the onions turn a deep, golden brown, stirring from time to time until they start to colour, then stirring more frequently and scraping the bottom of the pan as they begin to stick (see Cook's Tip).

3 Sprinkle over the flour and stir to blend. Stir in the white wine and bubble for 1 minute. Pour in the stock and bring to the boil, scraping the bottom of the pan and stirring to combine well. Reduce the heat to low, add the Cognac or brandy and simmer gently, stirring occasionally, for 45 minutes.

4 Toast the bread under a preheated hot grill (broiler) on one side. Turn over and top with the cheese, dividing it evenly. Grill (broil) until the cheese melts.

5 Place a piece of cheese toast in each of the 6 warmed bowls, then ladle the hot soup over. Serve at once.

Jerusalem Artichoke Soup

Select artichokes with the fewest knobs, as there is less waste and they will be easier to peel.

NUTRITIONAL INFORMATION

Calories 337   Sugar 7g

Protein . . . . .6g   Fats 28g

Carbohydrates . . .19g   Saturates 12g

 20 MINS   30 MINS

SERVES 4

INGREDIENTS

500 g/1 lb 2 oz Jerusalem artichokes

2 tsp butter

1 onion, finely chopped

115 g/4 oz peeled swede (rutabaga), cubed

1 strip pared lemon rind

700 ml/1¼ pints/3 cups chicken or
   vegetable stock

3 tbsp double (heavy) cream

1 tbsp fresh lemon juice, or to taste

4 tbsp lightly toasted pine kernels (nuts)

1 Peel the Jerusalem artichokes and cut large ones into pieces. Drop into a bowl of cold water to prevent discoloration.

2 Melt the butter in a large saucepan over a medium heat. Add the onion and cook for about 3 minutes, stirring frequently, until just softened.

3 Drain the Jerusalem artichokes and add them to the saucepan with the swede (rutabaga) and lemon rind. Pour in the stock, season with a little salt and pepper and stir to combine. Bring just to the boil, reduce the heat and simmer gently for about 20 minutes until the vegetables are tender.

4 Allow the soup to cool slightly, then transfer to a blender or food processor and purée until smooth. (If using a food processor, strain off the cooking liquid and reserve. Purée the soup solids with enough cooking liquid to moisten them, then combine with the remaining liquid.)

5 Return the soup to the saucepan, stir in the cream and simmer for about 5 minutes until reheated. Add the lemon juice. Taste and adjust the seasoning, adding more lemon juice if wished. Ladle the soup into warm bowls and very gently place the pine kernels (nuts) on top, dividing them evenly. Serve at once.

Roasted Garlic Soup

The combination of potato, garlic and onion works brilliantly in soup. In this recipe the garlic is roasted to give it added dimension and depth.

NUTRITIONAL INFORMATION

Calories	247	Sugar	.........7g
Protein	.........8g	Fats	..........10g
Carbohydrates	...34g	Saturates	......5g

🍲 15 MINS   🕐 1 HOUR

SERVES 4

INGREDIENTS

1 large bulb garlic with large cloves, peeled (about 100 g/3½ oz)

2 tsp olive oil

2 large leeks, thinly sliced

1 large onion, finely chopped

3 potatoes, diced (about 500 g/ 1 lb 2 oz)

1.2 litres/2 pints/5 cups chicken or vegetable stock

1 bay leaf

150 ml/5 fl oz/ ⅔ cup single (light) cream

freshly grated nutmeg

fresh lemon juice (optional)

salt and pepper

snipped fresh chives, to garnish

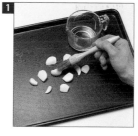  

1 Put the garlic cloves in a baking dish, lightly brush with oil and bake in a preheated oven at 180ºC/350ºF/Gas Mark 4 for about 20 minutes until golden.

2 Heat the oil in a large saucepan over a medium heat. Add the leeks and onion, cover and cook for about 3 minutes, stirring frequently, until they begin to soften.

3 Add the potatoes, roasted garlic, stock and bay leaf. Season with salt (unless the stock is salty) and pepper. Bring to the boil, reduce the heat, cover and cook gently for about 30 minutes until the vegetables are tender. Remove the bay leaf.

4 Allow the soup to cool slightly, then transfer to a blender or food processor and purée until smooth, working in batches if necessary. (If using a food processor, strain off the cooking liquid and reserve. Purée the soup solids with enough cooking liquid to moisten them, then combine with the remaining liquid.)

5 Return the soup to the saucepan and stir in the cream and a generous grating of nutmeg. Taste and adjust the seasoning, if necessary, adding a few drops of lemon juice, if wished. Reheat over a low heat. Ladle into warm soup bowls, garnish with chives or parsley and serve.

Saffron Mussel Soup

Mussels are easy to prepare, economical and very tasty. This soup has pure, delicate flavours and the fresh aromas of the sea.

NUTRITIONAL INFORMATION

Calories	381	Sugars	3g
Protein	16g	Fat	29g
Carbohydrate	11g	Saturates	17g

  15 MINS   40 MINS

SERVES 4

I N G R E D I E N T S

2 kg/4 lb 8 oz mussels

150 ml/5 fl oz/⅔ cup dry white wine

1 tbsp butter

2 large shallots, finely chopped

1 leek, halved lengthways and thinly sliced

pinch of saffron threads

300 ml/10 fl oz/1 ¼ cups double (heavy) cream

1 tbsp cornflour (cornstarch), dissolved in 2 tbsp water

salt and pepper

2 tbsp chopped fresh parsley

3 When they are cool enough to handle, remove the mussels from the shells, adding any additional juices to the cooking liquid. Strain the cooking liquid through a muslin-lined sieve. Top up the cooking liquid with water to make 1 litre/1¾ pints/4 cups.

4 Melt the butter in heavy-based saucepan. Add the shallots and leek, cover and cook until they begin to soften, stirring occasionally.

5 Stir in the mussel cooking liquid and the saffron. Bring to the boil, reduce the heat and simmer for 15–20 minutes until the vegetables are very tender.

6 Add the cream, stir and bring just to the boil. Stir the dissolved cornflour (cornstarch) into the soup and boil gently for 2–3 minutes until slightly thickened, stirring frequently. Add the mussels and cook for I–2 minutes to reheat them. Taste and adjust the seasoning, if necessary. Stir in the parsley, ladle into warm bowls and serve.

1 Discard any broken mussels and those with open shells that do not close when tapped. Rinse, pull off any 'beards', and if there are barnacles, scrape them off with a knife under cold running water.

2 Put the mussels in a large heavy-based saucepan over a high heat with the wine and a little pepper. Cover tightly and cook for 4–5 minutes, or until the mussels open, shaking the pan occasionally.

Watercress Vichyssoise

Traditional vichyssoise is simply cold leek and potato soup flavoured with chives. The addition of watercress gives it a refreshing flavour and lovely cool colour.

NUTRITIONAL INFORMATION

Calories .... 149 Sugars 3g
Protein .... 4g Fat 9g
Carbohydrate ... 13g Saturates 4g

 15 MINS   40 MINS

SERVES 4

I N G R E D I E N T S

1 tbsp olive oil

3 large leeks, thinly sliced (about 350 g/12 oz)

1 large potato, finely diced (about 350 g/12 oz)

600 ml/1 pint/2½ cups chicken or vegetable stock

450 ml/16 fl oz/2 cups water

1 bay leaf

175 g/6 oz prepared watercress

200 ml/7 fl oz/¾ cup single (light) cream

salt and pepper

watercress leaves, to garnish

1 Heat the oil in a heavy-based saucepan over a medium heat. Add the leeks and cook for about 3 minutes, stirring frequently, until they begin to soften.

2 Add the potato, stock, water and bay leaf. Add salt if the stock is unsalted. Bring to the boil, reduce the heat, cover and cook gently for about 25 minutes until the vegetables are tender. It may be difficult to find the bay leaf, however it is best removed.

3 Add the watercress and continue to cook for a further 2–3 minutes, stirring frequently, just until the watercress is completely wilted.

4 Allow the soup to cool slightly, then transfer to a blender or food processor and purée until smooth, working in batches if necessary. (If using a food processor, strain off the cooking liquid and reserve. Purée the soup solids with enough cooking liquid to moisten them, then combine with the remaining liquid.)

5 Put the soup in a large bowl and stir in half the cream. Season with salt, if needed, and plenty of pepper.

6 Refrigerate until cold. Taste and adjust the seasoning, if necessary. Ladle into chilled bowls, drizzle the remaining cream on top and garnish with watercress leaves. Serve at once.

Piquant Oatmeal Soup

This unusual soup, of Mexican origin, is simple and comforting. It has a hint of chilli heat, but its character is more sweet than spicy.

NUTRITIONAL INFORMATION

Calories 137	Sugars 4g	
Protein 3g	Fat 8g	
Carbohydrate ...14g	Saturates 4g	

 10 MINS   35 MINS

SERVES 4

INGREDIENTS

80 g/3 oz/1 cup porridge oats (rolled oats)

3 tbsp butter

1 large sweet onion

2–3 garlic cloves

350 g/12 oz tomatoes, skinned, deseeded and chopped

1.4 litres/2½ pints/6 cups chicken stock

⅛ tsp ground cumin

1 tsp harissa, or ½ tsp chilli purée (paste)

1–2 tbsp lime juice

salt and pepper

chopped spring onions (scallions), to garnish

1 Place a heavy-based frying pan (skillet) over a medium heat. Add the oats and toast for about 25 minutes, stirring frequently, until lightly and evenly browned. Remove the oats from the pan and allow to cool.

2 Heat the butter in a large saucepan over a medium heat. Add the onion and garlic and cook until the onion is softened.

3 Add the tomatoes, stock, cumin, harissa or chilli purée (paste) and a good pinch of salt to the softened onion and garlic.

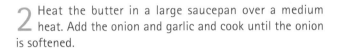

4 Stir in the oats and bring to the boil. Regulate the heat so that the soup boils gently and cook for 6 minutes.

5 Stir in 1 tablespoon of the lime juice. Taste and adjust the seasoning. Add more lime juice if desired. Ladle the soup into warm bowls and sprinkle with spring onions (scallions), to garnish.

COOK'S TIP

This soup is very quick to prepare once the oats are toasted. The oats could be prepared in advance at a convenient time.

VARIATION

Substitute lemon juice for the lime juice, using a little less.

Cucumber & Salmon Soup

When cucumber is cooked it becomes a much more subtle vegetable, perfect to set off the taste of smoked salmon.

NUTRITIONAL INFORMATION

Calories	308	Sugar	.........7g
Protein	........13g	Fats	..........22g
Carbohydrates	...15g	Saturates	.....12g

 15 MINS   25 MINS

SERVES 4

INGREDIENTS

2 tsp oil

1 large onion, finely chopped

1 large cucumber, peeled, deseeded and sliced

1 small potato, diced

1 stalk celery, finely chopped

1 litre/1¾ pints/4 cups chicken or vegetable stock

150 ml/5 fl oz/ ⅔ cup double (heavy) cream

150 g/5½ oz smoked salmon, finely diced

2 tbsp chopped fresh chives

salt and pepper

fresh dill sprigs, to garnish

1 Heat the oil in a large sauce-pan over a medium heat. Add the onion and cook for about 3 minutes until it begins to soften.

2 Add the cucumber, potato, celery and stock, along with a large pinch of salt, if using unsalted stock. Bring to the boil, reduce the heat, cover and cook gently for about 20 minutes until the vegetables are tender.

3 Allow the soup to cool slightly, then transfer to a blender or food processor, working in batches if necessary.

4 Purée the soup until smooth. If using a food processor, strain off the cooking liquid and reserve it. Purée the soup solids with enough cooking liquid to moisten them, then combine with the remaining liquid.

5 Transfer the puréed soup into a large container. Cover and refrigerate until cold.

6 Stir the cream, salmon and chives into the soup. If time permits, chill for at least 1 hour to allow the flavours to blend. Taste and adjust the seasoning, adding salt, if needed, and pepper. Ladle into chilled bowls and garnish with dill.

Spicy Icy Red Pepper Soup

This brilliantly coloured soup makes a great summer starter, especially when peppers are abundant in markets – or in your garden.

NUTRITIONAL INFORMATION

Calories	97	Sugars	........13g
Protein	.........3g	Fat	..........3g
Carbohydrate	...15g	Saturates	......0g

 15 MINS   50 MINS

SERVES 4

INGREDIENTS

1 tbsp olive oil

450 g/1 lb leeks, thinly sliced

1 large onion, halved and thinly sliced

2 garlic cloves, finely chopped or crushed

6 red (bell) peppers, cored, deseeded and sliced

1 litre/1¾ pints/4 cups water

½ tsp ground cumin

½ tsp ground coriander (cilantro)

1 tsp chilli purée (paste), or to taste

1–2 tsp fresh lemon juice

salt and pepper

finely chopped spring onion (scallion) greens or chives, to garnish

2 Stir in the (bell) peppers and cook for a further 2–3 minutes. Add the water, cumin, ground coriander (cilantro) and chilli purée (paste) together with a large pinch of salt. Bring to the boil, reduce the heat, cover and simmer for about 35 minutes until all the vegetables are tender.

3 Allow the soup to cool slightly, then transfer to a blender or food processor and purée until smooth, working in batches if necessary. (If using a food processor, strain off the cooking liquid and reserve. Purée the soup solids with enough cooking liquid to moisten them, then combine with the remaining liquid.)

4 Put the soup in a large bowl, then season with salt and pepper and add lemon juice, to taste. Allow to cool completely, cover and chill in the refrigerator until cold.

5 Before serving, taste and adjust the seasoning, if necessary. Add a little more chilli purée (paste) if a spicy taste is preferred. Ladle into chilled bowls and garnish with spring onion (scallion) greens or chives.

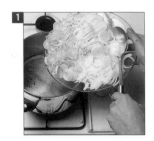

1 Heat the oil in a large saucepan over a medium heat. Add the leeks, onion and garlic and cook, covered, for about 5 minutes until the onion is softened, stirring frequently.

Melon & Ginger Soup

Almost any variety of melon is appropriate, including Honeydew, Galia, Ogen, Charentais or Cantaloupe, but it is essential that the melon is ripe.

NUTRITIONAL INFORMATION

Calories 179   Sugars 16g
Protein ....2g   Fat 12g
Carbohydrate ...16g   Saturates 7g

15 MINS   0 MINS

SERVES 4

INGREDIENTS

1 large ripe melon (about 1 kg/2 lb 4 oz)

¾ tsp grated peeled fresh ginger root, or more

1 tbsp fresh lemon juice, or to taste

1 tsp caster (superfine) sugar

120 ml/4 fl oz/½ cup whipping cream

salt

snipped fresh chives, to garnish

1 Halve the melon, discard the seeds and scoop the flesh into a blender or food processor. Purée until smooth, stopping to scrape down the sides as necessary. (You may need to work in batches.)

COOK'S TIP

To determine the ripeness of melon, gently press the end opposite the stem – it should give a little, and there is usually a characteristic aroma on pressing that helps to confirm the verdict.

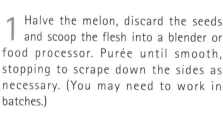 

2 Add the grated ginger, lemon juice and sugar with a pinch of salt and process to combine. Taste and add a little more ginger, if wished. Scrape into a bowl, cover and chill completely, usually for about 30 minutes, or until cold.

3 Add the cream and stir to combine well. Taste and adjust the seasoning, adding a little more salt and lemon juice if necessary.

4 To serve, divide the melon purée among four chilled bowls and garnish with chives.

Cucumber & Walnut Soup

Parsley tames the pungent garlic flavour of this traditional Balkan soup. The cucumber and yogurt make it a refreshing summer starter.

NUTRITIONAL INFORMATION

Calories	254	Sugars	.........4g
Protein	.........8g	Fat	..........23g
Carbohydrate	....4g	Saturates	......6g

20 MINS   0 MINS

SERVES 4

INGREDIENTS

1 large cucumber

60 g/2 oz/½ cup walnut pieces, toasted (see Cook's Tip)

15 g/½ oz parsley, leaves only

1 small garlic clove, very finely chopped

2 tbsp olive oil

4 tbsp water

1 tbsp fresh lemon juice, or to taste

300 ml/½ pint/1¼ cups strained Greek yogurt

salt and pepper

fresh mint leaves, to garnish

1 Peel the cucumber, slice lengthways and scoop out the seeds with a small sharp spoon. Cut the flesh into 2.5 cm/1 inch pieces.

2 Put the walnuts, parsley leaves, garlic, oil and water in a blender or food processor with half of the cucumber and purée until smooth, stopping to scrape down the sides as necessary.

3 Add the remaining cucumber to the blender or processor with a pinch of salt and the lemon juice. Purée until smooth.

4 Scrape the purée into a large bowl and stir in the yogurt. Season to taste with salt and pepper and add a little more lemon juice, if wished.

5 Cover and chill for about 30 minutes, or until cold. Taste and adjust the seasoning, if necessary. Ladle into chilled bowls and garnish with mint leaves.

COOK'S TIP

Toasting the walnuts gives them extra flavour. Just heat them in a dry frying pan (skillet) over a medium-low heat until they begin to colour and smell aromatic.

Cold Fresh Coriander Soup

This soup brings together Thai flavours for a cool refreshing starter. It highlights fresh coriander, now much more widely available.

NUTRITIONAL INFORMATION

Calories 107	Sugars 5g
Protein 4g	Fat 2g
Carbohydrate . . .19g	Saturates 0g

 15 MINS   35 MINS

SERVES 4

INGREDIENTS

2 tsp olive oil

1 large onion, finely chopped

1 leek, thinly sliced

1 garlic clove, thinly sliced

1 litre/1¾ pints/4 cups water

1 courgette (zucchini), about 200 g/7 oz, peeled and chopped

60 g/2 oz/4 tbsp white rice

5 cm/2 inch piece lemon grass

2 lime leaves

60 g/2 oz fresh coriander leaves (cilantro) and soft stems

chilli puree (paste), (optional)

salt and pepper

finely chopped red (bell) pepper and/or red chillies, to garnish

2 Add the water, courgette (zucchini) and rice with a large pinch of salt and some pepper. Stir in the lemon grass and lime leaves. Bring just to the boil and reduce the heat to low. Cover and simmer for about 15–20 minutes until the rice is soft and tender.

3 Add the fresh coriander leaves (cilantro), pushing them down into the liquid. Continue cooking for 2–3 minutes until they are wilted. Remove the lemon grass and lime leaves.

4 Allow the soup to cool slightly, then transfer to a blender or food processor and purée until smooth, working in batches if necessary. (If using a food processor, strain off the cooking liquid and reserve for later. Purée the soup solids with enough cooking liquid to moisten them, then combine with the remaining liquid.)

5 Scrape the soup into a large container. Season to taste with salt and pepper. Cover and refrigerate until cold.

6 Taste and adjust the seasoning. For a more spicy soup, stir in a little chilli purée (paste) to taste. For a thinner soup, add a small amount of iced water. Ladle into chilled bowls and garnish with finely chopped red (bell) pepper and/or chillies.

1 Heat the oil in a large saucepan over a medium heat. Add the onion, leek and garlic, cover and cook for 4–5 minutes until the onion is softened, stirring frequently.

Shrimp Dumpling Soup

These small dumplings filled with shrimp and pork may be made slightly larger and served as dim sum on their own, if you prefer.

NUTRITIONAL INFORMATION

Calories 311	Sugars 2g
Protein 18g	Fat 8g
Carbohydrate . . .41g	Saturates 2g

 20 MINS   10 MINS

SERVES 4

I N G R E D I E N T S

DUMPLINGS

150 g/5½ oz/1⅜ cups plain (all-purpose) flour

50 ml/2 fl oz/¼ cup boiling water

30 ml/1 fl oz/⅛ cup cold water

1½ tsp vegetable oil

FILLING

125 g/4½ oz minced (ground) pork

125 g/4½ oz cooked peeled shrimp, chopped

50 g/1¾ oz canned water chestnuts, drained, rinsed and chopped

1 celery stick, chopped

1 tsp cornflour (cornstarch)

1 tbsp sesame oil

1 tbsp light soy sauce

SOUP

850 ml/1½ pints/3¾ cups fish stock

50 g/1¾ oz cellophane noodles

1 tbsp dry sherry

chopped chives, to garnish

1 To make the dumplings, mix together the flour, boiling water, cold water and oil in a bowl until a pliable dough is formed.

2 Knead the dough on a lightly floured surface for 5 minutes. Cut the dough into 16 equal sized pieces.

3 Roll the dough pieces into rounds about 7.5 cm/ 3 inches in diameter.

4 Mix the filling ingredients together in a large bowl.

5 Spoon a little of the filling mixture into the centre of each round. Bring the edges of the dough together, scrunching them up to form a 'moneybag' shape. Twist the gathered edges to seal.

6 Pour the fish stock into a large saucepan and bring to the boil.

7 Add the cellophane noodles, dumplings and dry sherry to the pan and cook for 4–5 minutes, until the noodles and dumplings are tender. Garnish with chopped chives and serve immediately.

Prawn Gumbo

This soup is thick with onions, red peppers, rice, prawns and okra, which both adds flavour and acts as a thickening agent.

NUTRITIONAL INFORMATION

Calories	177	Sugar	.........5g
Protein	........12g	Fats	...........8g
Carbohydrates	...15g	Saturates	......1g

1 HOUR   45 MINS

SERVES 4–6

INGREDIENTS

1 large onion, chopped finely

2 slices lean bacon, chopped finely (optional)

1–2 garlic cloves, crushed

2 tbsp olive oil

1 large or 2 small red (bell) peppers, chopped finely or minced coarsely

850 ml/1½ pints/3½ cups Fish or Vegetable Stock (see pages 14–15)

1 fresh or dried bay leaf

1 blade mace

good pinch of ground allspice

40 g/1½ oz/3 tbsp long-grain rice

1 tbsp white wine vinegar

125–175 g/4½–6 oz okra, trimmed and sliced very thinly

90–125 g/3–4½ oz/½–⅔ cup peeled prawns (shrimp)

1 tbsp anchovy essence (paste)

2 tsp tomato purée (paste)

1–2 tbsp chopped fresh parsley

salt and pepper

TO GARNISH

whole prawns (shrimp)

sprigs of fresh parsley

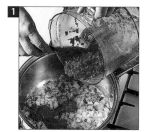  

1 Gently fry the onion, bacon (if using) and garlic in the oil in a large saucepan for 4–5 minutes until soft. Add the (bell) peppers to the pan and continue to fry gently for a couple of minutes.

2 Add the stock, bay leaf, mace, allspice, rice, vinegar and seasoning and bring to the boil. Cover and simmer gently for about 20 minutes, giving an occasional stir, until the rice is just tender.

3 Add the okra, prawns (shrimp), anchovy essence (paste) and tomato purée (paste), cover and simmer gently for about 15 minutes until the okra is tender and the mixture slightly thickened.

4 Discard the bay leaf and mace from the soup and adjust the seasoning. Stir in the parsley and serve each portion garnished with a whole prawn (shrimp) and parsley sprigs.

Index